LESLEY CHESTERMAN

Make Every Dish Delicious

Modern Classics and Essential Tips for Total Kitchen Confidence

PUBLISHED BY SIMON & SCHUSTER

New York   London   Toronto   Sydney   New Delhi

SIMON &
SCHUSTER
CANADA

Simon & Schuster Canada
A Division of Simon & Schuster, Inc.
166 King Street East, Suite 300
Toronto, Ontario M5A 1J3

First published in 2020 as *CHEZ LESLEY Mes secrets pour tout réussir en cuisine* by Éditions Cardinal.

This Simon & Schuster Canada edition October 2022

SIMON & SCHUSTER CANADA and colophon are trademarks of Simon & Schuster, Inc.

For information about special discounts for bulk purchases, please contact
Simon & Schuster Special Sales at 1-800-268-3216 or CustomerService@simonandschuster.ca.

Interior design by Quatre par Quatre, Catherine Gravel, and Emilie Deshaies

Manufactured in China

1   3   5   7   9   10   8   6   4   2

Library and Archives Canada Cataloguing in Publication
Title: Make every dish delicious : modern classics and essential tips
for total kitchen confidence / Lesley Chesterman.
Other titles: Chez Lesley. English
Names: Chesterman, Lesley, 1967– author.
Description: Simon & Schuster Canada edition. | Translation of: Chez
Lesley: mes secrets pour tout réussir en cuisine.
Identifiers: Canadiana (print) 20210394285 | Canadiana (ebook) 20210394293
| ISBN 9781982196370 (hardcover) | ISBN 9781982196387 (ebook)
Subjects: LCSH: Cooking. | LCGFT: Cookbooks.
Classification: LCC TX714 .C5413 2022 | DDC 641.5–dc23

ISBN 978-1-9821-9637-0
ISBN 978-1-9821-9638-7 (ebook)

*To my sister, Lorraine, my mother, Sylvia, and my grandmother Lillian,
the three women who always encouraged me and inspired me in the kitchen*

FOREWORD

Lesley Chesterman is a food and media rock star in Quebec, in both English and French. Apart from her twenty years of influential and informative restaurant reviews in the *Montreal Gazette*, she had a weekly reporting gig on Radio-Canada for a decade and continues to make countless other radio and television appearances as judge, commentator, and reporter. Lesley is so well known and so respected in French-speaking Canada that *Chez Lesley*, the award-winning French edition of this book, sold more than 20,000 copies thus far.

And now, at last, the English-speaking world has access to her wit and kitchen wisdom. At last, I say, for Lesley is a brilliant home cook and one of the most deeply knowledgeable food people I know. She's fueled by a deep curiosity about food and guided by her excellent palate.

We first met when I was on a book tour in Montreal about twenty years ago. I spent an afternoon cooking in her kitchen as we chatted about my book and many other things; the result was a long article in the *Montreal Gazette*. But better than the publicity for the book was the friendship that took root. Over the years since, we've spent time together in Montreal, Toronto, and elsewhere, in the kitchen and at the dinner table—talking, sometimes disagreeing, learning from each other, and laughing. When Lesley's around, the conversation is lively, opinionated, and informative.

A generous teacher, she wants us all to enjoy cooking, and to be confident in our kitchens. She's been a big help to me, most recently by explaining the mysteries of flan and custard, the technicalities of which I really did not understand.

What's special is the energy Lesley puts into everything she takes on. Her recipes are tested and retested until she is satisfied that she's figured out how to squeeze the maximum flavor from her ingredients. Once the dish is where she wants it, she writes the recipe and explanations so clearly that they're easy to follow and reliable. This urge to get it right means that her recipes, like the food at her table, are a real pleasure for cook and eater.

—Naomi Duguid, 2022

DO YOU REALLY NEED
ANOTHER COOKBOOK? YES!

Ten years ago, when I was approached to write a cookbook, I laughed. "The last thing the world needs is another recipe for carbonara," I told the editor who contacted me. I'll never forget her reply: "Maybe not. But I think they might like *your* recipe for carbonara." Perhaps she had a point, because carbonara, like so many dishes, is a recipe I have worked on tirelessly to get right. All those hits, misses, and little adaptations I've made over the years have transformed that classic into a very personal dish. That quest for fitting a recipe into my dream of what it should taste like extends to most everything I make.

How long have I been on the quest for delicious? Forever. Not that I was telling my mother her baby cereal wasn't right ("You call this oatmeal?"), but for as long as I can remember, I have been trying to figure out how to make the most of a dish. And once that interest took hold, I tackled everything from quiche to croquembouche. Not only was it fun and challenging, I got to feed my friends, family, and myself along the way. I was hooked.

This food fascination of mine turned into a career. In the early '90s, I attended cooking school for three years and became a professional pastry chef. For someone who found broccoli exciting, imagine my thrill at making chocolates, ice cream, and croissants from scratch. We'd make spongy genoise cakes, pipe delicate cookies, ice birthday cakes, and roll up thousands of cocoa-coated truffles. This opportunity to create something beautiful out of simple ingredients was endlessly stimulating. Somewhere along the way, though, between making sugar paste flowers and hundreds of mousse cakes, I realized a lot of the desserts I was making as a pastry chef looked great but didn't always taste great. Pastry making is so entrenched with technique, alas, that the flavour often gets lost along the way.

At the height of my pastry chef years, I headed to Los Angeles to eat at Campanile, a restaurant co-owned by chef Nancy Silverton. A week before I had been immersed in nougatine, multitiered wedding cakes, and finicky French pastries. But at Campanile, the dessert I ordered was a sourdough molten chocolate cake served with vanilla bean ice cream. I scoffed at the presentation. With no quenelles on the plate, fruit fans, or sugar roses, it looked like something a home cook would make. But after the first bite, I had an epiphany. Silverton's cake didn't look like much. But what it lacked in looks, it made up for in spades with taste. The sophistication was in the incredible flavours: intensely chocolate and boldly vanilla. The hot and cold temperature contrast was amazing, and the textures, from the crisp shell of the cake to the lusciousness of the ice cream, had me transfixed.

That dessert changed my whole outlook on food. All the innovative techniques and Marie-Antoinette presentations are pointless if the food isn't delicious. The challenge in a dish isn't making it pretty, but finding the balance between flavour, texture, even temperature. I don't think I made another sugar flower from that day forward. From then on, my only goal was finding a way to make every dish delicious.

From 1998 to 2018, that mindset continued when I worked as the fine-dining critic for the *Montreal Gazette*. I was fortunate enough to not only taste the food of some of the world's greatest chefs but to share my impressions with readers as well.

Comparing home cooks to chefs is like comparing the tortoise to the hare. Chefs live and breathe cooking. Most begin their profession at a young age and work long hours in a competitive environment. Their creativity is on call constantly, having to entice customers with every morsel on that plate. To do that, they rely on complex techniques, exquisite ingredients, expensive machinery, and a team of hands to help them realize their vision. It's a huge challenge.

That said, their goal is the same as that of the best home cooks: to serve food that will make people happy. But despite all the hoopla and posh surroundings, chefs don't always succeed. Some overthink it, some underthink it. Even at the highest level of cooking, finding that perfect balance of flavours isn't all that different from deciding how much sugar to add to your morning cup of coffee.

The longer I worked as a restaurant critic, the faster my interest in fancy food waned. Don't get me wrong: I love meticulous knife cuts, the snap of well-tempered chocolate, a perfectly balanced sauce, and a flaky-as-all-get-out croissant. But the priority must be flavour. We can't all cook like chefs, but anyone can make a delicious meal.

When planning out this book, I thought of it as a sort of guide to get novice cooks into the kitchen and offer experienced cooks new recipes to play with—with plenty of suggestions and hand-holding along the way. My goal was to offer a well-rounded repertoire of dishes you could make for many occasions. The recipes are both sweet and savoury, because the sweet really do require specific instructions, and as a former pastry chef, I couldn't resist! Nothing here is too complicated, though I do understand words such as "easy" and "advanced" are relative to one's cooking experience.

These aren't *all* of my favourite recipes, but a good part of my home repertoire, and most important, they hit the delicious mark every time.

PART 1

SET UP YOUR KITCHEN

STOCKING YOUR PANTRIES

Your kitchen is your domain, and the way you stock it dictates the way you will be cooking.

The contents of your pantry and refrigerator—which is really your cold pantry—make up a sort of wardrobe of basics and accessories that you use to dress up the meats, vegetables, or baked goods you're cooking. Add the freezer to that, and you have not one, but *three* pantries to keep stocked and organized.

Few of us have the time to food shop daily, so the goal is to always have enough staples between the pantry, fridge, and freezer to whip up a last-minute meal. What you don't want is an excess of produce dying in the crisper waiting to be cooked or, on the flip side, a fridge that looks full yet contains few items that can be pulled together to make a meal. The key is to find a balance between ingredients that have a long shelf life and those that must be used quite quickly.

It's the versatile basics (like lemons, butter, onions, potatoes . . .), in addition to the kitchen-cupboard staples, that enable you to turn out a meal without having to stop off at the grocery store. Take carbonara, for example: all you need are pasta, cheese, eggs, and bacon. In a well-stocked kitchen, you would have them all on hand.

Here are the essentials of my kitchen wardrobe. (And as none of us dress the same way, we don't cook the same way, either, so your choices will certainly differ from mine.) This list covers most of the basics you will need for the recipes that follow.

In the Fridge

Ah, the fridge, that destination for the midnight snacker, the ravenous teen home from school, the celebrant in search of the Champagne kept in the door in case of good news.

The fridge is the heart of the kitchen, and the place from whence the best ingredients spring. But the fridge can also be a nightmare, reeking of onions and filled with moldy yogurt and neglected condiments. Aim to keep your fridge items in constant rotation and avoid crowding the shelves with rarely used or almost-finished foodstuffs.

I would suggest focusing on these three categories:

1. Long-term: ingredients that have a long fridge shelf life

Anchovies, preferably packed in salt

Preserved lemons

Tube of tomato paste

Harissa

Sriracha

Mustard: yellow and Dijon

Ketchup

Dill pickles, cornichons, pickled onions

Capers

Egg whites (leftover, these keep a really long time)

Tahini

Commercial mayonnaise

Almond flour

Maple syrup

Butter

2. Mid-term: ingredients that keep for about a month

Dry salami, vacuum-packed

Parmesan and/or pecorino cheese

Buttermilk

Apples, lemons, ginger

Celery, carrots, leeks

Hot peppers

Fresh thyme

3. Short-term: ingredients that keep for about 2 weeks

Dairy: milk, sour cream, heavy cream, yogurt

Cheddar cheese

Bacon

Eggs

Assorted olives

Endives

Scallions

Parsley

Rosemary

Lemons

In general, meats, lettuce, vegetables, limes, tender herbs, and charcuterie should be kept for a week or less.

Ingredients that should never be refrigerated: onions, garlic, coffee, dry shallots, potatoes and—especially—tomatoes! Stone fruit should be kept on the counter until ripe, as refrigeration halts the ripening process.

In the Pantry

The pantry should always be kept well organized. Ensure every package and container is well sealed and expiry dates are respected.

Dry pasta

Rice: Arborio, basmati

Dried lentils

Vinegars: sherry, rice, white wine, red wine, apple cider, distilled white

Oils: vegetable, peanut, olive (regular and extra-virgin)

Canned tomatoes: whole and diced

Canned legumes: chickpeas, white beans, three-bean mix

Onions, garlic, shallots

Potatoes

Fish sauce

Soy sauce

Chicken bouillon cubes

Coconut milk

Coconut oil

Commercial mayonnaise (unopened)

Molasses

Vanilla extract

All-purpose flour

Sugar: granulated white, icing, brown

Baking soda

Baking powder

Cornstarch

Unsweetened chocolate, semisweet chocolate, chocolate chips

Granola, oatmeal, cereal

Spices: fine sea salt, fleur de sel, black pepper, cinnamon, nutmeg, ginger, cumin, cayenne, smoked paprika, curry powder, garam masala, garlic powder, steak spice, etc. . . .

In the Freezer

Ice

Ice cream

Chicken stock

Pesto

Nuts: walnuts, pine nuts, pecans, almonds, etc.

Frozen whole fruit or fruit purees

Frozen peas and corn

Homemade spaghetti sauce

An emergency loaf of bread

Pre-cooked legumes

Cookie dough

Sausages

1 whole chicken

Bottle of vodka (for the pasta sauce, of course . . .)

Food Storage 101

Food storage may not be the sexiest of topics, but knowing where to store ingredients is key to an organized kitchen and preventing needless waste. Consider these suggestions:

— **Bread:** Because bread molds faster in a humid environment, never store it in the fridge. Bread boxes help keep an unwrapped, crisp-crusted loaf fresh for a good 3 days. Just don't overcrowd the box or forget about the ancient bagels at the bottom.

— **Honey:** Keep your honey at room temperature; it may crystallize at cooler temperatures. If it does, just place it in a bowl of hot water and it will liquefy again. To avoid altering the flavour, never put top-quality honey in the microwave.

— **Onions, garlic, French shallots, and potatoes:** Always store these ingredients separately in a dry, dark corner of your cupboard. And never buy these ingredients refrigerated at the store, especially garlic.

— **Oils:** Never store oils (especially olive oil) in the fridge, as moisture can cause condensation in the neck of the bottle, and even a drop of water in your oil can make it go rancid.

— **Flavoured oils:** Nut oils, citrus oils, and truffle oil should be stored in a dark, dry place. Try to buy them in small quantities (8 ounces/250ml or less), as they go rancid quite quickly.

— **Nuts:** When possible, buy vacuum-packed nuts from a reputable dry-goods store rather than a supermarket.

— **Dried beans:** Store in well-sealed containers in the pantry. And buy in small quantities; when they are old, they take longer to cook.

— **Specialty and organic flours:** Always buy in small quantities and, if possible, store in the freezer to avoid moth infestations.

— **Bananas:** Never refrigerate bananas, or they will blacken. When bananas are too overripe for eating, they can be frozen, either peeled or unpeeled, to use in recipes later. Tip: Wrap the stems of your bananas in plastic wrap to extend their shelf life by a few days.

— **Tomatoes:** Always store at room temperature. When refrigerated, they lose their flavour and become mushy.

— **Chocolate**: Wrapped well, dark chocolate and chocolate chips can be kept in the pantry indefinitely. However, milk chocolate contains powdered milk and should be eaten within 6 months of purchase because it will go rancid. White chocolate should also be eaten within 6 months of purchase, but avoid keeping it for extended periods of time, as it easily absorbs surrounding pantry odours (even the smell of plastic wrap).

— **Peanut butter and other nut butters**: Store for up to 3 months at room temperature but refrigerate organic/natural butters to prevent them going rancid, and always store natural nut butters upside down to prevent the oil from accumulating at the top of the container.

— **Coffee**: Whole beans should be kept at room temperature in an airtight container. Same for ground coffee, which loses its flavour quickly, so try to use it up within a week. Freeze any coffee beans meant to be used more than 2 months after roasting. For best results, vacuum-pack the beans before freezing, and defrost only when you intend on using it. Avoid freezing and refreezing beans.

— **Wine**: Always refrigerate any leftovers after opening a bottle. To prolong the life of your wine, transfer the wine to a half bottle (375ml) and cork it. Port, sherry, and sweet wines will keep for several weeks in the fridge. Spirits should be stored at room temperature away from light, especially whisky, which is best stored in its original box.

Tools and Appliances

Pastry chefs love their blowtorches, piping bags, dockers, and spatulas, while chefs are obsessed with knives, Japanese mandolines, and multicoloured cutting boards. To each his or her own!

Much of the equipment used by professional chefs is ill-suited for amateur cooks, but there are some items that can really help you up your home-cooking game. Here are some suggestions for tools beloved by chefs that should find a place in your kitchen cabinets, too:

— **Digital scale:** Liquid and dry measures may be convenient, but a scale is not only more precise, but faster. If I had only one item to recommend above all, this would be it.

— **Storage containers:** Home kitchens are filled with plastic storage containers of all sizes, but for larger needs like storing flour or sugar, head to a restaurant supply store and look for large square containers.

— **Ice cream scoops:** Professional ice cream scoops are studier than others, and are ideal not only for scooping ice cream, but for scooping out even portions of everything from meatball mix to cookie dough.

— **Silicone baking mats (Silpats):** These mats are used to line sheet pans, which means no greasing and no parchment paper. They are pricey, but they are also sturdy and can be used over and over—just wash or wipe them clean and use again.

— **Various metal spatulas:** You can ice a cake with a butter knife, but spatulas will make the job easier and can be used for all sorts of kitchen tasks, from spreading to flipping to icing to lifting. Look for both straight and offset spatulas, as well as wider cookie spatulas.

— **Tongs:** Chefs love tongs, and you will, too, because they are just the right tool for stirring pasta, flipping meat and/or vegetables, and lifting anything that is too hot to handle. Look for heavy-grade tongs in both small and large sizes.

— **Dough scraper:** This flexible, horn-shaped soft plastic scraper (called a *corne* in French) is handy not only for getting every last bit of batter out of your bowl, but for scraping your work surface clean afterwards.

— **Japanese mandoline:** When you have plenty of onions to slice or potatoes to cut, or are looking for thin and precise slices of anything in abundance, a Japanese-made mandoline slicer (Benriner is a common brand) is the tool chefs turn to most. Just watch your fingers; the blades are razor-sharp.

— **Blowtorch:** The pastry chef's tool of choice, a blowtorch is great for heating up the sides of a bowl when you are beating a butter-based preparation or giving crème brûlée an evenly caramelized topping. Best of all, blowtorches aren't expensive and can be used for myriad tasks around the house, including lighting the candles on the dinner table. Just keep it away from the curtains and the kids.

— **Thermometers (preferably digital):** I still rely on a stainless-steel Polder candy thermometer I've been using for thirty years, but it's also worth investing in a digital probe thermometer for increased accuracy when checking internal temperatures for everything from crème caramel to côte de boeuf.

Appliances: My Favourites

Do you need a bread maker? Or an Instant Pot? Is it worth investing in a panini machine? Everyone has their pet kitchen appliances. I do, too, but sadly, there are plenty gathering dust in my basement, including a Crockpot, an Instant Pot, a deep-fat fryer, an air fryer . . . Obvious appliances like a microwave, toaster, and coffee machine aside, here are the eleven kitchen appliances I recommend most:

— **Stand mixer:** This is the most beloved appliance in my kitchen, and it never leaves the counter. I use it to make bread dough, cookie dough, cakes, meringue, compound butter, and so much more. Stand mixers do not come cheap, but they are definitely worth the investment, and the better brands should last a lifetime. If a big mixer is not for you, a handheld mixer is still a great tool and, save for kneading bread, will get many of the same jobs done—it's even preferable for whipping up small portions.

— **Immersion blender:** Also known as a hand blender, this tool is a great asset for the home cook. Ideal for blending soups and sauces right in the cooking pot, it's also great for making emulsified sauces from mayonnaise to lemon cream. I still use a regular blender on occasion to make extra-velvety soup in large quantities or maybe cocktails with ice, but otherwise, my go-to is the immersion blender.

— **Food processor:** I don't use my food processor often, but when I do, it's because it's the appliance that works best when making the likes of pie dough, cake batter, pesto, and bread crumbs, and especially for grating vegetables and cheese.

— **Inverted blender:** Small but powerful enough to pulverize small quantities of ingredients like nuts, fruit, or spices quickly, an inverted blender is one handy gadget. I pulverize sugar in it, combine liquid ingredients for muffins and cakes, and whiz up marinades and vinaigrettes. If you're a smoothie maker, this is the machine for you.

— **Panini press:** Paninis are hugely popular, but as most commercial sandwiches are pretty awful, consider making your own. Almost anything can be grilled between two pieces of bread, from the classic ham-and-Gruyère croque monsieur to a modern mix of caramelized onions, basil, prosciutto, and Parmesan. With models that can also be used to grill meat and fish, it's a great tool for getting teenagers to cook for themselves.

— **Ice cream maker:** There are many fancy ice cream machines on the market now with self-contained refrigerated units, but the ones I prefer are those with a removable freezing container that gets placed in the freezer overnight. The next day, you simply insert the container in the base of the machine, add your ice cream mix, churn, and in less than 20 minutes, you have homemade ice cream. It's also a cinch to clean up.

— **Soda maker:** The newest appliance on my counter and one I use often to make—instead of buy—carbonated water. Not only is it economical, it's environmentally friendly as well.

— **Juicer and juice extractor:** If you make a lot of juice, an electric juicer is a time-saver for juicing everything from lemons to pomegranates. I also have a juice extractor, which I rarely use, save for those days I feel the need for an apple, carrot, and celery juice or invigorating morning shot of ginger juice.

— **Waffle iron:** I'm more of a pancake person, but I cannot deny that I love a good waffle. An electric waffle iron makes it a pleasure to whip up a batch of waffles for a weekend breakfast—and this is another great appliance for getting kids to cook.

— **Coffee grinder:** If you're a coffee lover, the first step in producing a better brew is grinding your own beans. The fresher the grind, the more flavourful the coffee. I keep mine right on the counter, grind my coffee for every cup or pot, and now that I'm used to coffee made with freshly ground beans, I would never go back to buying pre-ground. Try it.

— **Rice cooker:** Rice cookers are fabulous for not only cooking rice to perfection but keeping it warm for hours. Just be aware that it takes longer to cook rice in a rice cooker than by stovetop methods, so plan to start your rice a good hour before serving.

Ready, Set, Cook! (But First, Some Tips)

Whenever people tell me they're depressed, stressed, or going through a tough time, I always say, "Try cooking." Usually, they follow up by telling me cooking stresses them out, too, and that they feel overwhelmed by the amount of knowledge it takes to be a good cook. Granted, some people aren't in the least bit interested in getting behind the stove, but eating? That's another story. Today, knowing exactly what we are putting into our mouths is something that should concern us all. And there's no better way to control that than by cooking for ourselves. Sure, a store-bought salad dressing or a takeout pizza are on occasion great time-savers, but I believe that very few daily activities are as rewarding as cooking. From planning a meal to making it to sharing the results with friends and family, the act of feeding people fills the heart with joy. If that has not been your experience in the kitchen, allow me to be your guide. I promise that the following tips will make the process a pleasure.

— **Set the scene:** Before you even slice an onion . . . put on an apron, clean up the kitchen, and clear off as much counter space as possible. Roll up your sleeves, tie back your hair, and wash your hands. Set up your cutting board and place a damp towel underneath to keep it from slipping. Pull out your favourite chef's knife. Set a pot of water on to boil. Preheat the oven. Turn on the stereo and pour yourself a glass of wine, if you like.

— **About those knives:** It's essential to keep your knives sharp, but you also need the right knife for each job. A good paring knife and a chef's knife are essential for cutting an onion. A bread knife (serrated knife) is irreplaceable for slicing, and a vegetable peeler with a fixed blade (*économe* in French) is preferable to a knife for peeling your vegetables. And when you start chopping, always plan the surface space you need. A large cutting board gives you the space to cut several ingredients at once. And always think about proportions: small knife, small cutting board . . . big knife, big cutting board.

— **Choose the right pan for the right task:** Select a pan that is too large to fry that chopped shallot, and you risk scorching it before it browns. Use too small a pan to fry those mushrooms, and they will take forever to develop any colour. As for the pans themselves, that old scraped up nonstick skillet should be replaced with a new one, or better yet, a thick-bottomed skillet that offers even heat. If you're looking for good pots and pans, department stores sell sets at very reasonable prices, especially after the holidays. Avoid using a nonstick pan for everything. It's ideal for eggs and fish fillets, but for meat, the caramelization of the crust is more effective when done in a stainless-steel or—especially— cast-iron pan.

— **Don't be a recipe rebel:** Sure, it's tempting to freestyle your way through a recipe, but that heap of ginger you added to your Bolognese might not be as glorious as you imagined. Do your best to follow a recipe the first time around and save your creativity for the next time.

— **Be smart about food preparation:** Do not use the same cutting board for onions and melon, or fish and meat. Do not prepare food on a surface where you were recently working with raw meat. Do not place cooked meat on a plate that previously held raw meat.

— **Rest your meat:** A roast chicken will lose its juices if carved immediately after cooking. Let it sit for 15 to 20 minutes to allow the meat to reabsorb the cooking juices. For steaks and roasts, tent with aluminum foil and let them rest for at least 10 minutes before slicing to facilitate the heat redistribution to the center of the meat.

— **When frying:** To prevent your butter from burning, use either clarified butter or a mixture of butter and vegetable oil. When frying meat, make sure your pan is very hot, and your cooking oil, too, then add the meat (if it has skin, start skin-side down) and give it a slight swirl around the pan to absorb some of the fat. Then leave it for between 2 and 4 minutes to form a crust before turning it over. If your piece of meat is sticking to the pan, give it a few more minutes to colour instead of trying to turn it too quickly and risking ripping the skin. Also, try not to crowd the pan too much or the temperature will lower and the meat will take longer to sear—if at all. The pieces should not touch, so be sure to either cook in batches or use two pans at the same time. Be patient!

— **About salting:** Salt wisely, and by that I mean pay attention to extremes. Salt is a great ingredient for making flavours come alive, but too much salt means your dish just tastes like salt. It is always easier to add than to take away, so salt lightly and regularly, and taste as you go. Always be sure to salt the cooking water for pasta and vegetables generously.

— **When food shopping:** Upgrade your food shopping by heading to specific stores that specialize in certain ingredients. I love a good supermarket, but there is no denying that a farmers' market offers a better choice of produce, often at a lower price. Likewise, a good butcher can give cooking tips and offer specific cuts you won't find at your supermarket meat counter. Of course, this goes for the cheese monger, fishmonger, baker, and specialty gourmet shops, too. It's time-consuming to shop at many different stores, but you will find better products and ingredients.

— **Take the time to read your recipe:** To avoid surprises mid-recipe, always read the recipe from beginning to end before proceeding and scan that ingredient list twice to make sure you won't need to run out halfway through to pick something up. We've all been there!

— **Have fun with it!** Find recipes to make homemade versions of the products you've been buying, like Ranch dressing, hummus, or tomato sauce. Once you develop a taste for homemade food, the less appealing processed foods will become. Also, get out of your cooking comfort zone and cook new things. Why not try your hand at making a curry (see page 216), a pizza (see page 185), or a fancy cake (see page 288)? Even if it's not a success, big whoop, it will be better next time.

— **When cleaning up:** Avoid pouring grease down the sink. Instead, transfer it to a small bowl, let it cool and then discard in the garbage or even bury it in your flower beds. Clean your oven and stove often to avoid fire hazards. Don't leave sharp knives in soapy water where the person using the sink after you risks cutting themselves if they hit the hidden blade. Also, never put kitchen knives in the dishwasher, nor any kitchen tools made of wood, copper, or cast iron.

— **And finally, avoid the kitchen-hog syndrome:** Do not monopolize the cooking duties. Share the space with others who want to cook. Get the children out of their rooms and into the kitchen to start cooking. The significant other, too. A meal is always more convivial when it is prepared by a team. And why not let children plan the dinner menu more often? (Just insist on a minimum of research on the internet or in cookbooks—otherwise, you risk eating pizza and pasta a little too often.)

But Hold On, I'm Useless in the Kitchen!

For several years I have heard people say things like, "I'm so bad at cooking, I don't know how to boil water" or "I'm useless in the kitchen, I can't even make a sandwich," or "I'm unable to scramble an egg!" Ugh.

I understand that making a gourmet meal is a challenge, but making a sandwich? Scrambling an egg? Is it so difficult? Really?

If we eat three meals a day every day, for our entire lives, isn't it in our own best interests to make food for ourselves? For our family? For our friends? Is it indifference, laziness, or fear? Perhaps the processed foods industry is to blame? Enticing us with addictive foodstuffs, bombarding us with advertising, and leading us to believe cooking's hard, time-consuming, and way beyond our skills?

I say FALSE!

For those who tremble at the idea of preparing a simple meal, here are some tips to rid yourselves of the idea that you are worthless in the kitchen:

— **Even if you do not like cooking**, you eat, so processed foods are surely present in your life. Do not let go of these foods right away, but eliminate the worst, like frozen meals, boxed macaroni, hot dogs, and commercial salad dressings. Try to incorporate at least one item you made yourself into your meals, be it a homemade salad with dressing or spaghetti sauce. And as for processed foods, find the most practical, the ones that you can add to something you've made from scratch: say, pesto, pre-marinated meat, or even a good-quality potato salad. No harm there. The next step, try out those meal kits, complete with recipes and all the ingredients required to make a meal. They're great confidence builders!

— **Look for inspiration.** Buy a new pot, pan, or kitchen tool that gives you pleasure to use. Nobody wants to cook in a bare kitchen without proper cookware. Invest in your kitchen, and if you choose wisely, your equipment will last a lifetime.

— **Appliances can make a difference.** I'm not big on slow cookers, but if they can inspire you to try new recipes, why not? The day I bought a panini press, I made sandwiches for a dozen people. It's always a treat to find an appliance that can both inspire you and help minimize your effort.

— **Find a kitchen "role model,"** a TV chef or cookbook author who inspires you. Jamie Oliver and Nigella Lawson have inspired me at times when I was in a cooking rut.

— **Cook with a more experienced friend.** The love of cooking is contagious. They'll help you out in the kitchen and share their tips, and before you know it, you'll be converted!

— **Cake mixes are great for kids, but you can do better.** To start, try a quick-to-make weekend cake (see page 296) or strawberry shortcake (see page 309).

— **"But hold on a minute . . . I don't have the time!"** A pork chop can be pan-seared in 6 minutes, and a chicken can be roasted in an hour. Cooking isn't necessarily about time, it's about practice.

So enough talking—let's get cooking!

When Using This Book

All recipes were tested using the standard bake setting on a residential oven. For convection baking, decrease the oven temperature given in the recipe by 25°F (about 10°C) or cut your baking time by about 5 minutes. If you are not sure about the variations of temperature in your oven, consider purchasing an oven thermometer. They are inexpensive and extremely helpful.

All eggs are large.

All butter is unsalted.

All salt is fine sea salt.

All pepper is freshly ground black pepper.

All flour is all-purpose, unless otherwise stipulated.

All sugar is granulated white, unless otherwise stipulated.

All brown sugar is either light or dark.

Whenever possible I try to purchase humanely raised meats, sustainable seafood, and organic and fair-trade produce. Not only do they tend to taste better, but the people involved in their production are not working in inhumane conditions or with life-threatening chemicals.

Salt: The Most Important Seasoning

Most recipes include some variation of the line "Season to taste." Easy enough, but when it comes to seasoning, there's much to consider.

In the home kitchen, salting is one of the most important steps in any recipe, and that goes for everything from salting cooking water to salting yeast doughs. In professional cooking, salting is one of the factors that separates the good chefs from the great. Under-salt food and it tastes bland; over-salt, and your dish is kaput.

Getting that balance right is an operation as precise as boiling caramel to the correct colour, roasting lamb to a perfect pinkness, and baking a crème brûlée until the nanosecond when the egg yolks coagulate. In the highest realms of cooking, salting is about enhancing to the hilt while not drowning out the host ingredient. This explains not only why chefs freak out when they see customers salting their food, but why gastronomic restaurants offer salt only upon request.

French chefs are famous for their love of salt. If you tried to sell the same duck confit made in France to North Americans, they would probably find it too salty. There's even a French saying that goes, *"Plat trop salé = cuisinier amoureux"* (Dish oversalted = chef is in love). Yet such generalizations don't really fly because salting is not so much a regional trend as a personal preference. Smokers are known to crave more salt than nonsmokers, and those who grew up eating salty food will reach for the saltshaker more often than those who did not. And if you are a "super-taster"—that is, someone who experiences taste more intensely than so-called "non-tasters"—you probably consume more salt to block out bitterness.

The key when salting is to do it progressively until the taste is enhanced—not trounced—by the salt. In cold preparations, excess salt is manageable, but in something hot like a sauce, it can be overwhelming. When salting at the outset of a recipe, consider the other salty elements in the makeup of the dish, such as cheese, bacon, sausage, fish sauce, soy sauce, miso, anchovies, olives, and pickles. Add salt to dishes that already count one or more of these ingredients and you risk overdoing it.

There's also the grain of salt to consider. Fine sea salt and kosher salt are best used in recipes, whereas "finishing salts," like flaky Maldon salt and delicate French fleur de sel, offer bonus bursts of salty flavour and the tiniest touch of crunchy texture to a finished dish. These are my favourites to serve at the table, though I cringe at the food-snob habit of bringing luxury salts (BYOS?) to restaurants.

Salt is always a hot topic in the food world, but judging by the number of pepper mills in restaurants, pepper is the seasoning of choice. Waiters in upscale Italian establishments have long been famous for their balletic pepper mill moves, but now servers in brasseries and bistros hover over the plate, ready to grind on command as well. I always decline, for the same reason I don't see the need for saltshakers on tables: in a serious restaurant, the seasoning is done in the kitchen. But if you're a pepper lover, keep in mind that there are other heat sources to explore, like Piment d'Espelette, cayenne, or a shot of Tabasco.

Before going in hard with the S&P, take a taste of the flavours in your dish and ask yourself how they could best be enhanced. Would they benefit most from salt, pepper, or something even more potent, like a shot of acidity in the form of lemon juice or vinegar? That drab cream sauce probably won't benefit from more salt and pepper, but a shot of lemon juice might brighten things up.

Those grilled vegetables doused in olive oil, too. Lime is also surprisingly brilliant squeezed over meat, so don't just keep it for the guacamole, mojitos, and key lime pie. Same goes for vinegar, an underappreciated flavour booster if ever there was one. Case in point: Greek salad. Instead of lemon, do as the Greeks do and add a drizzle of red wine vinegar over the top.

PART 2

MY RECIPES FOR SUCCESS:
THE FOUNDATIONS

EGGS: THE PERFECT INGREDIENT

EGGS: THE PERFECT INGREDIENT

So simple in appearance yet so complex in structure, the miraculous egg offers much potential within that little shell. Frothy soufflés, rich crème brûlées, and spongy cakes owe their magnificence to the humble egg. And when separated into yolk and white, the culinary possibilities become limitless.

However, looks are deceiving. Boiling an egg may be considered the most basic of kitchen tasks, yet mastering egg cookery takes time. The first dish you ever attempted was probably scrambled eggs. It's easy enough—crack, whisk, and fry. Poaching, frying, boiling, beating, and meringuing (yes, meringuing!) take practice, as does making the perfect omelet—often used as a test when hiring professional cooks. The great chef Paul Bocuse once told me that the most difficult dish to make perfectly was *deux oeufs au plat* (two fried eggs, sunny-side up), explaining, "Everyone overcooks them. Avoid high heat when frying eggs. It is best to go low and slow."

When heated, eggs coagulate (go from liquid to solid) at exactly 149°F (65°C). Getting to that temperature in the manner required by the recipe is what makes eggs so fascinating, and sometimes frustrating. This process results in the thickening of custards, the binding of ingredients in baked goods and casseroles, and the clarifying of consommés. Eggs also provide an emulsifying agent when you're making sauces such as mayonnaise and hollandaise, but once again, it's tricky to get things exactly right. They are also an important leavening agent, especially when beaten to a light froth or folded into a thick batter, such as for a soufflé. (Pitfalls here, too!)

Despite the complicated chemistry, however, you know that eggs are amazing, and you can cook them successfully, with just a little care.

Good to Know . . .

— Fried eggs and omelets are best cooked on medium heat to avoid a rubbery consistency that comes from overcooking.

— When baking, let your eggs come to room temperature before using, especially egg whites for meringues.

— When making meringue, it's essential that your bowl and beaters are clean and grease-free, as any impurities will prevent the whites from rising to their full potential. The egg whites must also be pure, with no stray yolk or any form of grease. This goes for the sugar as well.

— If any yolk gets into the white when separating an egg, use the edge of the broken shell, instead of your hands or a spoon, to retrieve the wayward yolk— works like a charm. It's not essential, but when you separate eggs, pinch the chalaza (the stringlike membrane) off the yolk so it drops into the whites.

— To avoid "burnt" lumpy yolks, never let sugar or salt sit on egg yolks without immediately whisking the mixture.

— When purchasing eggs for baking, large is the size that works best in most recipes, with the yolks weighing in at 20 grams and the whites at 30 grams.

— European egg farmers do not wash their eggs, so their shells retain their natural protective coating and can be stored on the counter. As North American producers generally do wash their eggs (thus removing the protective film), these should be kept refrigerated.

— The colour of the shell is determined by the breed of bird and has no effect on flavour.

— Organic eggs do not necessarily taste better, but as the birds are kept in more humane conditions, I try to buy organic as often as possible.

— Eggs are an excellent source of protein and are high in vitamin A, calcium, magnesium, iron, and riboflavin. They are low in fat as well: one large egg contains only 75 calories and 5 grams of fat.

— There are two ways to judge an egg's freshness, regardless of the expiration date on the side of the carton: A fresh egg will sink in a glass of cold water, and an old egg will float to the top. The porous shell absorbs air over time, which causes the egg's buoyancy. Alternatively, crack an egg onto a plate and observe its structure. If the yolk is well rounded and the white appears to be in two parts—a thick circle around the yolk and a second layer around the edge—your egg is fresh. Try to use your eggs within 2 weeks of purchase, especially for poaching, frying or soft-boiling.

— Keep your eyes out for small, speckled quail eggs. They are a gourmet treat, either poached or boiled.

Quick Recipes

Poached Eggs: Bring a small pot (for one egg) or deep skillet (for several) of water to a boil, then reduce the heat to maintain a simmer. Stir in 1 teaspoon white vinegar (use 2 teaspoons for a larger amount of water). Break one of your eggs into a small mesh strainer and swirl to remove the more liquid egg white while retaining the thicker white around the yolk. Carefully slide the egg into the water, and if you see the white begin to scatter, spoon the white back towards the yolk while making sure it isn't sticking to the bottom. (If you are cooking more than one egg, add the rest in the same fashion.) Poach for 3 minutes, then, using a slotted spoon, lift the egg out of the pot and transfer it to a paper towel. Serve immediately. Poached eggs can also be immersed in cold water and refrigerated for up to 2 days. To reheat, slide the poached egg into a small saucepan of simmering water for a good minute before serving.

Hard-Boiled Eggs: I recently swapped my usual egg cooking method with this technique by chef J. Kenji López-Alt: Bring an inch of water to a boil in a pot large enough for the eggs to fit snugly in a single layer. With the aid of a spoon, carefully lower the eggs into the boiling water and cover the pot. Set your timer for 11 minutes (for a soft-boiled egg, 6 minutes is sufficient). When the time is up, remove the eggs from the water and plunge them into a bowl filled with ice and water. Peel and enjoy, or refrigerate in the shell for up to a week.

Danièle's Scrambled Eggs: This method was inspired by the French chef Danièle Mazet-Delpeuch: Whisk eggs with milk, using 1 tablespoon of milk per egg (you can approximate here). Season with salt and pepper. For every 2 eggs, set an extra yolk aside to whisk into the mix at the end. Heat a skillet over medium heat and add a spoonful of butter. Swirl to coat the bottom of the pan. When the butter begins to foam, pour in the eggs and, using a whisk, gently stir the eggs as they form curds. When the eggs are still glistening but no longer runny, remove the pan from the heat and immediately whisk in the reserved yolk(s) and, if you're up for it, a spoonful of heavy cream. Check the seasoning and serve immediately. For a large quantity of creamy scrambled eggs, cook in a bowl over a pot of lightly simmering water (a bain-marie) while whisking continuously to break up the curds. Remove from the heat and proceed as above.

Classic French Omelet: Heat an 8-inch (20cm) nonstick skillet, preferably with sloped sides, over medium-high heat. In a small bowl, whisk 3 eggs until very smooth, adding a pinch each of salt and pepper, as well as 1 tablespoon chopped fresh chives, if you like. Add 2 teaspoons butter to the hot pan and when it begins to bubble and foam, pour in the eggs. Immediately start whisking vigorously with the back of a fork until the eggs form small curds, then lift the pan up on an angle towards you and begin to roll the omelet as it sets to the base of the pan. Check to see if the eggs are set to your liking (I like it moist) and then fold the bottom lip of the omelet over the seam in the middle. Invert onto a dinner plate and reshape to make it pointy on each end. Rub with a pat of cold butter to give it a nice sheen and serve immediately.

Basic Egg Salad: For egg salad, use 2 hard-boiled eggs per portion and mash well in a bowl with the back of a fork. Add 1 tablespoon mayonnaise per egg, along with fresh herbs like dill, chives, or parsley, or a combination. A few tablespoons of chopped celery work well here, too. Stir to blend, adding salt and pepper to taste along with a pinch of cayenne. Serve on deeply toasted bread, open-faced or in a sandwich. For an added bit of crunch, arrange a layer of thinly sliced radish or arugula over the top.

Mayonnaise: Place a large egg yolk in a medium bowl and let it come to room temperature. Whisk in a large pinch of salt as well as pepper (preferably white pepper to keep the mayonnaise a uniform colour, or cayenne), followed by 1 teaspoon Dijon mustard and 1 teaspoon white wine vinegar. Very gradually whisk in ¼ cup olive oil. Begin with a few drops at a time to establish the emulsion and then pour it in in a thin stream while you whisk. Once the olive oil is incorporated, gradually whisk in ½ cup vegetable oil until the mayonnaise thickens. For a bit of tang, whisk in a spoonful of fresh lemon juice at the end; for a garlic mayonnaise, add a minced clove of garlic to the ingredients before incorporating the oil. You can mix up the oils here, using all olive oil or all vegetable oil. Fresh mayonnaise is best used immediately but can be refrigerated in an airtight container (with plastic film pressed against the surface of the mayonnaise) for up to 2 weeks. *Makes ¾ cup*

—

Regarding Salmonella

Although chances of salmonella poisoning by a Canadian egg are about one in a million, according to the Canadian Egg Marketing Agency, there are precautions to be taken to avoid this potentially fatal bacteria. Always discard any broken or cracked eggs in the carton. Wash your hands and any utensils, such as knives and cutting boards, used in the preparation of eggs before reusing them for other foods. Do not allow foods prepared with eggs to sit at room temperature for too long, and discard any buffet leftovers. Only eggs that are cooked thoroughly are considered risk-free. It is not advisable to serve raw or partially cooked eggs to small children, pregnant women, or anyone weakened by illness. It is entirely up to you whether you are willing to take the small risk of eating a runny-yolked soft-boiled egg. Traditional chocolate mousse, homemade mayonnaise, and pasta carbonara are made with raw egg yolks, but since they happen to be three of my favourites, I am always careful to use the freshest eggs possible.

SHREDDED EGG SOUP WITH SPINACH

SERVES 4

This soup, better known as stracciatella, *is a Roman specialty to which I have added spinach, not only because of its nutritional value, but also to liven things up a bit. It's a great pick-me-up at the end of a hard day or when you're feeling a little under the weather. Using a good chicken stock for this recipe is imperative.*

4 cups (1L) Chicken Stock, (page 82) or store-bought, unsalted

4 large eggs

1 tablespoon semolina flour or fine cornmeal

⅓ cup (about 20g) freshly grated Parmesan cheese, plus more for serving

½ teaspoon fine sea salt

Pinch of grated nutmeg

Freshly ground black pepper

3 cups (about 85g) fresh spinach, thick stems removed

Squeeze of fresh lemon juice

- In a medium pot, over medium heat, bring the stock to a slow boil.

- In a small bowl, whisk together the eggs, semolina, Parmesan, salt, nutmeg, and pepper. Pour 1 cup of the hot stock into the egg mixture and whisk until smooth. Gently pour the egg mixture into the pot with the rest of the stock and, with a wooden spoon, stir the mixture slowly until the eggs break up into shreds. Coarsely chop the spinach, stir into the soup, and simmer for another minute. Check the seasonings and serve the soup piping hot, topping each bowl with a spoonful of Parmesan and a squeeze of fresh lemon juice.

RICOTTA, PARMESAN, AND ZUCCHINI FRITTATA

SERVES 1 GENEROUSLY

Frittata is a common Italian egg dish that I came to know through the cookbooks of London's River Cafe. I think of it as a baked omelet that makes for the perfect quick lunch or light dinner. Feel free to double the recipe and add fresh tomatoes and/or sautéed mushrooms, if you like.

3 teaspoons olive oil

1 small zucchini, sliced on an angle

¼ red bell pepper, thinly sliced

1 small garlic clove, minced

Fine sea salt and freshly ground black pepper

2 large eggs

1 large egg yolk

3 tablespoons ricotta cheese

3 tablespoons grated Parmesan cheese

Handful of chopped fresh parsley, basil, or thyme

- Preheat the oven to 375°F (190°C).

- In a small ovenproof skillet, heat 2 teaspoons of the olive oil over medium heat. Add the zucchini and bell pepper and sauté until they begin to brown. Add the garlic, sauté a minute more, and season well with salt and black pepper. Remove from the heat and transfer to a plate.

- In a small bowl, whisk together the eggs, egg yolk and 2 tablespoons each of the ricotta and Parmesan. Return the pan to medium heat and add the remaining 1 teaspoon oil, swirling it over the entire surface of the pan. When the oil has warmed, pour in the egg mixture and reduce the heat to low. When the mixture begins to set underneath, arrange the zucchini and bell pepper mixture over the top, dot with the remaining ricotta and scatter over most of the herbs. Season with salt and black pepper.

- Place in the hot oven and bake for about 3 minutes. Remove from the oven, loosen the sides of the frittata with a spatula and transfer to a plate, flipping it over if you like. Sprinkle on the remaining Parmesan and herbs. Serve immediately.

SHAKSHUKA

Second in popularity only to avocado toast, this North African egg dish is all the rage on the brunch circuit. There are all sorts of variations, but this is the way I enjoy it, be it for brunch, lunch, or even a light supper, with some good crusty bread alongside. This recipe can easily be doubled or tripled.

1½ tablespoons olive oil

1 small red onion, thinly sliced

1 small red bell pepper, thinly sliced

1 fat garlic clove, chopped

½ teaspoon ground cumin

¼ teaspoon smoked paprika

½ teaspoon ground coriander

Pinch of cayenne pepper

1 (14-ounce/398ml) can chopped tomatoes

Fine sea salt and freshly ground black pepper

About 2 cups chopped fresh spinach (tough stems removed and chopped)

4 large eggs

½ cup (60g) crumbled feta cheese

A few tablespoons chopped fresh cilantro, parsley, and/ or dill

- In a deep medium saucepan, heat the oil over medium heat. Add the onion and bell pepper and cook until softened but not browned, about 5 minutes. Add the garlic and cook for a minute more, then stir in the cumin, paprika, coriander, and cayenne pepper until well blended. Add the tomatoes in one shot, then fill the can halfway with water and add that as well. Season with a good pinch of salt and a few grinds of black pepper and stir to combine. Simmer the sauce until it just begins to thicken, 7 to 10 minutes. If it gets too thick, stir in a bit of water. It should be quite loose but not soupy. Add the spinach and stir for a minute more, or until the greens are wilted.

- Remove the pan from the burner and make four indentations in the sauce. Crack an egg into each hollow and sprinkle over the feta. Cover and place over medium heat. Cook for 4 to 5 minutes, until the egg whites are firm. Remove from the heat, sprinkle over the herbs, and serve immediately.

CRÈME BRÛLÉE

SERVES 6

Crème brûlée is a hugely popular dessert made famous in New York's most celeb-filled restaurant of the '80s, Le Cirque. It's surprisingly easy to make at home, though a blowtorch is required to make the ideal caramel topping. The cooking times here are long, but with crème brûlée, it's important to go low and slow, and I bake the individual portions at an even lower temperature so that the texture of the cream remains as velvety as possible.

½ cup (125ml) whole milk

1½ cups (375ml) whipping cream

½ vanilla bean, split lengthwise and seeds scraped out, or
1 tablespoon grated orange zest

½ cup (100g) sugar, plus more for sprinkling

5 large egg yolks

* **Note about sizes:** It's important to bake your crème brûlée(s) in low ramekins, about 1 inch (3cm) in depth, because you want a large surface to caramelize. I use either six small round ramekins (4½ × 1 inches/10 × 3cm) or one large dish (9 × 1½ inches/23 × 4cm).

• Preheat the oven to 250°F (125°C) if making one large crème brûlée or 225°F (110°C) if making individual portions. Place the oven rack in the middle position.

• In a medium saucepan, stir together the milk, cream, vanilla seeds (or zest), and half the sugar and bring to a boil. Meanwhile, in a large bowl, whisk the egg yolks with the remaining sugar until thick and creamy.

• Gradually pour the hot milk mixture over the egg mixture, whisking all the while, then strain the mixture through a fine sieve into a large (9 × 1½-inch/23 × 4cm) porcelain ramekin or six small (4½ × 1-inch/10 × 3cm) ones and place immediately in the oven. If making one large crème brûlée, bake for about 1 hour 15 minutes, until the cream is set and doesn't jiggle in the center. If making smaller ones, bake for 1 hour 30 minutes (add 10 minutes more if the ramekins are a bit deep).

- Let cool to room temperature and then chill for at least an hour before finishing and serving. (At this point, the crème brûlée can be wrapped well and refrigerated for up to 5 days.)

- Sprinkle a fine layer of sugar over the cooked cream, then, using a blowtorch, caramelize the sugar by moving the flame around, holding it about 5 inches (12.5cm) from the surface, until the sugar is evenly melted and caramelized all over. This can also be attempted under a hot broiler, but be sure your cream doesn't begin to bubble before the sugar caramelizes. Serve immediately, or chill for up to 1 day; after that, the caramel will start to melt.

ORANGE CRÈME CARAMEL

SERVES 6

*When talking egg recipes, there is no way you can omit crème
caramel. Problem is, so many people find this classic French dessert
"too eggy." To offset that egginess, I cook it at a lower temperature
and flavour it with vanilla or orange zest. And for special occasions,
I sometimes pour a little orange liqueur over the top.*

Caramel

¾ cup (150g) sugar

6 tablespoons (90ml) water

Flan

Grated zest of 1 bright-
skinned orange, or ½ vanilla
bean, split lengthwise and
seeds scraped out

½ cup (100g) sugar

2 cups (500ml) whole milk

4 large eggs

2 tablespoons orange
liqueur, such as Grand
Marnier, triple sec, or
Cointreau for serving
(optional)

- Preheat the oven to 325°F (160°C). Pour a bit of water into the base of a deep roasting pan in which six ramekins will fit snugly (I use a 9 × 13-inch/23 × 33cm pan) and place a cotton napkin, kitchen towel, or a few layers of paper towel over the top. Place your six ramekins on the towel.

- **Make the caramel:** In a small, heavy saucepan, combine the sugar and water, stir a few times, then bring to a boil over medium-high heat. Let the mixture boil—untouched—until it begins to colour, about 6 minutes. When a whiff of smoke comes up from the pot, turn off the heat and just swirl the mixture until the bubbles subside and the sugar solution reaches a nice golden caramel. Pour immediately into the ramekins, swirling them if necessary to make sure the caramel covers the bottom.

- **Make the flan:** Put a full kettle of water on to boil.

- In a large bowl, rub together the orange zest and sugar with your fingers until the sugar takes on an orange hue (or a beige hue, if you're using the vanilla beans instead). Scald the milk (you can use the pot you used for the caramel) with half the sugar and whisk the eggs into the remaining sugar. Pour the hot milk into the egg mixture, whisking well, then strain the mixture into a large measuring cup.

Divide the mixture evenly among the ramekins, then pour enough boiling water from the kettle into the roasting pan to come up almost to the top of the ramekins.

- Carefully slide the roasting pan into the oven. Bake until the flan is set, about 35 minutes (if using a thermometer, the internal temperature should be 176° to 180°F/80° to 82°C). Carefully lift the ramekins out of the pan and set on a wire rack to cool, then refrigerate until ready to serve. (Well covered, they will keep refrigerated for up to 5 days.)

- To serve, dip the bottom of each ramekin in a bowl of hot water for about 30 seconds to loosen the caramel, then run a small knife just around the rim of the flan. Invert onto a serving plate and pour over the orange liqueur, if desired.

MERINGUE TORTE

SERVES 10

As a kid, this meringue cake was known in my house as the "Forgotten Torte,"
since it's left in the oven overnight to bake. My mother made it constantly in
the '70s and all her friends did, too, so it was literally the only dessert I saw
at parties for a good decade. Not only is it easy to make, but the cake offers
a fun contrast of textures between its frothy interior and crusty exterior.

9 large egg whites (270g),
at room temperature

1 teaspoon cream of tartar

Pinch of fine sea salt

2¼ cups (450g) sugar

1½ teaspoons vanilla
extract

½ teaspoon almond extract

1 recipe Crème Chantilly
(page 308)

Fresh strawberries or
raspberries, for garnish

Strawberry Coulis
(page 308), for serving

- Preheat the oven to 425°F (220°C). Place the oven rack in the lower third position. Butter only the base of a two-piece 10 × 4-inch (25 × 10cm) tube pan.

- In a large bowl using a handheld mixer, or in the bowl of a stand mixer fitted with the whisk attachment, beat the egg whites with the cream of tartar on medium speed until frothy, about a minute. Increase the speed to medium-high, add the salt, and beat for a few minutes more, until the whites form soft peaks.

- While beating, gradually sprinkle in the sugar a few tablespoons at a time, waiting until each addition is well incorporated before adding the next spoonful (take your time). Once all the sugar has been added, scrape the bowl, increase the speed to high, and beat for a few minutes more, until the meringue forms very stiff peaks. Add the vanilla and almond extract, then turn off the beaters.

- Spoon one-third of the meringue into the bottom of the prepared pan. Using a spoon or rubber spatula, spread the meringue into the corners of the pan. Repeat two more times, pressing down lightly between layers to eliminate any air pockets. When all the meringue is in the pan, smooth the top into an even layer.

- Run your finger around the edge of the pan to create a crevice between the rim of the pan and the meringue (this is a crucial step that will help the cake to rise straight).

- Place the pan in the oven and immediately turn the oven off. Do not open the oven door for at least 6 hours. After 6 hours, remove the cake from the oven, but do not refrigerate yet. If the top crust rises above the top of the pan, lightly press it down with your fingers. Remove the torte by pushing the bottom of the pan up, away from the sides. Run a knife under the torte to release it from the pan bottom. Or you can unmould it, upside down, onto a dessert platter, then flip it right side up to serve with the crisp shell on top (which is my preference, because the cake is less likely to slip off the serving plate)—any surrounding crispy bits can be secretly devoured while no one is looking.

- To finish, dollop the Chantilly cream on the top of the cake, or pipe it into large rosettes using a pastry bag fitted with a fluted tip, if you like. Arrange the berries over the cream and refrigerate until ready to serve (no longer than a day). Slice into generous portions and serve with plenty of strawberry coulis.

About Vanilla

Vanilla is an ingredient we know so well, from the ice cream flavour that out-sells all others to the bottle in the cupboard we secretly sniffed as kids. It's familiar in our breakfast yogurt or seed-speckled crème brûlée, yet the product itself could not be more exotic, hailing from faraway places like Tahiti, Madagascar, New Guinea, Indonesia, Uganda, French Polynesia, and Mexico.

Chances are, if you have vanilla in your home, it's in the form of vanilla extract, either pure or artificial, a pantry staple if ever there was one. Because pure vanilla extract has become exorbitantly expensive of late, you may have been holding back and opting for imitation. Do not feel guilty. Studies show the difference between pure vanilla extract and artificial in baked goods is almost impossible to detect. But when I have a recipe where vanilla is the star of the show, I'll opt for either the pure stuff or the ne plus ultra, a vanilla bean.

In most cases, the vanilla bean you find for sale in North America is from Madagascar as 80 percent of the world's vanilla crop hails from that country. Vanilla vines originated in Mexico, yet Mexico's production remains small, which means those bottles of vanilla extract you find at the Cancún duty free probably don't contain much in the way of real vanilla. FDA standards dictate that vanilla extract must be made with 13.35 ounces (380g) of chopped vanilla beans per gallon (4.5L) of extract. Considering the amount of extract sold in Mexico, there is no way local vanilla production could come close to covering that amount.

Vanilla beans have always been the second most expensive spice after saffron. When production is high, prices are so low you can find vanilla beans at your local supermarket. But when production is paltry, as has been the case for the past few years, vanilla can set you back $10 per bean—or more.

Considering the labour involved, vanilla beans *should* be expensive. The beans are the fruit of the vanilla orchid (*Vanilla planifolia*) whose vines are grown around trees in plantations. It takes four years for the plants to give fruit. And when it blossoms, the vanilla orchid bloom lasts but a day, and on that day, the orchid must be hand-pollinated—in the morning—to produce a vanilla bean. After nine months on the vine, the pods are harvested, boiled, and then wrapped in jute to sweat out the humidity. A few days later, the beans begin to ferment, giving them their chocolate-brown colour. Two weeks of sun-drying follow to halt the fermentation process, and finally, the beans are graded according to size and quality. And production is small: eight vines produce 13 pounds (6kg) of green vanilla beans, which amount to but 2.2 pounds (1kg) of dried and cured beans.

When you spot whole beans sold at a decent price, stock up. Kept sealed in a plastic bag (avoid bending them) in a dark pantry, vanilla beans have an endless shelf life. Use to infuse vanilla flavour in liquids like milk, cream, or even a simple syrup for cocktails. To get the most out of your bean, split the pod lengthwise and scrape out the pulpy seeds. Add the seed pulp to the mixture, as well as the scraped pod. When you strain the mixture, remove the vanilla pod, rinse clean, and let air-dry, then take your bean and place it in a mason jar, pour over enough sugar to cover, and seal shut. In a few weeks, that sugar will become vanilla sugar, which can be sprinkled over a fruit tart or crumble, or used in any vanilla-friendly recipe. With an ingredient this precious, it's crucial to exploit it to its fullest.

BUTTER: THE INDISPENSABLE FAT

BUTTER:
THE INDISPENSABLE FAT

I have spent years interviewing chefs and food personalities about their food preferences. One question I could never resist was what ingredients they always had in their fridge. They'd list off lemons, kimchi, Parmesan cheese, schmaltz, capers, eggs, and a host of other foodstuffs. But the one staple that was never mentioned was butter . . . and I always wondered why. Did they simply take it for granted? Or was there something uncool and old school about admitting that you cook with butter over, say, olive oil or coconut oil? I've concluded that it was a bit of both, because unless you follow a vegetarian or vegan regime, butter is an absolute *must*. Salty, sweet, clarified, local or imported . . . butter is the key ingredient in many of my favourite dishes, sauces, pies, and pastries.

I always have butter on hand: unsalted butter in the fridge for baking and cooking, and semi-salted on the counter for daily use. I bet there's butter in most of your kitchens, too. When butter is on sale, I stockpile it in my freezer. And when I'm feeling flush, I'll splurge on artisanal butter for eating in fat slivers, a bit like cheese, on a cracker or slice of fresh baguette. Butter adds texture, tenderness, and above all flavour to our food. Few would deny that one of life's great pleasures include a fresh-from-the-oven muffin slathered with butter, a steak topped with a round of melting *beurre maître d'hôtel,* or a mille-feuille made with shattering sheets of buttery puff pastry. Yes!

The late, great British food writer A. A. Gill was once asked, "If you could eat anything, what would it be right now?" He replied: "Two soft-boiled eggs in a blue-and-white egg cup. A baguette with pale white, sweet, cool butter, and runny wild-strawberry jam. A bowl of coffee with just a touch of chicory. A jug of hot milk."

I could not agree more.

Good to Know . . .

— With so many new butters flooding the market these days, when in search of a good brand, taste it straight. What you're looking for is the flavour of fresh cream. It's worth sampling several—you will taste a difference.

— Butter has a long shelf life. It can be kept refrigerated for 6 to 9 months, and even then, taste it to see where it's at before tossing it, because it can last beyond the expiry date on the package. As butter absorbs smells, store it away from the rest of your ingredients. As for butter on the counter, I keep it in a lidded butter dish; those Breton butter crocks, where the butter is submerged in water, work well, too. Just be careful about how long you keep butter unrefrigerated because it will oxidize and go rancid at some point. When it starts to smell or taste a bit rank (this can take about 10 days), it's time to say goodbye. As butter starts melting at 90°F (32°C), you should always keep it refrigerated in hot weather.

— About salted butter: Many of us grew up eating salted butter, so unsalted butter seems dull in comparison, yet salted butter is often so salty that I find the taste of the cream is overwhelmed by the salt. Salted butter can also ruin a recipe for a sauce or baked good. To solve such issues, try semi-salted butter and save the unsalted butter for recipes where salt is a no-no, like buttercream or icing.

— It is worth seeking out imported butters, such as the French brands Échiré and Isigny Ste Mère, and the most famous brand, Le Beurre Bordier from Saint-Malo. The texture is quite dense, and the flavour is complex—verging on cheesy (especially if you are buying cultured butter). European salted butters are often even saltier than North American, so consider opting for unsalted, known as *beurre doux* in French. Keep in mind, though, that these butters can cost up to $50 per pound, ten times the price of standard supermarket butter, so use sparingly and be sure to check expiry dates to avoid getting saddled with a less-than-stellar product.

— According to Canadian regulations, butter must contain at least 80 percent fat, about 16 percent water, and about 3 percent milk solids. Specialty butters often have a fat content between 83 and 90 percent, which offers not only a more concentrated taste, but a "drier" butter. This makes it better for baking, though the price is so high that you might want to check your bank balance before using it for pie dough.

— Butter can change colour from summer to winter, but not to worry—this just depends on the feed of the cows.

— Butter burns at 350°F (175°C), so you have two options for cooking at high temperatures: First, use butter in tandem with oil so the butter does not burn as quickly. Second, use Clarified Butter (page 57), butter with the milk solids filtered out so that the remaining clear liquid (the butterfat) can be heated as high as 450°F (230°C) without risk of burning. Clarified butter keeps longer than regular butter, too, though with the milk solids removed, it's less flavourful.

— Often associated with Indian and Middle Eastern cuisine, ghee is another form of clarified butter that is simmered even longer over low heat to remove moisture and develop flavour from the lightly caramelized milk solids, which are filtered out before use.

— Also commonly used in cooking is Browned Butter (below), known in French as *beurre noisette* ("hazelnut butter"), which describes the nutty flavour it develops. Here the caramelization of milk solids is taken even further, until they begin to brown on the bottom of the pan and the remaining liquid butter takes on a beige hue. It is often used in cakes and sauces, over fish or pasta—even in ice cream.

— Try making butter at home, a fun project to try with kids. You may have already made butter accidentally by overwhipping cream. Simply beat 1 cup (250ml) or more heavy cream in a large bowl using a handheld mixer on high speed. Once the cream reaches the stiff peak stage, keep beating until you see a yellow mass form on the beaters with a pool of liquid beneath. Squeeze in cheesecloth or a paper towel to remove as much liquid as possible (this step is important because the liquid will otherwise cause your butter to spoil quite quickly). Use as is or knead in a bit of sea salt to taste.

Quick Recipes

Clarified Butter: Place your butter in a small pot and melt very slowly over low heat, until the milk solids sink to the bottom and foam forms on the top. Skim off the foam and gently strain the butter through a fine sieve or cheesecloth to separate the liquid butter fat from the milk solids.

Browned Butter: In a small pot, deep enough to allow the butter to bubble up, melt the butter over medium-low heat. Watch it carefully; after a good 5 minutes, the milk solids will rise to the top. When these solids begin to brown, carefully move them aside with a spoon to see whether the butter has started to darken. When it has taken on a deep golden colour, remove from the heat. Let cool slightly, then strain through a fine sieve or cheesecloth to remove the browned milk solids. Try out the browned butter in recipes like the vinaigrette on page 64. It's also a treat drizzled over popcorn.

Hollandaise Sauce: An old-school favourite that still holds up, hollandaise can be used over freshly steamed asparagus, a fillet of fish, or a poached egg for eggs Benedict. It can be made by hand, but it is far easier to whip up in a blender. For the smoothest sauce, use clarified butter.

In a small saucepan, melt ½ cup (1 stick/110g) unsalted butter (clarified or regular) over medium heat, and heat until bubbling. Place 3 egg yolks, a large pinch of salt and 2 tablespoons fresh lemon juice in a blender and blend on high speed. With the machine running, pour in the hot butter, starting with a few drops at a time to create an emulsion, then gradually streaming in the rest until you have a creamy sauce. Use immediately or transfer to a bowl set over another bowl of hot (not boiling!) water. Do not overheat the sauce or it will separate. To maintain the sauce's pale yellow colour, season with white pepper instead of black. To add an extra bit of pep, sprinkle cayenne or paprika over the hollandaise after pouring.

Compound Butters

Fats are a great transporter of flavour, and butter works well at dispersing all sorts of tastes throughout a dish. A great way to take advantage of butter's flavour-delivery abilities is to make compound butter, simply butter to which other ingredients have been added. The additions can vary from herbs to onions, even sugar and spice. Here are a few of my favourite compound butters—feel free to play around with the mixes to make your own signature butter. Also, consider doubling the recipe for any of these butters, as the extra portion can be rolled into a cylinder and frozen for later use.

Escargot Butter: This is the butter traditionally used to top snails when making *escargots à la bourguignonne*, but it's also great on grilled steak, fish, or vegetables. It's also the butter I use to make garlic bread. Just slice a baguette in half lengthwise, spread the butter on thickly, and broil until golden.

Beat ½ cup (1 stick/110g) room-temperature unsalted butter until creamy, then add 2 tablespoons chopped fresh parsley, 1 minced large garlic clove, 1 tablespoon fresh lemon juice, ¼ teaspoon salt, and a few turns of the pepper mill of black pepper.

Kiev Butter: Make Escargot Butter as directed, but substitute chopped fresh dill for half the parsley.

Béarnaise Butter: In a small saucepan, sauté 2 tablespoons finely chopped shallot in 2 teaspoons butter over medium heat. When the shallots have softened (but before they brown), add 1 tablespoon white wine vinegar and stir until the shallots have absorbed the vinegar. Remove from the heat and let cool.

Beat ½ cup (1 stick/110g) room-temperature unsalted butter until creamy, then add the cooled shallots, 2 tablespoons chopped fresh tarragon leaves, ¼ teaspoon salt, and a few turns of the pepper mill of black pepper.

Mushroom Butter: I like this butter added to a plain risotto or most any pasta, or on grilled meats. It can also be used to add a jolt of flavour to mushroom soup or a dish of sautéed mushroom caps.

Soak ½ cup (10g) dried porcini mushrooms in a cup of warm water until softened through, about 30 minutes. Remove the mushrooms and squeeze out any liquid. Finely chop. Melt 1 tablespoon butter in a small skillet over medium heat and fry up 2 teaspoons minced garlic (about 1 large clove) for 30 seconds, then add the mushrooms. Sauté until they release some liquid, then remove from the heat and let cool to room temperature.

Beat ½ cup (1 stick/110g) room-temperature unsalted butter until creamy, then add the mushroom mix in small bits at a time, followed by 1 teaspoon fresh lemon juice, ¼ teaspoon salt, and a few turns of the pepper mill of black pepper. Truffle oil haters can abstain, but to boost the mushroom flavour, I like to add a few drops of truffle oil to this butter, but no more or it will take over.

Pumpkin Pie Spiced Butter: I hate to jump on the crowded pumpkin pie spice bandwagon, but this butter is just so great at adding a pleasant autumnal sweetness to a simple scone, muffin, or toasted slice of baguette.

Beat ½ cup (1 stick/110g) room-temperature unsalted butter until creamy, then blend in ½ teaspoon ground cinnamon, ¼ teaspoon grated nutmeg, ¼ teaspoon ground ginger, ¼ teaspoon ground allspice, a pinch of ground cloves, and 1 tablespoon brown sugar.

Suzette Butter: Drop a couple of tablespoons of this butter in a hot pan, add one crêpe at a time, turn it over and then fold into quarters. Serve about 3 crepes per person, and you're looking at quite the posh dessert. This butter's also delicious spread on French toast, pancakes, or any breakfast bread.

Beat ½ cup (1 stick/110g) room-temperature unsalted butter until creamy, then add a pinch of salt, ⅓ cup (45g) icing sugar, and 1 tablespoon finely grated orange zest. Drizzle in ¼ cup (60ml) fresh orange juice and 1 tablespoon Grand Marnier (or other orange liqueur), cognac, or brandy.

To store compound butters: Spoon the compound butter into the center of a large sheet of parchment paper, wax paper, or plastic wrap, forming a log about 1½ inches (4cm) in diameter. Fold the wrap over the butter and gently push in and under to form a smooth cylinder. Twist the ends to seal and refrigerate until firm, about 1 hour, before use. The wrapped butter can be refrigerated for up to 1 week or frozen for up to 1 month.

BROWN BUTTER VINAIGRETTE

MAKES ABOUT ½ CUP (125ML)

This elegant and nutty dressing is not for everyone or every salad, but it's hard to beat drizzled over white asparagus or bitter salad greens like endives or a peppery mesclun mix. It's also great on roasted carrots, parsnips, and potatoes, or try it on delicate white-fleshed fish like cod, halibut, or sole.

½ cup (1 stick/110g) unsalted butter

1 small shallot, minced

2 tablespoons fresh lemon juice

Fine sea salt and freshly ground black pepper

¼ cup chopped fresh parsley

• Following the instructions on page 57, brown the butter, then strain it into a bowl over the shallot and whisk well. When warm, add the lemon juice and season with salt and pepper. Use as desired, and be sure to top whatever you drizzled it over with some parsley, which adds a welcome bitter taste to cut the richness of the butter. Refrigerate any leftover vinaigrette; reheat it slightly before using to make it pourable.

BÉARNAISE SAUCE

MAKES ABOUT ½ CUP (125ML)

This is the classic Béarnaise, an emulsified butter sauce that can be used on a myriad of dishes from meats to vegetables but is especially wonderful with a côte de boeuf (see page 240). Purists strain the sauce, but you can certainly skip that step if you don't mind the shallots in there. If you are at all nervous about making this sauce over high heat, transfer the shallot-vinegar mix to a heatproof bowl, place it over a pot of simmering water and follow the rest of the instructions. This all but guarantees your sauce will not overheat and split, but if it does, you can quickly whisk in a few tablespoons of cold water to try to save it. And if you're too late, serve it anyway—it won't look great, but it will still taste good.

2 tablespoons minced French shallot

3 tablespoons white wine vinegar

Fine sea salt and freshly ground black pepper

½ teaspoon dried tarragon

2 large egg yolks

1 tablespoon fresh lemon juice

½ cup (1 stick/110g) unsalted butter, cut into cubes, at room temperature

2 tablespoons finely chopped fresh tarragon

• Place the shallot and vinegar in a small saucepan. Add a pinch each of salt and pepper and cook over medium heat until the vinegar has almost completely evaporated, 3 to 4 minutes. Reduce the heat to low and whisk in a tablespoon of water along with the dried tarragon, followed by the egg yolks and lemon juice. When the sauce begins to thicken slightly, begin adding the butter in increments, whisking vigorously after each addition. Continue whisking in the butter until it's all incorporated, being sure to remove the pot from the heat if the mixture comes close to a boil, then whisk until a smooth, creamy sauce forms, 2 to 3 minutes. Strain the sauce into a small bowl, stir in the fresh tarragon and season to taste with salt, pepper, and a touch more lemon, if desired. Use immediately or keep in a warm place for about 10 minutes until ready to serve.

NO-FUSS CHICKEN KIEV

SERVES 4

Chicken Kiev was my Ukrainian grandmother's favourite dish, and she was extremely particular about its makeup. The star ingredient of a proper chicken Kiev is dill, and the chicken breast must be pounded and rolled around a knob of cold butter, which should (fingers crossed) explode out when the crisp chicken ball is pierced. My first intention was to include the authentic recipe, but as it's quite fiddly to make, I've come up with a plan B, a sort of chicken schnitzel topped with Kiev Butter. Of course, you'll be missing out on the butter volcano, but the taste will be just as good, and your stress level will be significantly diminished. I like this served with rice, but mashed potatoes or boiled egg noodles also do well at absorbing all that dilly butter.

4 chicken breasts, about 6 ounces (180g) each

Fine sea salt and freshly ground black pepper

1 recipe Kiev Butter (page 62), chilled

1 cup (140g) all-purpose flour

3 large eggs, beaten

2 cups bread crumbs, panko bread crumbs, or a combination

½ teaspoon cayenne pepper

Oil, such as peanut, canola, or sunflower, for frying

Dill sprigs, for serving

Lemon wedges, for serving

- Remove the inner filet from each chicken breast and set aside. Slice each chicken breast in half (it can be horizontally or vertically, whichever you're most comfortable with). Place each chicken breast and filet between two sheets of plastic wrap, and using a mallet, pound them until they reach an even ¼-inch (6mm) thickness. Season with salt and pepper and transfer to a large plate and refrigerate. Cut the chilled Kiev butter into ¼-inch-thick (6mm) rounds.

- **Prepare your frying trio:** place the flour on one plate, the eggs in a shallow bowl next to it, and the bread crumbs on another plate next to that. Season the flour by blending in about a teaspoon of salt and the cayenne (you can do this with your fingers) then dredge each piece of chicken in the flour to cover all the surfaces. Next, dip into the egg mixture, and finally dredge the chicken pieces in the bread crumbs, pushing them well into the mix to get a good, even coating. Shake off any excess crumbs and refrigerate the paillards for at least 20 minutes before frying (the chicken can be prepared up to this point a few hours in advance).

- Preheat the oven to 300°F (150°C).

- Pour enough oil into a large, deep skillet for a shallow fry (about ½ inch/1½cm) and heat over medium-high heat. When the oil is hot but not smoking (aim for about 325°F/163°C if using a thermometer), add the chicken breasts and fry, turning over after about 2 minutes, until they are a nice golden colour. Do not overcrowd the pan so the temperature remains constant and the chicken cooks evenly. Using tongs, transfer the chicken to a plate lined with paper towels to absorb any excess oil. If not serving immediately, place in a warm oven until ready to serve.

- To serve, place the hot chicken paillards in an even layer on a serving platter. Arrange a few rounds of the butter over each (I place at least two rounds per piece) and then scatter generously with dill springs. Do not be stingy with the dill—it makes all the difference. Right before serving, squeeze lemon juice over the chicken or, better yet, pass lemon wedges at the table and let the guests do it themselves.

MAPLE AND PECAN SHORTBREADS

MAKES ABOUT 48 COOKIES

Yes, maple sugar is pricey, but this recipe is hard to beat, and I seem to have an abundance of it in my pantry (always saving it for a special occasion). Feel free to substitute granulated sugar for the maple sugar, resulting in equally delicious pecan shortbread.

1 cup (2 sticks/225g) unsalted butter, at room temperature

⅔ cup (110g) maple sugar

¼ cup (50g) brown sugar

2 teaspoons vanilla extract

½ teaspoon fine sea salt

¼ cup (30g) cornstarch

1½ cups (210g) all-purpose flour

1½ cups (165g) pecans, coarsely chopped

1 egg, for egg wash

About ½ cup (100g) turbinado or raw sugar

- In the bowl of a stand mixer fitted with the paddle attachment, or in a large bowl using a handheld mixer, cream the butter, maple sugar, brown sugar, vanilla, and salt until very fluffy and smooth. Scrape down the sides of the bowl. Add the cornstarch and flour all at once and mix just until it forms a dough, then add the pecans. Turn the dough out onto a clean work surface and knead lightly until smooth. Divide the dough into two pieces and roll each into a 12-inch-long (30cm) log. Roll each log onto a sheet of parchment paper and use the paper (folded over) to help shape the dough, trying to get it into as even a cylinder as possible. Refrigerate to harden, at least 3 hours. (At this point, the logs of dough can be wrapped well and frozen for later use.)

- Remove the dough from the refrigerator about 20 minutes before slicing and preheat the oven to 375°F (190°C). Place the oven rack in the middle position. Line several baking sheets with parchment paper.

- In a small bowl, whisk the egg until smooth and pour the turbinado sugar onto a square plate or bread mould. Using a pastry brush and working with one log at a time, brush the entire surface of each log with the whisked egg and then roll it in the sugar. Transfer the logs to a cutting board and, using a sharp knife, slice into ½-inch-thick (1.5cm) rounds. You should get about 24 slices per log. Transfer the rounds to the prepared baking sheets, placing them a few inches apart. Bake for 15 to 18 minutes, until they are deep golden brown. Transfer to a wire rack to cool.

SALTED BUTTER CARAMEL SAUCE

MAKES 1½ CUPS (375ML)

This universally loved sauce is easy to make and just the thing drizzled over ice cream, a fruit crumble, or a lemon tart, or enjoyed straight from the jar. Feel free to play with the flavourings, too, adding lime zest or orange zest, half a vanilla bean, or a teaspoon of instant espresso powder to the cream. You can even add up to ¼ cup (50ml) of alcohol, be it Cointreau, kirsch, rum, or even bourbon. As caramel is blisteringly hot, this is not a good recipe to make with children.

¾ cup (150g) sugar

¼ cup (85g) white corn syrup

1 cup (225ml) whipping cream

4 tablespoons (½ stick/55g) salted butter, cut into pieces

Fine sea salt

- Rinse a thick-bottomed medium pot, but don't dry it. Add the sugar and corn syrup. Place over medium-high heat and whisk just to combine, then allow to bubble away, untouched. Meanwhile, in a small pot, bring the cream to a boil, then turn off the heat and set aside.

- When the sugar is fully melted and begins to colour around the edges, start to lightly swirl the syrup as it bubbles away until it becomes an even golden brown, about 4 minutes. Now watch the mixture carefully. As soon as it releases a first burst of smoke, turn off the heat and whisk in half the cream. Add the remaining cream and then whisk in the butter. When all the butter is melted, turn the heat back on to high, bring the sauce to a rolling boil and boil for about 30 seconds (it should reach 222°F/106°C on a candy thermometer, but you really don't have to bother). Remove from the heat and strain the caramel into a clean jar. Let cool, then add a pinch of salt; taste and add more if you'd like it saltier (don't add too much or you'll ruin the caramel sauce). Cover and keep refrigerated until ready to use. The sauce will solidify when cold, so reheat it on the stove or in the microwave to reach a pourable consistency.

CHOCOLATE CHIP COOKIES

MAKES THIRTY 2½-INCH (5CM) COOKIES OR FIFTEEN 4-INCH (10CM) COOKIES

The key ingredient in the best chocolate chip cookies is butter, and this recipe is no exception. I wanted to have a chocolate chip cookie recipe in this chapter, but I dislike so many of them, finding them either too greasy, half-baked, or overwhelmed with too much chocolate or salt. After consulting several pastry chefs and testing a dozen recipes, I came up with one that made me fall in love with this classic cookie all over again. When baking my last batch, I sent my kids out to get more chocolate chips, and to my dismay they brought back the mini kind. But the results were so good that I now recommend them over standard chips any day.

1½ cups (210g) all-purpose flour

½ teaspoon baking powder

½ teaspoon baking soda

¼ teaspoon fine sea salt

½ cup (1 stick/110g) unsalted butter, at room temperature

⅓ cup (75g) brown sugar

½ cup (100g) granulated sugar

1 large egg

1 teaspoon vanilla extract

1½ cups (240g) mini chocolate chips or regular chocolate chips

- In a small bowl, whisk together the flour, baking powder, baking soda, and salt. Set aside.

- In the bowl of a stand mixer fitted with the paddle attachment, or in a large bowl using a handheld mixer, beat together the butter and both sugars on high speed until creamy. Add the egg and vanilla and beat until light and creamy, about 3 minutes. Blend in the dry ingredients on low speed, beating just until the flour disappears, then add the chocolate chips and mix just to combine. Do not overwork the dough.

- Using a 2-inch-diameter (5cm) ice cream scoop for smaller cookies or a 4-inch (10cm) scoop for larger ones (or just use two spoons), portion the dough into balls (30 balls for regular cookies or 15 for larger ones), placing them on a tray as you go, and refrigerate for 30 minutes.

- After 20 minutes, preheat the oven to 350°F (180°C). Line two baking sheets with parchment paper.

- Place the dough balls on the prepared baking sheets, leaving a few inches between each, and bake for 12 to 15 minutes, until they just begin to colour around the edges. Let cool on a wire rack before eating.

* **Note:** You can also freeze the dough once it is portioned out. Just be sure to defrost the cookies on the baking sheets at room temperature for about 20 minutes before baking.

VARIATIONS

- **For double chocolate cookies:** Reduce the flour to 1¼ cups (175g) and sift together with ¼ cup (25g) unsweetened cocoa powder. Increase the amount of brown sugar to ½ cup (100g) and instead of chocolate chips, add ¾ cup (150g) chopped bittersweet chocolate. *Makes 30 regular or 15 large cookies*

- **For oatmeal chocolate chip cookies:** Reduce the flour to 1 cup (140g), reduce the brown sugar to ¼ cup (50g) and add ⅔ cup (70g) rolled oats along with the dry ingredients. *Makes 30 regular or 15 large cookies*

SOUPS AND STOCKS:
THE SOUL OF THE KITCHEN

SOUPS AND STOCKS:
THE SOUL OF THE KITCHEN

Making homemade stock is a lot of work. You will be chopping, sautéing, skimming, straining, and storing. You will need lots of bones, a mound of vegetables, and plenty of fresh herbs, as well a massive stockpot to cook it in and containers in which to store it. Ouf! Why go to all the trouble? Why not just buy powdered stock or bouillon cubes? The answer: flavour. An authentic homemade stock, made by simmering bones, vegetables, and seasonings in water, is the base for soups, sauces, stews, gravies, and rice dishes. French chefs refer to a stock as a *fond*, which means foundation. The success of a simple onion soup depends entirely on its richly flavoured veal, beef, or chicken stock. Bland Arborio rice needs an excellent stock to transform it into an elegant risotto. And meats braised in stock result in stews with rich flavours and silky textures. Commercial powdered bouillons produce stocks that taste harsh and salty by comparison.

Homemade stock is also inexpensive. Call your butcher ahead of time to ask for any available bones. The charge is minimal, and many friendly butchers have given me bones free of charge. Once your stock is done, you can fill your freezer for the months to come, then pull out this veritable liquid gold next time you want to whip up a soup, risotto, or so much more.

Good to Know . . .

— A large, tall stockpot will allow you to make plenty of stock at once and keep evaporation to a minimum. It will eliminate the need to add water throughout the cooking process. Some evaporation is required, so the pot should be kept uncovered.

— Don't make stock with a mixture of many kinds of bones. You will end up with a stock with no distinct flavour.

— Use cold water to cover the bones. When the water is brought to a boil, the gradual heat will solidify the impurities and aid in extracting the flavours.

— Clarity is the hallmark of a good stock. Stocks will become cloudy when brought to a rolling boil. A slow bubbling is adequate. Avoid stirring and skim the surface often while the stock is simmering. If it does become cloudy, don't worry; it's still perfectly delicious, just not aesthetically ideal.

— Always wrap herbs and other seasonings in cheesecloth or a coffee filter to make a bouquet garni; otherwise, the herbs will break up and cloud the stock. Use whole peppercorns in the bouquet garni, since ground pepper can turn bitter over long cooking periods.

— Never add salt. When salted stock is added to a soup, concentrated into a sauce, or stirred into a risotto, the resulting dish could end up being too salty. Keep in mind that stock is a component of a dish, not a soup.

— When your stock is finished cooking, taste it, being careful to avoid the layer of fat on the top. If the flavour is weak, reduce the stock further until it's more concentrated and flavorful.

— Never use freshly made stock directly from the pot. It must be degreased first by either skimming off the hot fat or, preferably, chilling the stock for 24 hours and removing the layer of fat that rises to the top.

— Never refrigerate hot stock. Cool it to room temperature first. You can speed up the cooling process by setting bowls of hot stock in a sink full of cold water. Never cover warm stock. Covering will slow down the cooling process.

— Stock should be refrigerated for no more than a few days. If refrigerated stock begins to bubble, throw it out immediately. Stock can be frozen for several months, but it should be defrosted in the refrigerator and brought to a boil before use.

— If you see a recipe that calls for "brown" chicken stock, the only difference is that the chicken bones and vegetables were roasted in the oven first. Brown stock is more deeply flavoured and dark golden in colour.

— Once you've mastered chicken stock, try others, like veal stock, fish stock, brown chicken stock, or vegetable stock.

CHICKEN STOCK

MAKES ABOUT 24 CUPS (6L)

Chicken stock is a good project for beginners because it's simple to make and it's the stock you'll probably use most in everything from soup to sauce to risotto. It's also a lighter alternative to beef stock for onion soup (see page 125). If you don't have a large stockpot, you can halve the recipe.

About 5 pounds (2.3kg) raw chicken carcasses, backs, wings, or necks

3 celery stalks, chopped

1 medium leek, washed and chopped

5 large carrots, chopped

1 large yellow onion, chopped

8 ounces (250g) white mushrooms, cleaned and quartered

½ head garlic, sliced in half horizontally

Small handful of thyme sprigs

Large handful of fresh parsley

2 bay leaves

1 teaspoon whole black peppercorns

- Place the chicken carcasses in a large stockpot and add enough cold water to cover. Bring to a boil, skimming off any impurities (scum) that rise to the surface. Add the celery, leek, carrots, onion, mushrooms, and garlic and bring to a boil again, then immediately reduce the heat to the slowest of simmers. Skim again.

- **Prepare the bouquet garni:** Wrap the thyme sprigs, parsley, bay leaves, and peppercorns in a small piece of cheesecloth or a paper coffee filter, and secure tightly with kitchen string. Add the bouquet garni to the pot.

- Simmer, skimming the top occasionally, for 4 hours. Remove from the heat and let cool slightly, about 15 minutes. Strain the stock through a fine sieve into a large bowl (or several bowls) and let cool to room temperature, then cover and refrigerate overnight. The next day, remove the layer of solidified fat from the top of the stock (this can be kept to make rendered chicken fat). The stock can be used right away, or poured into containers and refrigerated for up to 2 days or frozen for up to 3 months.

VEGETABLE STOCK

MAKES ABOUT 8 CUPS (2L)

The secret to making vegetable stock with pizzazz is to brown the vegetables before adding the water. When it comes to quantities, feel free to add more vegetables if you're looking to clean out your fridge—just avoid strong vegetables like cabbage, turnips, rutabaga, or squash.

2 tablespoons vegetable oil or olive oil

2 medium onions, quartered

4 large carrots, cut into 1-inch (2.5cm) pieces

4 celery stalks, cut into 1-inch (2.5cm) pieces

1 large leek, washed and cut into 1-inch-thick (2.5cm) pieces

8 ounces (250g) white mushrooms, cleaned and quartered

1 head garlic, sliced in half horizontally

2 teaspoons whole black peppercorns

½ teaspoon whole allspice berries

Handful of fresh parsley

A few sprigs of fresh thyme

1 bay leaf

Fine sea salt

- In a large stockpot, heat the oil over medium heat. Add the onions, carrots, celery, leek, mushrooms, and garlic and sauté until they begin to brown (do not let them burn, or your stock will be bitter). Wrap the peppercorns, allspice, parsley, thyme, and bay leaf in a square of cheesecloth or a paper coffee filter and secure tightly with kitchen string to make a bouquet garni. Add the bouquet garni to the pot. Add about 12 cups (3 liters) cold water and bring to a boil, then reduce the heat to maintain a simmer. Cook, uncovered, for a good hour, occasionally skimming off any scum or foam that accumulates on the surface.

- Strain the stock through a colander lined with cheesecloth into a clean container, then press down on the vegetables with the back of a spoon to squeeze out any remaining liquid. (You can discard the vegetables.) Season to taste with salt. Let the stock cool to room temperature, then refrigerate or freeze until needed.

MUSHROOM SOUP

SERVES 4

This elegant mushroom soup is sophisticated enough to serve at a dinner party yet simple enough to enjoy solo on a winter afternoon.

¼ cup (7g) dried porcini or other wild mushroom mix

4 tablespoons (½ stick/55g) unsalted butter, divided

1 medium yellow onion, chopped

Fine sea salt and freshly ground black pepper

1 teaspoon fresh thyme, or ½ teaspoon dried

1 pound (450g) button mushrooms, cleaned

2 small or 1 large garlic clove(s), finely chopped

2 tablespoons all-purpose flour

3 cups (750ml) Chicken Stock (page 82) or Vegetable Stock (page 84)

¼ cup (60ml) whipping cream (optional)

2 tablespoons chopped fresh parsley or chives

A few drops of truffle oil (optional)

- Place the porcini in a small bowl and pour over 1 cup (250ml) warm water. Leave to soak.

- In a medium saucepan, melt 3 tablespoons of the butter over medium heat, and when it froths, add the onion, a pinch of salt, a little pepper, and the thyme. Cook, stirring from time to time, until the onion is softened but not browned. Meanwhile, set 6 large mushrooms aside, slice the rest, then add them to the pan and fry over high heat until they release their liquid.

- Being careful to keep the soaking water, drain the rehydrated dry mushrooms, coarsely chop, and add them to the pan along with the garlic. Continue to sauté the mixture over high heat for a couple of minutes, then add the flour. Fry it all together a minute more, then gradually stir in the porcini liquid (avoiding any sediment), followed by the stock. Bring to a boil, stir, then lower the heat and let simmer for 25 to 30 minutes.

- While it's cooking, slice the reserved mushrooms into thick slices and sauté them in a small pan with the remaining tablespoon of butter over high heat until browned. Set aside.

- To finish the soup, puree the hot mixture in a blender (or with an immersion blender), then return it to the pot and stir in the cream, if desired. Bring to a boil, then remove from the heat.

- Ladle the soup into bowls and serve, garnished with the sautéed mushrooms and parsley or chives.

JEAN'S MINESTRONE

SERVES 6

Every time I ask my boyfriend, Jean, what he would like for dinner, he answers, "How about something light, like a minestrone?" I nod, and then go off and make a cream-sauce pasta. It's kind of a running joke around here. Anyway, here is a minestrone for all the light eaters out there. Minestrone is really just a simple vegetable soup, but what makes all the difference is the quality of the olive oil and cheese you add at the end. You can also add in a spoonful of Pesto (page 157). Guess my version isn't all that light after all!

2 tablespoons olive oil

1 large celery stalk, diced

1 medium onion, finely chopped

2 carrots, diced

1 garlic clove, crushed

3 tablespoons chopped fresh parsley

1 bay leaf

1 (14-ounce/398ml) can or container chopped tomatoes, drained

8 cups (2L) Chicken Stock (page 82) or Vegetable Stock (page 84)

1 (14-ounce/398ml) can or jar borlotti or cannellini beans, drained and rinsed

$\longrightarrow$

- In a large saucepan, heat the olive oil over medium-low heat. Add the celery, onion, carrots, and garlic. Cook until golden, about 5 minutes.

- Add the parsley, bay leaf, tomatoes, stock, and beans, and slowly bring to a simmer. Reduce the heat slightly and simmer for 45 minutes to an hour, adding a little boiling water if needed every so often to maintain a soupy consistency.

⅔ cup (90g) uncooked short pasta (like macaroni or ditalini)

About 4 large handfuls of fresh spinach, leaves stemmed

Fine sea salt and freshly ground black pepper

Extra-virgin olive oil

Freshly grated Parmesan cheese or fresh pesto, for serving

- Add the pasta and simmer for about 6 minutes more. Stir in the spinach and remove from the heat, season with salt and pepper and let rest for 10 minutes. Serve warm, with a drizzle of your best olive oil and a handful of grated Parmesan or, if you have some handy, a spoonful of fresh pesto.

CHEDDAR VEGETABLE SOUP

SERVES 6 AS A MAIN COURSE OR 8 AS AN APPETIZER

I updated this soup from a vintage Gourmet *magazine recipe. The inclusion of flour as a thickener and the large amount of cheese added at the end might give pause to those of you looking for something light. While making it, you also might be worried that it looks a bit grey and murky. But when you stir in the cheese at the end, it all brightens up and comes together. I like to serve this for a family-dinner main course, but it's sophisticated enough to serve for guests. If you use vegetable stock, it's a good option for vegetarians, too.*

2 zucchini

3 tablespoons vegetable oil, plus more as needed for rubbing

1 large onion, chopped

1 large red bell pepper

1 pound (450g) small new potatoes, preferably red-skinned, scrubbed and quartered

2 cups (about 280g) fresh corn kernels (from 3 large ears)

⅓ cup (45g) all-purpose flour

4 cups (1L) Chicken Stock (page 82) or Vegetable Stock (page 84)

2 cups (500ml) milk

⅛ teaspoon cayenne pepper, or to taste

→

- Top and tail the zucchini, slice them each lengthwise into 3 strips, rub lightly with oil, season with salt and black pepper and grill on a grill pan until golden. Let cool, then slice into 1-inch (3cm) pieces and set aside.

- Place the bell pepper on a gas flame or under the broiler to roast, then wrap in a paper towel and let cool. When cool, rub off the skin, discard the seeds, and cut the flesh into ¼-inch (6mm) strips.

- In a large, heavy saucepan or Dutch oven, sauté the onion in the 3 tablespoons oil over medium heat until it softens, about 5 minutes. Stir in the potatoes and corn and cook for another 3 minutes, stirring gently. Add the flour and cook for another 3 minutes. Slowly add the stock in a stream, stirring continuously, followed by the milk, the roasted pepper, and cayenne. Season with salt and black pepper to taste. Bring the mixture to a boil, then reduce the heat to maintain a simmer and cook until the potatoes are tender and the broth has thickened.

Fine sea salt and freshly
ground black pepper

2½ cups (about 280g)
grated extra-sharp Cheddar
cheese

- If you are not serving the soup immediately, cover and set aside.

- When ready to serve, bring the soup back to a boil and gradually stir in the Cheddar, adding it in about five batches and stirring well after each addition until melted. Do not let the soup come back to a boil, or the cheese will separate. Serve immediately, with the grilled zucchini pieces spooned over the top.

* **Note:** If reheating leftovers, be sure not to bring the soup to a boil or it will separate.

How to Keep Food Waste at Bay

It is estimated that 32 percent of the world's food is wasted; that's 109 million tons annually in North America, or about 650 pounds (296kg) per person. With numbers this startling, the question is begged, how can this be?

Well, consider this: As consumers, we have become unrealistically demanding, reaching for the most perfectly shaped fruit, the luxury cuts of meat, the freshest everything. Food is a large expense in most of our lives, and with high prices come high expectations of quality. Understandable, but this relentless pursuit of produce perfection has made us shun anything overripe, unpopular (like offal), or anywhere near its expiry date. If we grew our own vegetables and raised our own animals, we would be hard-pressed to throw out that chicken neck or those browning green beans. If we made the processed foods we buy at home, we would think twice about tossing them so easily. Because we have so little invested in what we eat (besides money), we don't think twice about letting the bread go mouldy, the lemons get soft, the lettuce wilt, the ham rot, and the nuts go rancid. Instead, we pile it into our already heaving landfills—and not only that food we could have eaten, but all the plastic wrapped around it. Out of sight, out of mind.

We all waste too much food. If you don't, bravo! For the rest of us, here are some tips to avoiding food waste in our kitchens:

— **Yes, that best-before date is important,** but your nose and taste buds are equally effective in determining if a food is still good. Unless the product is visibly rotten, take a good whiff and then a small taste to judge whether the food is truly "off." Human beings have an incredible capacity to judge whether they will be poisoned, so if the food tastes awful or fizzes on your tongue, chances are, it's done. Just don't automatically throw it away because the "best before" date tells you to.

— **Think like a chef!** Before you throw out anything, consider whether it can be used again. Okay, you don't have to candy all your orange peels, but why not keep an empty carton of milk in the freezer and use it to store bits of carrot, leek tops, celery leaves, onion trimmings, or any herbs you can use later to flavour your stocks? And for those black bananas? Banana bread! Sour milk? Pancakes! Parmesan rinds? Soup! Egg whites? Pavlova! Roast leftovers? Pasta sauce! Soft vegetables? Vegetarian lasagna!

— **Take a tour of your fridge daily.** Ideally, your fridge should be kept as empty as possible, instead of turning into a storage container for long-lost condiments and yogurt containers. Rotate your stock of perishables, placing all the newer containers behind the older ones. Have a good look at the state of everything in there. It's a shame to find a package of rotting whatever that you can't recall even buying.

— **Consider investing in a freezer for storing extras** like bread, meat, bacon, stocks, soups, cheese, spaghetti sauce, and more. Just don't let your freezer turn into a dumpster for leftovers like that half-eaten tourtière you shoved in there last Christmas.

— **Go grocery shopping often** instead of filling up your fridge once a week with items that will perish before you get to them, and purchase items with a short shelf life—like meat, herbs, and delicate greens—on the day you need them. And when you go shopping, never arrive at the store hungry, or chances are, you'll buy double what you need.

— **At restaurants, ask for a doggy bag**—even for bread. You paid for that food, so don't be afraid to ask to take it home for tomorrow's lunch.

— **Dry bread?** Croutons! Not just for your Caesar salad, but sliced in rounds and toasted to serve with cheese or pâté. If it's too hard to slice, pop it in the microwave for 20 seconds to soften it up. Pulverize especially dry bread in a food processor or blender to make crumbs to use for breading in dishes like No-Fuss Chicken Kiev (page 68), or sauté in butter until crisp and use as a topping for vegetable gratins or white-sauce pastas.

— **Plan your meals.** If you are the planning type, you can plan your meals in advance and shop for exactly what you need each week or every few days. That way, everything in your fridge corresponds to a dish you have a recipe for in advance. I admire people who do this, though I cannot say I am always that disciplined.

— **Pamper your herbs:** I use herbs endlessly in summer, so I prefer to grow as many as I can in a large pot by my back door. In the winter, I buy the potted herbs sold in my supermarket instead of loose herbs, the best being thyme and basil. If you take care of them, they will grow new shoots and last for months. I even transplant them into bigger pots, especially in summer, when smaller pots dry out quickly in the sun.

— **Develop a relationship with your food.** Grow anything you can (cherry tomatoes and herbs can easily be grown on an apartment balcony), purchase your meat directly from a farmer, or look into receiving boxes of produce from an organic farm in your area. Once you feel more tied to your food, you'll have a much tougher time tossing it out.

SALADS AND VINAIGRETTES: MASTERING SIMPLICITY

SALADS AND VINAIGRETTES: MASTERING SIMPLICITY

When I was a kid, salad meant chopped iceberg lettuce and cucumbers doused in commercial salad dressing. As awful as that sounds, I loved it. The crunch of the lettuce, the refreshing bitterness of the cucumber skin, the jolt of acidity and saltiness from the dressing . . . such a treat. Time went on, and so did the trends: I remember the early Caesar salads, blanketed in thick dressing with dusty croutons and Day-Glo bacon bits. In contrast came spinach salads laden with raisins and pecans and chunky Greek salads crowned with blocks of feta. Somewhere along the way, salads took a turn for the sweet, with raspberry vinegar and orange segments mixed into this new mix of greens called mesclun. Meanwhile, balsamic vinegar was being drizzled over everything and extra-virgin olive oil replaced all those flavourless oils of the past. Arugula tossed with Parmesan curls was *the* Italian restaurant appetizer. A decade later, good luck finding a restaurant that didn't feature some form of the beet-and-goat-cheese duo.

Still, I love a good salad, be it a deconstructed *salade niçoise* or a grain bowl filled with lentils and quinoa. Truth be told, though, the vast majority of salads are dreary. This is especially true in restaurants, where salad is too often an afterthought. I still recall my cooking school teacher telling the class, "Undressed lettuce is for rabbits!" So true. Worse yet are salads made with commercial mesclun mix so insipid it makes me long for the iceberg of my youth. As salads are the backbone of their business, vegetarian and vegan restaurants are the exception, but even then you can hit some duds. And that's a shame, because salads aren't just healthy (generally speaking . . .) but a great opportunity to enjoy a multitude of textures and flavours in one dish.

Not only is the dressing key, but the base ingredients—from greens to chopped parsley—must be vibrant and handled with care. The same rule of thumb applies for any add-ins, be they croutons, nuts, cheese, or sprouts. Also, be mindful not only of what you put in, but how much. Proportions can make or break a salad. As salad is generally an inexpensive dish, it's worth spending extra for quality condiments, starting with a single-estate extra-virgin olive oil, a fancier wine vinegar (try a potent sherry vinegar or delicate champagne vinegar), as well as an IGP (Indicazione Geografica Protetta, or Protected Geographical Indication) balsamic vinegar of Modena. Before you know it, your pantry will be filling up with specialty items like white balsamic, cold-pressed sunflower oil, tarragon vinegar, and French walnut oil . . . Let the experimentation begin!

Good to Know . . .

— Avoid purchasing bagged salads. Not only are they more expensive than heads of lettuce, but the greens in the bag are also picked at different times, which means some leaves will rot faster than others and affect the taste of the entire mix.

— When washing lettuce, fill the sink or a large bowl with very cold water. Slice off the core, separate the leaves and plunge them into the water. Let them sit for about 10 minutes, then lift out the leaves, a few handfuls at a time, spin dry in a salad spinner and lay them out on a clean towel to dry completely. This method is also a good way to revive heads of lettuce that have been languishing in the crisper for a few days.

— Never refrigerate your lettuce damp or in water. Either store it in a plastic bag or, better yet, a large plastic container with a snap top with a few sheets of paper towel at the bottom. This way, the leaves stay crisp for a good week. This is also the method I use to clean and store fresh herbs.

— Once your dressing is mixed, test the seasonings using a lettuce leaf instead of your finger to gauge whether it is well-balanced and well-seasoned.

— When dressing salads, pour a few tablespoons of your dressing into the bottom of the bowl, add the salad greens, then pour dressing on top progressively and toss very well before adding any more. Salads are often over- or underdressed, and the reason for that can be that they're not tossed thoroughly.

— When dressing grain salads, be aware that the grains will absorb some of the dressing, so you might want to add two-thirds of the dressing at first and then the rest right before serving.

—

What's Blanching?

Blanching is the process of flash-cooking items in salted boiling water or steam and then quickly cooling them down to stop the cooking. This is a great technique to use when cooking vegetables in general, especially anything green to maintain the colour and al dente texture. This is the technique used for preparing vegetables for freezing or pre-cooking leafy greens like rapini or spinach. Blanching vegetables like string beans, celery root, broccoli, asparagus, cauliflower, peas, and corn is often recommended when they will be added to salads. Yes, they can be used raw, but a quick cook softens their texture for the better. Consider this technique for preparing vegetables beforehand, too. Vegetables can be blanched and kept refrigerated until ready to serve, at which point all you have to do is sauté them in a bit of hot butter or oil and season.

How to: Bring a good quantity of generously salted water to a rolling boil and prepare a bowl of ice and water. Add the vegetables to the boiling water and cook for a few minutes, or until they just begin to soften. Immediately drain the vegetables and plunge them into the ice water. Once they have cooled down completely, drain again and let air-dry or even spread them out on paper towels to speed up the operation.

BASIC VINAIGRETTE

Always work with the basic ratio of 1 part vinegar to 4 parts oil or, when using lemon, 2 parts lemon juice to 5 parts oil. With balsamic vinegar, the proportion is still 1 to 4, but if you prefer a stronger flavour, try 1 part vinegar to 3 parts oil.

Always add salt directly to the vinegar or lemon juice before adding the oil so it can dissolve.

As for the oil, it can be olive oil or a neutral oil like canola or sunflower, or a combination of both.

To boost the flavour, add some minced garlic or French shallot. A bit of Dijon mustard will add sharpness and help emulsify the mix. For a touch of sweetness, add honey or maple syrup, but sparingly. Chopped fresh parsley or chives work well in a vinaigrette, but you can also add them directly to the salad.

The easiest way to make vinaigrette is to measure out the ingredients in a jar and shake to combine. When making by hand, place the vinegar and salt in a bowl and whisk to dissolve. Add the onion, shallot, or garlic, followed by any seasonings (spices, mustard, etc.). Gradually whisk in the oil to create an emulsion and finish by adding any fresh herbs. Vinaigrette recipes can easily be doubled (or more). Any leftover vinaigrette should be kept in the fridge; if there's garlic in the mix, store it for no longer than a week.

APPLE CRANBERRY VINAIGRETTE

MAKES ABOUT ¾ CUP (180ML)

This vinaigrette adds an excellent fruity flavour to Bibb lettuce and other tender greens. Use quality fruit juice (organic, if possible) for best results, and use a nonreactive metal pot (like stainless steel) to avoid the juice taking on a metallic taste when boiled.

1 cup (250ml) apple juice

½ cup (125ml) cranberry juice

2 teaspoons apple cider vinegar

Fine sea salt and freshly ground black pepper

¼ cup (60ml) extra-virgin olive oil

- In a small saucepan over medium heat, cook the apple and cranberry juices together at a low simmer until they are reduced by two-thirds (you'll end up with about ½ cup/125ml). Let cool.

- In a jar, combine the cooled juice mixture and the vinegar, and season with salt and pepper. Cover with the lid and shake until well combined. Pour in the olive oil and shake again. Serve immediately or cover and store in the refrigerator for up to a week.

RANCH DRESSING

MAKES 1¼ CUPS (310ML)

Ranch dressing can do no wrong, it seems, and this version certainly worked wonders at getting my children to eat salad. I've included a variation with blue cheese that's ideal poured over a fat slice of iceberg lettuce and then sprinkled with bacon bits and croutons to make an old-school wedge salad. I once served that to a group of French winemakers, who practically licked their plates clean.

⅓ cup (85g) plain yogurt

⅓ cup (85g) Mayonnaise (page 34) or store-bought (see Note)

½ cup (125ml) buttermilk

1 tablespoon finely grated onion

1 small garlic clove, minced

½ teaspoon fine sea salt

Freshly ground black pepper

1 tablespoon chopped fresh chives

1 tablespoon chopped fresh dill

1 tablespoon chopped fresh parsley

• Pour the yogurt, mayonnaise, buttermilk, onion, garlic, salt, a pinch of pepper, the chives, dill, and parsley into a jar, screw on the lid, and shake to blend. Keep refrigerated for up to a week; be sure to shake well before using.

Blue cheese dressing: Whisk in ½ cup (60g) crumbled blue cheese (like Roquefort) as well as 1 tablespoon fresh lemon juice and ¼ teaspoon Worcestershire sauce.

* **Note:** When using commercial mayonnaise, I recommend Hellmann's brand because it's not sweetened.

GREEN GODDESS DRESSING

This classic American dressing was a recent revelation to me and is now a favourite for gussying up salads or using as a dip or a flavour enhancer for a plate of sliced avocado or tomato. I also love it drizzled over Roast Potatoes (page 146), salmon, or chicken. I use quite a number of herbs here, but you can make your own combination, as long as you end up with a good cupful.

¼ cup fresh parsley leaves

¼ cup fresh chervil or dill sprigs

½ cup fresh basil leaves

2 tablespoons fresh tarragon leaves

2 scallions, chopped

1 small garlic clove, minced

2 anchovy fillets, chopped

2 tablespoons fresh lemon juice or white vinegar

¼ cup (60ml) canola oil or olive oil

½ teaspoon fine sea salt

½ teaspoon freshly ground black pepper

¼ cup (55g) mayonnaise

¼ cup (55g) sour cream or buttermilk

- In a blender, combine the parsley, chervil, basil, tarragon, scallions, garlic, anchovies, lemon juice, canola oil, salt, and pepper. Blend until smooth.

- Add the mayonnaise and sour cream. Blend again, taste, and adjust the seasonings to your liking. Use immediately or cover and store in the refrigerator for up to 5 days.

HONEY DRESSING

MAKES ¾ CUP (180ML)

My mother made a version of this vinaigrette when I was a kid and used it specifically for a very '80s salad of raw spinach, red onion, and orange suprêmes. It's just the thing when you're looking for a bit of sweetness to contrast bitter greens. I've even used it on fruit salad. You can use a neutral oil or olive oil here, or a combination of both. For a vegan version, replace the honey with maple syrup.

2 tablespoons apple cider vinegar

2 tablespoons fresh lemon juice

½ teaspoon fine sea salt

¼ teaspoon freshly ground black pepper

2 tablespoons honey

1 teaspoon Dijon mustard

1 tablespoon finely chopped onion or French shallot

⅓ cup (80ml) vegetable oil or olive oil

2 tablespoons chopped fresh parsley

- In a small bowl, whisk together the vinegar, lemon juice, salt, pepper, honey, mustard, and onion, pouring the vegetable oil in a slow steam while whisking quickly to emulsify and adding the parsley at the end.

- Alternatively, you can blitz everything together in the blender to make a smooth sauce. Refrigerate any leftovers, covered, for up to a week.

QUICKIE CAESAR DRESSING

With so many recipes around for Caesar salad, I figured the world didn't need another. But this is the dressing I probably make most because my kids beg for it, but also because it works so well not just on Caesar salad but in potato salad, over grilled vegetables, and even with something that needs a boost like a pork chop.

1 to 2 garlic cloves

½ teaspoon fine sea salt

2 anchovy fillets

1 large egg yolk, or
1 tablespoon Mayonnaise
(page 34), or store-bought

½ teaspoon freshly ground
black pepper

2 tablespoons fresh lemon
juice

1 teaspoon Worcestershire
sauce

2 dashes of Tabasco sauce

½ teaspoon Dijon mustard

⅓ cup (80ml) extra-virgin
olive oil (or a mix of half
vegetable oil and half
olive oil)

- On your cutting board, peel and smash the garlic clove(s), sprinkle over the salt and chop together with the anchovy fillets until it all forms a paste.

- Place the paste in a medium bowl (or in your salad bowl), and whisk in the egg yolk, pepper, lemon juice, Worcestershire, Tabasco, and mustard until smooth, then gradually whisk in the olive oil to emulsify. Use immediately or keep covered and refrigerated for up to 3 days.

CAESAR SALAD

In my days as a restaurant critic, I ate my fair share of Caesar salads, and the good ones were few and far between. Though a steakhouse and Italian restaurant standby, the original Caesar salad was made in Tijuana, Mexico, and would be unrecognizable compared to what we see today: no anchovies, no capers, no bacon! It's quite a basic salad, so the secret is to use the best ingredients possible, especially when it comes to the olive oil. I like a few anchovies in the dressing for that umami punch, and if it's a main course salad, I'll add bacon. Homemade croutons are a must, and always toss the salad in a big bowl at the table right before serving. Bliss!

2 heads romaine lettuce, or 3 hearts of romaine

2 tablespoons unsalted butter, melted

2 tablespoons olive oil

1 garlic clove, chopped

2 to 4 thick slices sourdough bread

1 recipe Quickie Caesar Dressing (page 107)

1 cup (about 60g) grated Parmesan-Reggiano or Grana Padano cheese

6 slices bacon, fried and chopped (optional)

Freshly ground black pepper (optional)

- Using a bread knife, slice the romaine into bite-size pieces, removing the tips of the leaves if they are blemished. Wash in cold water, spin dry, wrap in a clean dish towel, and refrigerate.

- In a small saucepan, combine the butter and oil together over medium-high heat. Add the garlic, and when it sizzles, remove from the heat.

- Preheat the oven to 375°F (190°C).

- Slice the bread into 1-inch (3cm) cubes (you should get about 3 cups). Place on a small baking sheet, pour over the cooled butter-oil mixture, and toss well with your hands to coat. Spread out into an even layer and bake for about 20 minutes, stirring once or twice, until the croutons are well browned. Let cool completely.

- To serve, transfer the lettuce to a large salad bowl and add the dressing, croutons, cheese, and bacon (if using). Toss very well and taste for seasoning, adding a bit of freshly ground pepper, if desired. Serve immediately.

FOUR-BEAN SALAD

SERVES 4

*I love a good bean salad, but alas, many of them are no fun.
Beans need supporting players to shine, and this lineup of add-
ins results in a salad that can be made any time of year as a side
or full lunch. When doubling this recipe, consider using one can of
beans and one can of chickpeas, as they have the most flavour.*

1 (14-ounce/398ml) can
three-bean mix, drained and
rinsed

1 cup sliced (1-inch pieces)
green beans, blanched

½ large red bell pepper,
diced, or 1 large celery
stalk, diced

½ medium red onion, diced

¾ cup (110g) peeled,
seeded, and diced
cucumber

¼ cup chopped fresh
parsley

⅓ cup (80ml) Honey
Dressing (page 106)

½ teaspoon fine sea salt

Freshly ground black
pepper

Splash of red wine vinegar

½ cup (60g) crumbled feta
cheese

• In a large bowl, combine the bean mix, green beans,
bell pepper, onion, cucumber, and parsley, pour over
the dressing, and mix to combine well. Sprinkle over
¼ teaspoon of the salt and a couple turns of the pepper
mill, taste, and add the rest of the salt if needed. Finish
off with a splash of vinegar, which will give the salad a
nice lift. Refrigerate until ready to serve. You can eat it
right away, but it does get better after a few hours.

• Right before serving, check the seasoning again, then
crumble over the feta and enjoy.

GRILLED RATATOUILLE SALAD

SERVES 8 TO 10

A specialty of the city of Nice, ratatouille is a vegetable stew made with peppers, zucchini, onion, tomato, garlic, and eggplant. It's ideally made in late summer when all those vegetables are at their peak. This grilled salad is not what I'd consider an authentic ratatouille, but so what? It includes all the usual ratatouille suspects. The idea here is to create a harmonious blend, which means you should aim to have about the same quantity of each vegetable, and everything should be sliced about the same size. It's good to be flexible with this recipe; if you like more herbs, feel free to add more parsley, thyme, or basil to taste. Try, though, to combine everything while the grilled vegetables are still warm to help the flavours meld together. I like this served alongside grilled meats (lamb especially!) or fish, but it can also make a brilliant pasta sauce.

2 cups (400g) cherry tomatoes

Fine sea salt and freshly ground black pepper

2 yellow or Vidalia onions

Olive oil

3 medium zucchini

1 medium eggplant, or 2 small Japanese eggplants

2 red bell peppers

2 sprigs thyme

2 tablespoons fresh lemon juice

2 garlic cloves, finely chopped

¼ cup extra-virgin olive oil

Handful of fresh basil leaves, torn

- Slice the cherry tomatoes in half (or quarters, if they are large) and place in a large bowl. Sprinkle with a generous pinch of salt and a bit of black pepper, stir, and set aside.

- Slice the onions horizontally into rings about ½ inch (1cm) thick. Rub with oil, season with salt and black pepper, and set aside.

- Top and tail the zucchini and slice each lengthwise into 3 fat strips. Slice the eggplant the same way into strips about 1 inch (2.5cm) thick (try to slice the zucchini and eggplant strips to the same thickness). Lay the zucchini and eggplant slices down on a cutting board or plate, flesh facing up, and sprinkle generously with salt. This will help purge any bitterness and excess water in the vegetables. Let stand for a good 10 minutes, then, using a paper towel, sponge off the beads of water on the zucchini and eggplant. Place the slices in a bowl, drizzle over a bit of oil, and toss until they are glistening.

- Heat your grill or heat a grill pan on the stovetop over high heat. Get all your vegetables ready for grilling.

- Once the grill or grill pan is very hot, cook the vegetables: First, roast the bell peppers until they are charred all over and then immediately wrap them individually in a paper towel. Let cool completely. Next, grill the onion rounds until they are charred and tender. Finally, grill the zucchini and eggplant slices until they are deep golden and tender. Set all the vegetables aside.

- Discard the excess liquid that has accumulated under the salted tomatoes. Remove the leaves from the thyme sprigs, chop them lightly and stir them into the tomatoes. Chop the onions into 1-inch (2.5cm) pieces and add them to the tomatoes. Rub the skins off the charred bell peppers, slice them open, remove the seeds and white membranes, and cut the flesh into roughly 1-inch (2.5cm) pieces. Stir the roasted peppers into the onion-tomato mix. Slice the zucchini and eggplant strips into 1-inch (2.5cm) pieces and stir those in as well.

- In a small lidded jar, combine the lemon juice, garlic, and a pinch of salt. Cover and shake to combine. Add the olive oil, cover, and shake again.

- Pour the dressing over the mixed vegetables and stir well to combine. Add the basil leaves, season to taste with salt and black pepper, and give the salad another big stir, combining the ingredients without crushing the vegetables. Serve immediately, or cover and refrigerate to serve the next day, making it even more delicious. Kept any longer, it tends to get soggy.

COUSCOUS SALAD

SERVES 4 TO 6

I've been making this salad, adapted over the years from a Jamie Oliver recipe, for as long as I can remember. It's lovely served alone, but also makes an excellent side dish for grilled meat in summer. It's a wonderful way to incorporate a variety of flavours and textures into a meal, and it's just as delicious served hot or cold.

3 tablespoons fresh lemon juice

7 tablespoons (105ml) olive oil

Fine sea salt and freshly ground black pepper

1¼ cups (225g) couscous

1 cup plus 2 tablespoons (280ml) cold water

½ cup coarsely chopped fresh parsley, basil, mint, cilantro, or a mixture of all or some of these

4 scallions, finely chopped

1 to 2 fresh red chiles (optional)

Suggested mix-ins: drained and rinsed canned chickpeas (about 1 cup/175g); 2 zucchini or yellow squash, grilled and diced; 2 red bell peppers, grilled and diced (bottled work well here); halved cherry tomatoes (a scant cup/150g); and a handful of asparagus spears, grilled and sliced

Splash of balsamic vinegar

- In a small lidded jar, combine the lemon juice with the olive oil, season with salt and pepper, seal, and shake to combine. Set the dressing aside.

- Pour the couscous into a large bowl, cover with the water, and stir lightly with a fork to distribute the water. Set the couscous aside to absorb the water, about 15 minutes.

- Using a fork, fluff up the couscous, then add the herbs, scallions, chiles (if using), and any mix-ins. Pour over the dressing and mix well. Season again with salt and pepper as needed, as well as a few drops of vinegar. Serve immediately or keep refrigerated for up to 24 hours.

QUINOA WITH DRIED CRANBERRIES AND PECANS

SERVES 4 TO 6

I first tasted a version of this dish at a dinner party, served hot alongside meat. I asked for the recipe, which I later turned into a cold salad with much success. Quinoa not only has a delicious nutty flavour, but it is rich in fiber and other nutrients as well. To add a bitter edge, stir in a handful of torn arugula leaves right before serving.

2⅓ cups (580ml) water

1 cup (200g) quinoa

½ cup (50g) pecans, chopped

½ cup (70g) dried cranberries

1 French shallot, or 3 scallions

Leaves from ½ bunch cilantro

2 tablespoon extra-virgin olive oil

¼ cup (60ml) fresh lemon juice or orange juice

2 tablespoon red or white wine vinegar

Couple dashes of Tabasco

1½ teaspoons toasted sesame oil

1 teaspoon pure maple syrup

½ teaspoon fine sea salt

Freshly ground black pepper

- In a medium pot, bring the water to a boil. Stir in the quinoa, reduce the heat to medium-low, and cover. Cook until all the water is absorbed and the grains are soft, about 15 minutes. Remove from the heat, take off the lid, and fluff up the grains with a fork. Place a cotton napkin over the pot, put the lid back on, and let cool.

- Meanwhile, toast the pecans in a small skillet or in the oven. Chop the cranberries, shallot, and cilantro, but not too fine because you want a bit of texture here.

- In a small bowl, whisk together the olive oil, lemon juice, vinegar, Tabasco, sesame oil, maple syrup, salt, and pepper.

- Transfer the quinoa to a large bowl, fluff up the grains again, then stir in the toasted pecans, cranberries, shallot, and cilantro. Pour over two-thirds of the dressing, stir well, and check the seasonings. Set aside for 1 hour to allow the flavours to marry (or refrigerate if you're eating later in the day).

- Stir in the rest of the dressing and serve, or keep refrigerated for another day.

ONIONS, LEEKS, AND OTHER BEAUTIFUL BULBS: THE BUILDING BLOCKS OF FLAVOUR

ONIONS, LEEKS, AND OTHER BEAUTIFUL BULBS: THE BUILDING BLOCKS OF FLAVOUR

Of all the ingredients in my pantry, the one I reach for the most is the onion. That said, it's probably the one we take for granted most—ridiculous, considering how many dishes would fail without them. I'm not talking obvious choices like onion soup or onion rings, but dishes where onions work as a building block, a supporting player, like Bolognese, rice pilaf, chicken curry, or the Roman version of *pasta all'amatriciana*. Onions flavour stocks and vinaigrettes, sauces and marinades. Whenever I'm looking for an ingredient to enliven a green salad, red onions or shallots, thinly sliced, always save the day.

Onions play a huge role in European recipes, but they're omnipresent in all cuisines, as are their fellow bulbs in the allium family: garlic, scallions, shallots, leeks, chives, and those much-sought-after ramps. Sautéed, pickled, roasted, grilled, deep-fried, and especially raw, these bulbs are potent flavour boosters. I could cook without them, but no ingredient would be more missed.

Good to Know . . .

— People revert to all sorts of techniques to avoid tearing up while slicing onions. Ditch the ski goggles and instead light a candle next to your cutting board or, if you have a gas stove, light a burner and chop as close to it without risk of being burned. The flame will draw the sulfur to it and away from your eyes. Also, the sharper your knife, the sharper the cut, resulting in less sulfur being released from the onion.

— Never refrigerate French shallots, onions, or garlic, and avoid purchasing them refrigerated—especially garlic. Keep them in a cool, dark place to prevent sprouting. Only spring onions, scallions, garlic scapes, chives, ramps, and leeks need to be refrigerated.

— Raw onions are delicious, but the sulfur released when they are sliced makes them acrid. To avoid this dilemma, soak sliced onions in cold water with a shot of white vinegar for about 10 minutes. Drain and pat dry with a paper towel before serving.

— When sautéing onions, I always follow Nigella Lawson's suggestion to add a pinch of salt to the pan to help prevent the onions from browning too quickly. It works!

— When selecting onions, keep in mind that you will get a different taste depending on the variety. White onions are the mildest, a bit sweet and not especially flavourful. Vidalia onions are also a white onion, but markedly sweeter. I like them best grilled. A yellow onion (aka Spanish onion) is a favourite for cooking. It has the most intense flavour, which mellows and sweetens when cooked, especially when slow-cooked toward caramelizing. Yellow onions are too strong, really, to eat raw, and because they are so sulphurous, even keeping them in the fridge after slicing will overwhelm everything else with an onion flavour. My preferred all-around onion is the red onion. It's good both raw and cooked. Red onions have a mild flavour and a slight sweetness, and their deep magenta hue adds a pop of colour to everything from salads to hamburgers. They're also ideal for pickling. Their only downside is that they don't keep as long as yellow onions.

— French shallots are the most sophisticated of alliums. Their flavour isn't as sharp as that of a yellow onion, but is more complex, and preferable to garlic in most vinaigrettes. They also melt into a sauce beautifully, which makes them my top pick for risottos. Try them deep-fried and sprinkled over salads, flatbreads, soups, and gratinéed dishes.

— Garlic scapes are a great addition to this category. The flowering head of an immature garlic plant, garlic scapes are harvested in spring before the plants form garlic bulbs. Finely chop and use them in compound butters, salads, or pestos, but go easy because they're strong.

— Ramps, also known as wild leeks and wild garlic (*ail des bois* in French), have been banned for commercial sale in Quebec since 1995, when they were listed as a vulnerable species, though they are available for sale in other Canadian provinces, especially Ontario. Ramps look like scallions, but smaller, with a thinner bulb and a leafier head. Their flavour is more garlicky than a scallion and more potent than a leek. Wildly popular in foodie circles, ramps are the harbinger of spring on many restaurant menus. Slow-growing and increasingly rare, ramps have become an expensive delicacy and, unfortunately, a black-market food item. For this reason, I've abstained from offering ramp recipes. But if you have the chance to taste them where allowed, try them in soups, pastas, risottos, pizzas, and especially pickled.

— About garlic: If you tend to burn your garlic, here are four suggestions:

1. Use crushed whole cloves in stews or sauces, which will give garlic flavour without burning.

2. Infuse your cooking oil with coarsely chopped garlic and remove or strain out the pieces before cooking.

3. As garlic cooks much faster than onions and other vegetables, add chopped garlic towards the end of sautéing.

4. Roast a head of garlic and use the resulting less pungent garlic paste in place of fresh garlic. To roast garlic: Preheat the oven to 400°F (200°C). Slice the tops off a garlic head(s), drizzle with oil, season with salt and pepper, and wrap in foil. Place in the oven as it heats up and roast for 30 to 40 minutes, depending on the size of the head(s). Let cool; when ready to use, simply press out the flesh from the skins. You can keep the roasted garlic refrigerated for up to 2 weeks, or even frozen for a couple of months.

PICKLED RED ONION

MAKES ABOUT 1 CUP (250ML)

For a different taste, substitute 1 teaspoon cumin, coriander, or mustard seeds for the rosemary. Toast the seeds in a dry pan over low heat until fragrant, then add them to the jar with the onion. You can also add red pepper flakes for a hit of heat.

1 large red onion

1 garlic clove, sliced in half

1 sprig rosemary

¾ cup (180ml) red wine vinegar

¾ cup (180ml) water

2 tablespoons sugar

1 teaspoon fine sea salt

• Sterilize a pint (500ml) mason jar (see Note) and set aside.

• Slice the onion in half through the root, then lay the halves flat and slice them as thinly as possible into half circles (a mandoline comes in handy for this purpose; just watch your fingers). Fill the jar with the onion slices, then push the garlic and rosemary into the onion.

• In a small pot, combine the vinegar, water, sugar, and salt and bring to a boil. Stir well, then pour over the onion. Push the onion down into the vinegar mixture to make sure it is fully submerged, then clean the rim of the jar and seal shut. Refrigerate for at least a day before serving; it will keep, refrigerated, for several months and improve over time.

* **Note:** To sterilize jars, preheat the oven to 350°F (180°C). Wash the jars and lids in hot soapy water and rinse clean. While they are still wet, turn them upside down on a wire rack set over a baking sheet and place them in the oven for 15 minutes.

ONION MARMALADE

MAKES ABOUT 3 CUPS (750ML)

Onion marmalade is a treat served cold on a charcuterie board or cheese plate, or warm alongside roasted chicken, beef, or pork, raclette, or cheese fondue. It also makes a great gift. The recipe is time-consuming, but relatively simple to make. Don't hesitate to use a variety of different onions; whatever you have on hand will work.

4 tablespoons (½ stick/55g) unsalted butter

3 large Spanish onions or a combination of different onions (4 pounds/1.8kg total), thinly sliced

2 sprigs thyme

1 cup (225ml) dry white or red wine

½ cup (125ml) wine vinegar

2 tablespoons grenadine or pomegranate molasses

½ cup chopped fresh cilantro (optional)

Fine sea salt and freshly ground black pepper

• In a large, deep saucepan, melt the butter over medium heat. Add the onions and thyme and sweat, stirring occasionally, for 3 minutes until soft, covering the pan between stirs. Remove the lid and add the wine, vinegar, and grenadine. Cook until almost all the liquid is evaporated and the onions are soft and translucent, 20 to 30 minutes. Remove from the heat, add the cilantro, and season with salt and pepper. Serve at room temperature. Onion marmalade keeps refrigerated in a covered jar for up to 1 week.

ONION SOUP WITH GRUYÈRE DE GROTTE

SERVES 6

This recipe was given to me by Jean-François Vachon, the chef at the excellent Montreal bistro L'Express. The secret to his soup is the addition of vincotto (slow-cooked grape must), which gives the soup a rich flavour and touch of sweetness. You can find it at most gourmet shops and larger supermarkets alongside the vinegars, but if you can't find it, add a teaspoon of sugar when cooking the onions. Don't be alarmed by the number of onions; they cook down significantly.

1 tablespoon unsalted butter

3 large Spanish onions (about 4 pounds/1.8kg), thinly sliced

1 bay leaf

1 large garlic clove, minced

1 cup (250ml) dry white wine

2 tablespoons vincotto

6 cups Chicken Stock (page 82) or store-bought, unsalted

½ cup (125ml) port

Fine sea salt and freshly ground black pepper

12 thin slices toasted baguette

3 cups (about 300g) grated Gruyère de Grotte cheese, Gruyère, or any good-quality Swiss grating cheese

Chopped fresh parsley, for garnish

- In a large pot or Dutch oven, melt the butter over medium heat. Add the onions all at once and cook, stirring regularly and covering between stirs for the first 10 minutes, until they are very soft and lightly caramelized, about 45 minutes. You don't have to stir them continuously, but don't neglect them, either, or they will cook unevenly. You'll know they're ready when they begin to stick to the bottom of the pot and caramelize. Add the bay leaf, garlic, white wine, and vincotto and cook for another 5 minutes. Add the stock and simmer for 30 minutes.

- When ready to serve, preheat the broiler of your oven. Set six ovenproof soup bowls on a baking sheet.

- Remove the bay leaf from the soup, add the port, and season to taste with salt and pepper. Divide the soup among the bowls, cover each with 2 slices of toasted baguette, and top generously with the cheese. Place under the broiler for about 2 minutes, just until the cheese is melted and lightly golden. Sprinkle over a bit of parsley and serve immediately.

LEEK AND HAM SOUFFLÉS

SERVES 4

Soufflés can be a little intimidating. The key is not to overbeat the egg whites, which should only be whisked to soft peaks. The centers of the soufflés should be creamy, not dry, so be careful not to overcook them. The base and filling can be made in advance and reheated when you are ready to assemble the soufflés. These soufflés are not the ones that puff up high and collapse the minute they are served. They only puff up a bit, so you're missing out on a bit of pizzazz, but rest assured, they hold their shape very well. I like these best served for brunch or lunch.

5 large eggs

4 tablespoons (½ stick/55g) unsalted butter, plus more for greasing

2 tablespoons all-purpose flour

1 cup (250ml) milk

Fine sea salt and freshly ground black pepper

2 leeks, white parts only, washed and chopped into small dice

2 ounces (55g) smoked ham or prosciutto, cut into small dice

¼ cup (60ml) whipping cream

Pinch of grated nutmeg

1 cup (about 75g) grated Swiss cheese

- Separate the eggs and place the whites into a very clean, large metal or glass bowl; set the whites aside. Set aside 3 yolks for this recipe (the extra yolks can be used for another recipe).

- In a medium saucepan, melt 2 tablespoons of the butter over low heat. Add the flour and whisk to make a paste (this is called a roux). Cook the roux for 1 minute, then pour in ¼ cup (60ml) of the milk, whisking vigorously until smooth. Gradually pour in the rest of the milk, whisking continuously. Bring to a boil and let bubble at a full boil for a minute, then remove from the heat. Whisk in the 3 egg yolks one by one. Season the soufflé base with ½ teaspoon salt and a pinch of pepper and keep warm.

- In a large skillet, melt the remaining 2 tablespoons butter over medium heat. Add the leeks. Sauté until soft and transparent (you don't want them to brown), then stir in the ham. Pour over the cream, season with the nutmeg, and simmer until the cream reduces a bit. Set aside in a warm place. (If preparing the soufflés in advance, you can keep the soufflé base and sautéed leeks refrigerated until ready to finish the soufflés; let them come back to room temperature before proceeding.)

- Fifteen minutes before serving, preheat the oven to 400°F (200°C). Put a full kettle of water on to boil. Butter four 1½-cup (375ml) soufflé ramekins, dust them with some of the cheese, and set them in a deep roasting pan.

- In a large bowl, whisk together the soufflé base and the sautéed leek mixture. In a medium bowl, beat the egg whites with a pinch of salt until they hold soft peaks. Whisk one-third of the egg whites into the soufflé base. Then, using a spatula, gently fold in the remaining egg whites, along with half the cheese.

- Fill the prepared ramekins one-third full of the soufflé mixture and sprinkle about 1 tablespoon of the cheese over each. Top off the filling with the remaining soufflé mixture so that it comes just over the top of each dish. Sprinkle a large pinch of the remaining cheese over the tops.

- Pour enough very hot water from the kettle into the roasting pan to come halfway up the sides of the ramekins. Bake for 20 to 25 minutes, until puffed and golden. Serve immediately.

POACHED LEEKS WITH CURRY VINAIGRETTE

SERVES 4

This dish comes from the late, great Montreal restaurant Le Paris-Beurre, where Chef Hubert Streicher served this appetizer to legions of fans for over thirty years. The key here is the curry vinaigrette, which is also delicious served with steamed asparagus. It is best to use small leeks, which Streicher recommends tying into a bundle so they don't come apart when cooking. You can make this vegan by substituting Vegenaise for the mayonnaise.

½ cup (110g) Mayonnaise (page 34) or store-bought

2 teaspoons Dijon mustard

1 tablespoon fresh lemon juice

1 teaspoon mild curry powder

½ teaspoon ground turmeric

1 tablespoon hot water

5 small or 4 medium leeks

2 tablespoons coarsely chopped fresh flat-leaf parsley

¼ cup walnuts, toasted and coarsely chopped, or toasted bread crumbs

• In a small bowl, whisk together the mayonnaise, mustard, lemon juice, curry powder, turmeric, and hot water. Set aside.

• Trim the roots off the leeks and from there, measure 10 inches (25cm) from root to top and slice off the dark green tops. Peel off any withered or damaged outer leaves, then, starting about 1 inch (2.5cm) up from the base of the leek, halve the leeks lengthwise. Rinse under cold running water, getting well between the layers.

• Tie the leeks together in a bundle with kitchen string. Bring a pot (large enough to fit the leek bundle) of salted water to a boil. Add the leeks, reduce the heat to maintain a simmer, cover, and cook until the point of a knife pierces through the roots with little resistance, about 12 minutes. Remove from the water, cut off the string, and lay them in a single layer, cut-side down, on a baking sheet lined with paper towels. You can either serve them warm or chilled, covered, to serve later.

• Slice the leeks in half horizontally and place four halves on each plate (five if you are using small leeks) with the cut side facing up. Spoon 2 to 3 tablespoons of the vinaigrette onto the leeks and sprinkle over the parsley and walnuts. Serve immediately.

Little Extras: How to Enhance Dishes with Unexpected Ingredients

Adding flavour boosters to dishes is an essential part of the cooking process. And we do it all the time, be it a clove of garlic in vinaigrette, slices of pineapple atop pizza, a slick of wasabi on sushi, cherries alongside a duck breast, or balsamic vinegar drizzled over strawberries. And these days, it seems, sriracha everywhere! Those are the classics, but how about a dash of salt and pepper on your watermelon, or a spoonful of buckwheat flour in your buttermilk pancake batter? Here are some other unexpected enhancers to try:

— **Goat cheese and blue cheese:** I put goat cheese everywhere possible. In salads, gratinéed on tartines, as a filling for vegetable tarts, in savoury cheesecakes, folded into an omelet . . . Melt a round of goat cheese over a ladleful of ratatouille (see page 112), serve with crusty baguette and a chilled rosé, and you have a quick summer meal. As for blue cheese, with its intense, salty flavour, it's not everyone's favourite eaten straight up. But served crumbled or diluted in a dressing or a sauce, blue cheese revs up meats, salads, pasta, dips, and flatbreads.

— **Honey:** Used in everything from tea to tarts to toast, honey is also terrific drizzled over cheese, especially goat cheese and blue cheese.

— **Nuts:** Macadamia nut–crusted fish or chicken breast reads like the most '90s restaurant entrée ever, but I would never say no to walnuts in a salad made with beets, mâche, and goat's cheese, or toasted pine nuts in a pasta. With nuts, it's not only about flavour but the great added texture.

— **Sesame seeds:** Toast lightly and scatter over slices of fresh mango.

— **Lime:** Instead of the usual lemon, try lime squeezed over grilled meats. Or try marinating strawberries with a bit of lime juice and zest, a spoonful of sugar, a few torn basil or mint leaves, and a few drops of vanilla extract. Serve with cream (or yogurt) and sprinkle with chopped pistachios.

— **Preserved lemon:** A great addition to anything that would benefit from an intense lemon boost, like a salsa verde served with meat or grilled fish, grain salads, pastas, and risotto. Don't forget to remove the flesh and seeds and use just the rind.

— **Olive oil:** The best extra-virgin olive oils are not only ideally used as a condiment drizzled directly over vegetables, meats, pastas, and more, but also vanilla ice cream or a quenelle of chocolate ganache, sprinkled with a pinch of sea salt.

— **Truffle oil:** Probably the most controversial flavour enhancer, truffle oil was used heavily in the '90s to add a luxurious essence to everything from salmon tartare to wild mushroom risotto. I use it only in two instances: in preparations where mushrooms are the star of the show, and in Bolognese sauce enhanced with dried porcini. You can also add a few drops to a mushroom compound butter (see page 62), but the key is to always add truffle oil drop by drop. If you add too much, the truffle flavour will dominate, so use caution.

— **Fish sauce:** This condiment is widely used to flavour so many Southeast Asian dishes and sauces, but also, as my friend cookbook author Naomi Duguid suggests, a simple marinade rubbed into steak, especially bavette.

— **Grated fresh horseradish:** Far more intense than the bottled variety, fresh horseradish is great atop oysters, in a sweet potato gratin, grated over a tomato salad, or used to add a jolt to salad dressings.

— **Red chiles:** Prevalent in countless cuisines, I like chiles best chopped up fine and sprinkled over ingredients like fresh mozzarella, salsas, and cold soups, or infused into butter to give an unexpected but delicious hit of fruity heat to chocolate desserts.

— **Pink peppercorns:** Often used in cream sauces for meat or seafood, I like the gentle heat and floral hit of crushed pink peppercorns in fruit salad mixed with a bit of vanilla bean pulp and chopped mint leaves. Also lovely on vanilla ice cream with strawberries. When used in savoury recipes, always add at the end of cooking time, as heat destroys its flavour.

— **Garam masala:** This classic seasoning for curries also makes a great addition to lemon-based marinades for chicken.

— **Fennel seeds:** Wonderful to add an extra dimension of flavour to spaghetti sauce, especially when paired with red pepper flakes.

— **Rosemary:** This classic herb is always paired with lamb but wonderful in a syrup used for cocktails or poaching pears or peaches. And if not rosemary, try a pinch of saffron.

— **Booze:** Nothing boosts a red fruit dessert quite like a spoonful of kirsch, while rum, cognac, and bourbon are excellent enhancers for caramel or chocolate desserts. But for sipping with chocolate, Talisker single malt Scotch whisky is hard to beat.

POTATOES:
HUMBLE BUT HEAVENLY

POTATOES:
HUMBLE BUT HEAVENLY

Ah, the potato! The fortunes of this humble staple rise and fall on the wing of public opinion. Whether celebrated by renowned chefs or rejected by carb-loathing celebrities, the potato is comfort food par excellence, an ingredient without which I, personally, could never survive in the kitchen. No matter what the season, potatoes always have a place in my pantry. In late summer, they need little in the way of gussying up. In winter, however, gussying up is de rigueur for what can be a pretty tasteless out-of-season vegetable. Potatoes do very well with bulbs like garlic, shallots, and leeks, and it's worth spicing them up or throwing in a handful of fresh herbs before serving. All fats work well with potatoes: butter, of course, but also olive oil, bacon fat, and especially duck fat. The potato's versatility is nothing short of miraculous.

Countless textures can be achieved simply by changing cooking methods. When it comes to mashed potatoes, I only like them one way: buttery, silky, slightly salty, and more runny than stiff. Roast potatoes must be crisp and golden on the outside, creamy and fluffy within. Used as an ingredient, the potato has given us classic dishes such as potato pancakes, pierogi, and tartiflette. And no true potato lover would pass up the opportunity to elevate the ubiquitous French fry by paying homage to its predecessor, Belgian-style frites.

It might be difficult to imagine, but there was a time when the humble potato was rejected by the population and its consumption forbidden by law . . . But in France, in 1772, the government finally acknowledged the potato's nutritional value, and succeeded in introducing it to the kitchens of the masses, thanks to a cookbook called *La cuisinière bourgeoise*. From those twenty initial recipes, the mighty potato has yet to cease to inspire home cooks everywhere, including yours truly.

Good to Know . . .

— When purchasing, avoid potatoes with any black or soft spots and, if possible, consult the package to see if the potatoes are ideal for baking, roasting, or pureeing.

— The recipes that follow will state which potato is ideal, but if you're going to have just one variety in your pantry, I'd opt for Yukon Gold.

— In summer, it's worth buying new potatoes at a farmers' market for the freshest possible product, which, flavour-wise, will put those out-of-season spuds to shame.

Quick Recipes

Baked Potatoes: Use russet (Idaho) or Yukon Gold for best results. Preheat the oven to 400°F (200°C). Line a baking sheet with aluminum foil, if desired. Scrub your potatoes under cold water, dry well, and pierce the skin with a fork in several places. Rub with a little oil and bake on the prepared baking sheet or directly on the oven rack for 60 to 70 minutes, turning the potatoes over halfway through cooking. The potatoes should puncture easily when cooked through. To shorten the baking time, you can first microwave the potatoes on high for 5 minutes, then roast in the oven for about 30 minutes to finish cooking and crisp up the skins.

Sweet potatoes can be baked in the exact same way, but be sure to place them on a sheet of foil to catch any caramelized juices.

—

On Mashed Potatoes . . .

Mashed potatoes are one of the world's great comfort foods, yet when poorly made, there is little comfort to be found in a thick and lumpy mound of starch. The dreaded mashed potatoes of my youth benefitted from copious amounts of gravy, but happily, I experienced a mashed potato epiphany in my twenties when I tasted Chef Joël Robuchon's famous *purée de pommes de terre*. Cloudlike and silken, these were the mashed potatoes of my dreams. Your fork didn't get wedged into these spuds; instead, this puree actually sank through the tines. The texture was featherlight; it merely hit your palate with a burst of butteriness before dissolving in a sigh of potato flavour. Heaven!

Robuchon is heralded as one of the twentieth century's most creative chefs, and yet the dish he is famous for is mashed potatoes. I have made his recipe often, but with an eyebrow-raising 600 calories per serving, Robuchon's mash is a bit much. So I started working on a recipe of my own, inspired by his technique of first drying out the pureed potatoes, then slowly incorporating bits of cold butter followed by a stream of hot milk. I scaled back on the butter and added a touch of sour cream (or buttermilk) for extra tang.

ROBUCHON'S PUREE, MY WAY

The secret behind the famous mashed potatoes of Chef Joël Robuchon is butter—and lots of it—as well as the hot/cold method: cold butter, hot milk. My version is inspired by Robuchon's, but a tad less orgiastic. Notice the addition of white pepper, which is really just a matter of aesthetics.

2 pounds (900g) fingerling or yellow-fleshed potatoes, unpeeled

Fine sea salt

1 cup (250ml) milk

½ cup (1 stick/110g) unsalted butter, very cold, cut into small pieces

¼ cup (55g) sour cream or buttermilk

Freshly ground white pepper

• Scrub the potatoes, place in a large pot, add cold water to cover by 1 inch (2.5cm), and salt the water. Bring to a boil over high heat, reduce to medium heat, and simmer until cooked through, about 20 to 30 minutes. Drain, quickly rinse with cold water, then peel while still warm.

• In a small saucepan over medium heat, bring the milk to a simmer and set aside.

• Puree the potatoes through a food mill or ricer into a large clean pot, then place over medium-low heat and cook, stirring with a wooden spoon, for a few minutes to dry out the potatoes. Stir in the butter, a piece at a time, then gradually incorporate the hot milk, and finish by adding the sour cream. Season generously with salt, tasting as you go, as well as a bit of white pepper. The puree should drop easily from a spoon yet still hold its shape. To ensure the puree is extremely smooth, whisk quickly just before serving.

KARTOFFELSUPPE (POTATO SOUP WITH MARJORAM AND SMOKED DUCK BREAST)

SERVES 4

This hearty German classic, by Chef Hans Stefan Steinheuer of Steinheuers Restaurant Zur Alten Post, may seem more ideally suited to the cold winter months, but as potatoes are at their best in late summer, it's a soup worth serving in warm weather, too. For a twist, try serving it cold.

3 medium yellow-fleshed potatoes, peeled

2 French shallots, finely chopped

3 tablespoons unsalted butter

⅓ cup (80ml) white wine

2½ cups (625ml) Chicken Stock (page 82)

2 cups (500ml) whipping cream

½ cup (50g) chopped leek

¼ cup (30g) chopped celery

1 bay leaf

1 sprig thyme

1 sprig marjoram, plus extra leaves for garnish

1 garlic clove, smashed and peeled

1 tablespoon crème fraîche

Fine sea salt

Cayenne pepper

½ cup (about 70g) shredded smoked duck breast or prosciutto

- Bring a small pot of salted water to a boil. Meanwhile, chop two of the potatoes into large cubes and set aside. Cut the third potato into a small dice and add to the pot of boiling water. Cook until tender, then drain and set aside.

- In a Dutch oven or deep saucepan, sauté the shallots in the butter until tender. Pour over the wine, 2¼ cups (560ml) of the stock, and the cream. Add the large-cut potatoes, as well as the leek, celery, bay leaf, thyme, marjoram, and garlic. Simmer until the potatoes are tender, about 20 minutes. Remove the bay leaf, thyme, and marjoram and puree the mixture in a blender or with an immersion blender (for an even smoother soup, pass the mixture through a fine sieve). Pour back into the pot and whisk in the crème fraîche; add the remaining ¼ cup (60ml) stock if the soup seems too thick. Season with salt and a bit of cayenne.

- Just before serving, reheat the soup and stir in the reserved diced potatoes. Divide among four bowls and scatter over the duck meat and a few marjoram leaves. Serve immediately.

POTATO PANCAKES

MAKES 8 TO 10

This is a recipe from a friend and terrific cook, Ginette Chapdelaine, who serves these pancakes topped with sour cream and either caviar or smoked salmon as an hors d'oeuvre. They also make an elegant accompaniment to a meat dish.

1 large Yukon Gold potato, peeled and cut into large dice

¾ cup (180ml) Chicken Stock (page 82)

Fine sea salt and freshly ground black pepper

2 teaspoons vegetable oil, plus more for frying

½ large leek, white part only, washed and thinly sliced

½ cup (70g) all-purpose flour

1 teaspoon baking powder

⅓ cup (80ml) milk

1 large egg, separated

1 teaspoon Dijon mustard

¼ cup (about 15g) grated sharp Cheddar cheese

1 tablespoon chopped fresh chives

- Place the potato in a small saucepan along with the stock and a large pinch of salt and cook over medium-high heat until fork-tender.

- Meanwhile, in a skillet, heat the 2 teaspoons oil over medium heat. Add the leek and sauté until soft but not browned. Remove from the heat and set aside.

- Reserving ⅓ cup (80ml) of the cooking liquid, drain the potato and pass it through a ricer into a large bowl (or mash well in the bowl). Gently stir in the flour, baking powder, and reserved cooking liquid. Using a whisk, mix until smooth, then stir in the milk followed by the egg yolk, mustard, cheese, chives, sautéed leek, and a good pinch each of salt and pepper.

- In a small bowl, whisk the egg white to soft but firm peaks, then fold it into the potato mixture. Refrigerate until ready to fry.

- Preheat the oven to 300°F (150°C). In a large nonstick skillet, heat a bit of oil over medium-high heat. Drop large spoonfuls of the batter onto the hot pan and even them out with the back of the spoon. Cook for about 2 minutes on each side, until deep golden. Transfer to the warm oven and repeat with the remaining batter. Serve immediately.

TARTIFLETTE

Originating in the valley of Aravis, home of Reblochon cheese, tartiflette was created in the '80s by the Reblochon cheese trade union to increase sales. Like fondue and raclette, this calorie-rich dish is popular in ski resorts but also makes for a fine midweek meal, served with a baguette and green salad. Oka or raclette cheeses are fine substitutes for the Reblochon. In Quebec, look for Kenogami, Champfleury, or Le Rustique Camembert.

3 tablespoons unsalted butter, at room temperature

About 2½ pounds (1.1 kg) yellow-fleshed potatoes

Fine sea salt and freshly ground black pepper

12 ounces (about 350g) thick-cut bacon, cut into cubes (lardons)

1 large yellow onion, chopped

¼ cup (60ml) whipping cream

1 (1-pound/450g) wheel Reblochon cheese (see headnote)

- Preheat the oven to 450°F (220°C). Generously butter a 7 × 12-inch (18 × 30cm) gratin dish.

- Peel the potatoes and place in a large pot; add cold water to cover and salt the water. Bring to a boil over high heat, then reduce to a simmer until the potatoes can be easily pierced with a knife, about 20 minutes. Drain and let cool.

- Meanwhile, in a large skillet, cook the bacon over medium heat until just crisp. Drain on paper towels. Pour out all but 2 tablespoons of the bacon fat from the pan (don't bother measuring, just eyeball it), then add the onion and fry until it just begins to brown. Remove from the heat and set aside.

- Slice half the potatoes into 1-inch-thick (3cm) rounds and arrange them over the base of the prepared gratin dish. Scatter over half the bacon bits and then half the onion. Season lightly with salt and pepper. Repeat the process, then pour over the cream. If you have a wheel of Reblochon, slice it in half horizontally to make two rounds and lay them over the potatoes. If using another cheese, slice it into ½-inch (1cm) pieces and then place them strategically over the potatoes so that every area will be covered when they melt.

- Bake until the potatoes are brown and the cheese is melted and bubbling, about 30 minutes. Serve.

—

French Fries, the Belgian Way

Frites are omnipresent in Belgium, with friteries (*fritkot*) in every town and roadside stop. Belgian frites, or *fritten* in Flemish, are made following strict rules:

First, the potato of choice is the Bintje, renowned for its rich, tart taste and firmness when fried. Chances are you won't find them at your local market, so go for russet or Yukon Gold.

Second, to assure the ideal contrast between crisp exterior and soft interior, the cut is long and thick (½ inch/1cm on each side and 2 to 3 inches/5 to 7.5cm long).

Third, to help achieve the perfect crisp texture, the cut should be a little rough. But if cutting is not your forte, feel free to use a French fry slicing gadget, as I and many Belgians do.

Fourth, the two-step frying technique is a must. After a quick blanching in boiling water, the potatoes are first fried at a medium temperature to cook the inside. After a 30-minute wait, they are then plunged into very hot oil for a few minutes, until golden and crisp outside.

And fifth, the frying fat of choice is beef drippings or lard, resulting in rich and crisp fries that are worth the indulgence. But let's get real here: peanut oil or canola oil is the more realistic option.

To serve a crowd, count on ½ pound (225g) of potatoes per person, use the same amount of fat, and fry in batches. And finally, there's the accompaniment: mayonnaise, which can be customized with garlic, spices, herbs, mustard, mussel juice, liquor, pickles, or cream.

Making French fries at home can be tricky, even dangerous. If you don't have a fryer, take extra precautions by using a deep-fry thermometer to check for the correct frying temperature, and use a heavy pot or pan on a burner at the back of the stove.

BELGIAN FRITES
WITH MAYONNAISE DIPPING SAUCE

1 pound russet or Yukon Gold potatoes

6 cups (1.5L) peanut or canola oil

2 tablespoons Dijon mustard

2 tablespoons Mayonnaise (page 34) or store-bought

About 2 tablespoons whipping cream

Fine sea salt and freshly ground white pepper

- Bring a large pot of water to a boil.

- Peel the potatoes, wash them carefully, and dry with a kitchen towel. With a large knife, cut lengthwise into ½-inch-thick (1cm) slices, then turn them on their sides, cut into bâtonnets 2½ to 3 inches (6.5 to 8cm) long, and place in a large bowl of cold water.

- Working in batches, add the potatoes to the boiling water and blanch for a full minute after the water comes back to a boil. Remove with a slotted spoon and drain on paper towels while you prepare your oil.

- In a deep, heavy-bottomed pot or deep fryer, heat the peanut oil to 300°F (150°C). When the blanched potatoes are cool and thoroughly dry, plunge them into the hot oil for 8 to 10 minutes, until they just begin to colour. Remove from the oil and drain on fresh paper towels. Let rest for at least 30 minutes before proceeding. (At this point, the blanched potatoes can be frozen in a single layer on a sheet of parchment paper until solid, then piled into a plastic bag and frozen for up to 3 months; fry them directly from frozen.)

- Meanwhile, in a small bowl, whisk together the mustard, mayonnaise, and enough cream to liquefy the mix. Season with salt and pepper and serve with hot fries for dunking.

- When ready to serve, raise the oil temperature to 340°F (170°C). Plunge the blanched potatoes back into the oil and fry until golden, about 2 minutes. Remove with a slotted spoon and drain on a paper towel–lined plate, then quickly transfer to a bowl and toss with salt. Serve piping hot, with the dipping sauce alongside.

ROAST POTATOES

SERVES 4

For years, the dish that eluded me most was oven-roasted potatoes. Turns out, the secret, as I learned in Simon Hopkinson's book Roast Chicken and Other Stories, *is to parboil them, roast them at high heat, and not be shy with the oil. None of us wants to ingest a ton of oil, but the beauty of this recipe is that little of the oil is absorbed by the potatoes. In fact, there's enough left over to reuse for your next batch. For the ultimate in gourmet roast potatoes, substitute duck fat for the olive oil. I sometimes sprinkle the top with Gremolata (page 249) for extra oopmh.*

2 pounds (900g) Yukon Gold potatoes, peeled

Fine sea salt and freshly ground black pepper

¾ cup (175ml) olive oil or duck fat

A few sprigs of rosemary

A few pinches of dehydrated minced garlic

Squeeze of fresh lemon juice (optional)

- Preheat the oven to 450°F (230°C).

- Cut the potatoes on an angle into 2-inch (5cm) wedges, then place them in a large pot. Add water to cover by about an inch (2.5cm) and salt the water. Bring to a boil and cook for about 7 minutes, until the potatoes are almost cooked through. Drain carefully in a colander, give it a shake, and let them sit for a minute to dry.

- Meanwhile, heat a 9 × 13-inch (23 × 33cm) roasting pan or 10-inch (25cm) skillet over high heat. Pour in the olive oil, which should generously cover the base by about ½ inch (1cm). Add the rosemary sprigs and when they begin to sizzle, add the potatoes in one shot, being careful not to splatter any hot oil. Stir gently with a wooden spoon to coat them in the oil, add a generous sprinkling of salt, then immediately place the pan in the hot oven. Roast for about 45 minutes, turning the potatoes every 15 minutes or so, until they are crunchy and golden on the outside and velvety within.

- Use a slotted spoon to scoop the potatoes onto a warm serving dish. Season with salt and pepper, as well as a pinch or two of dehydrated garlic and a squeeze of fresh lemon juice, if desired, then serve.

PART 3

DINNER: SOLVED

PASTA:
MY PASSION AND PLEASURE

PASTA:
MY PASSION AND PLEASURE

Pasta is the dish I eat most often, for the simple reason that it makes me happy, and I absolutely *love* to make it. Having grown up like many people with spaghetti and meat sauce at the family table, my personal repertoire grew as I created pasta dishes of my own. One of my favourites was a recipe for penne with chicken, zucchini, and mushrooms that was doused in a full cup of cream and topped with a blanket of Parmesan. I impressed many a date with that one! Later I adopted a less-is-more approach, favouring lighter, more traditional pastas (though I have always had a habit of sneaking a shot of cream into the sauce when nobody's looking). When pressed for time, I often throw together a half pound of spaghetti dressed simply with the juice of three lemons, half a cup of grated Parmesan, and two-thirds of a cup of olive oil. It's the pasta I downed almost every morning for breakfast when I was pregnant to stave off morning sickness, and it's still a go-to. But when time is not an issue, I'll happily cook up an authentic Bolognese that, truth be told, takes longer to make than a three-tier wedding cake.

Slurping back a garlicky *spaghetti vongole* is one of life's great pleasures, feasting on rigatoni with sausage and rapini with a goblet of Chianti is my birthday treat of choice, and I have yet to pass up a slice of glistening lasagna verde. Be it a desert island go-to, a last meal before the apocalypse, or a dish I'd dive into with Brad Pitt, my answer will always be pasta. That said, there are so many excellent pasta recipes out there that it felt a bit silly for me to rewrite them with just a few tweaks of my own. Instead, I've chosen the ones that I eat at home on a regular basis. I've taken a few liberties with tradition, but before wagging your finger in disapproval, give them a try.

Good to Know . . .

— Pasta is pretty flavourless on its own, and therefore must be cooked in generously salted water. For every 4 quarts (4L) water, add about 2 tablespoons salt.

— All of these recipes call for dry pasta, though they could certainly be made with fresh pasta if that is your preference.

— A pound (450g) of dry pasta serves 6, or 4 generously (which is the case in my house).

— To prevent pasta from sticking together as it cooks, always give your pasta space in a large pot with plenty of water and stir well for the first few minutes of cooking. Do not add oil to the pasta water; it's a waste of good oil, and the excess oil on the pasta strands prevents them from absorbing sauces well later on.

— Always reserve a cup of the pasta cooking water before draining the pasta. The starch released into the water by the pasta helps thicken your sauce ever so slightly, and the salt in the water will help season the dish. Adding a few spoonfuls to your pasta once the sauce is stirred in helps meld the two together and prevents the dish from being too dry.

— Experiment with the cooking time of your pasta. Draining your pasta about a minute before the cooking time recommended on the package is ideal if your pasta will then simmer for a minute or two in a sauce.

— Fresh herbs can work miracles on many pastas. A handful of chopped fresh parsley and/or basil tossed in right before serving can enliven the simplest pastas, especially those with vegetables or seafood. A handful of torn arugula leaves is another great flavour booster.

— Regarding cheese: I use primarily freshly grated Parmigiano-Reggiano, but Grana Padano is an excellent alternative, and certainly less expensive. Pecorino Romano, made from ewe's milk, is sharper in taste and saltier than Parmesan, so use it more sparingly. It's the star of *cacio e pepe*, and is also traditionally used on spaghetti carbonara and *pasta all'amatriciana*, sometimes in combination with Parmesan. It's worth having both on hand to experiment with. Avoid adding cheese to seafood pasta. Debate all you want—to me, it just doesn't taste good.

— If you are someone who has always served pasta in a bowl with the sauce on top, try mixing them together in a large sauté pan with a bit of pasta water so the two elements become one. If there's one helpful hint to borrow from authentic Italian restaurant kitchens, this would be it.

— I'm a big fan of a final flourish when it comes to pasta. Grated cheese is a given, but I also love a drizzle of excellent olive oil, a torn ball of fresh mozzarella, or a spoonful of mascarpone or ricotta cheese.

— Play around! Pasta is one of the most forgiving dishes ever. Add grilled red bell peppers, sautéed zucchini, caramelized onions . . . but keep in mind that ingredients like ginger, spices, and yesterday's broccoli aren't necessarily going to do your pasta any favours.

BASIC TOMATO SAUCE

MAKES 6 CUPS (1.5L)

Because the canned tomatoes are the star of this show, look for the best quality you can find, such as Italian brands with San Marzano tomatoes, which can be identified with a DOP (Denominazione di Origine Protetta, or Protected Designation of Origin) stamp on the label. At their best, they are sweeter and less acidic. Feel free to enhance the sauce if you like with a couple of teaspoons of fennel seeds and/or chili flakes added to the sautéed onions. This sauce can be used in all the recipes in this chapter that call for tomatoes in the cooking. Just substitute an equal amount of sauce for the volume of tomatoes called for in the recipe.

1 (34-ounce/798ml) can plum tomatoes, preferably San Marzano, with their juices

About ⅓ cup (80ml) olive oil

1 medium onion, chopped

4 large garlic cloves, smashed and peeled but left whole

2 tablespoons tomato paste

1 (22-ounce/660ml) jar tomato passata

2 teaspoons fine sea salt

Freshly ground black pepper

Handful of fresh basil leaves

- Pour the plum tomatoes with their juices into a small bowl and crush with your hands or a potato masher.

- In a large, thick-bottomed pot or Dutch oven, heat the olive oil over medium-high heat. Add the onion. Sauté until it is soft and then add the garlic. Stir in the tomato paste and fry for a minute more.

- Carefully pour in the passata and the crushed tomatoes, being careful the oil doesn't bubble up and splatter. Fill the passata jar halfway with water, cover, shake, and pour the water into the pot as well. Stir the sauce, season with the salt and a little pepper, reduce the heat to medium-low, and simmer until it reaches the consistency of porridge (it should reduce by about one-third). Remove the garlic cloves from the sauce and crush them on a plate to make a paste. Stir the garlic paste back into the tomato sauce, along with the basil leaves.

- Simmer for a few more minutes, then remove from the heat. Use immediately or let cool and refrigerate in an airtight container for up to a week or freeze for up to 3 months.

PESTO

MAKES ABOUT 3 CUPS (750ML)

There are countless uses for pesto: spooned into soups and risottos, spread on pizzas and sandwiches, served alongside grilled meats and vegetables, folded into dips and salads, stirred into pastas or boiled new potatoes . . . the possibilities are endless! This recipe produces the most beautiful emerald-green pesto. The ascorbic acid here is optional, but it helps keep the pesto's bright colour for up to a week in the refrigerator. To make the ascorbic acid powder, just grind up a vitamin C tablet with a mortar and pestle.

6 cups lightly packed (about 110g) fresh basil leaves

2 cups lightly packed (about 30g) fresh parsley leaves

1 large garlic clove, chopped

¼ cup (35g) pine nuts, toasted

1 teaspoon fine sea salt

½ teaspoon freshly ground black pepper

1 generous cup (about 75g) freshly grated Parmesan cheese

¾ cup (180ml) extra-virgin olive oil

¼ teaspoon ascorbic acid powder (optional; see headnote)

- Bring a pot of water to a boil and fill a large bowl with ice and water for an ice bath. Plunge the basil and parsley into the boiling water, count 15 seconds, then plunge them immediately into the ice water. Drain, then place them in a clean dish towel and twist the towel to squeeze out any excess moisture. (It's important to get the herbs as dry as possible.)

- Place the blanched herbs in a food processor, along with the garlic, pine nuts, salt, and pepper, and process until the mixture forms a paste. Add the cheese, process again, and, while the machine is running, slowly pour in the olive oil and process until the mixture forms a thick paste (pesto should not be runny). Check the seasonings, then add the ascorbic acid (if using). Process the mixture one last time to incorporate. Store the pesto in a jar, topped with a thin layer of olive oil, in the refrigerator for five days. Pesto also freezes very well in ice cube trays to make individual portions.

MAX'S CARBONARA

SERVES 4 TO 6

I make this dish often for the sole reason that my eldest son, Max, would happily eat it every day. I usually use pancetta instead of the more authentic guanciale (cured pork jowl), which can be difficult to find. And when I don't have pancetta, I use—you guessed it—good ol' bacon. I've made countless versions of this dish, adding wine, cream, and even milk, which made all my Italian friends scream, "No dairy in carbonara!" But now I've settled on this recipe, the most authentic, really, and the one I make most often. It might take a few tries to get the texture of the sauce just right. But no worries, you'll nail it.

Fine sea salt

1 pound (450g) spaghetti or penne

1 teaspoon olive oil

5 ounces (140g) guanciale (or pancetta or bacon), cut into small dice

1 garlic clove, smashed and peeled

2 large eggs

2 large egg yolks (the freshest possible)

¾ cup (about 45g) finely grated Pecorino Romano or Parmesan cheese, or a mix of the two, plus more for passing at the table

Freshly ground black pepper

- Bring a large pot of salted water to a boil. Add the pasta to the boiling water, stir well, and cook according to the instructions on the box.

- Meanwhile, in a large and rather deep skillet, heat the olive oil over medium heat. Add the guanciale and the garlic and cook quite slowly until the guanciale releases most of its fat and just begins to crisp up. There should be about 2 tablespoons of fat accumulated around the fried meat. If there's more, you can remove some, but be sure to keep a few spoonfuls in the pan. Remove the garlic and reduce the heat to low.

- Meanwhile, in a small bowl, whisk together the eggs, egg yolks, and cheese. Add a few good grindings of pepper. Scoop out 1 cup (250ml) of the pasta cooking water and whisk about ¼ cup (60ml) into the egg-cheese mixture (reserve the remaining ¾ cup/180mL pasta water).

→

- When the pasta is cooked, drain it and immediately add it to the hot guanciale in the skillet. Toss well to coat the pasta with the guanciale and its fat, adding a few spoonfuls of the reserved pasta water if it looks dry. Remove from the heat, then pour over the egg mixture and toss well until the sauce thickens slightly, adding most of the reserved pasta water while tossing just until you achieve a glistening creamy sauce that coats the pasta evenly. It shouldn't be dry. Working quickly, transfer the spaghetti to a serving dish and top with a few more grinds of pepper. Serve immediately, with extra cheese, if you like.

QUICKIE BOLOGNESE

SERVES 6

This recipe was pulled together in about 30 minutes one night when all I had to make dinner were pantry staples and a pound of ground beef. I wasn't optimistic, but the resulting pasta was so good that it's now part of my repertoire. This can be made with ground turkey or lamb instead of the beef. A few slices of smoked bacon, chopped up and added before the vegetables, makes it even more lush. Substitute lentils for the meat and you have a delicious vegetarian version (see page 163). Beginner cooks, this one's for you!

3 tablespoons olive oil

1 medium red onion, diced

1 large carrot, diced

1 celery stalk, diced

Fine sea salt and freshly ground black pepper

3 garlic cloves, smashed and chopped

1 pound (450g) ground beef (or a combination of beef, pork, and veal)

1 teaspoon red pepper flakes

2 tablespoons tomato paste

A few sprigs of thyme

½ cup (125ml) red or white wine (optional)

1 (14-ounce/398ml) can diced tomatoes

$\longrightarrow$

• In a large skillet or Dutch oven, heat the olive oil over medium-high heat. Add the onion, carrot, celery, salt, and a few grinds of black pepper. Sauté until the vegetables soften and just begin to brown, then stir in the garlic. Fry for a minute more, being careful not to burn the garlic. Break the meat into small pieces while adding it to the pot. Cook, stirring frequently, until the meat is well browned and any liquid has boiled off. Add the red pepper flakes, tomato paste, and thyme and stir for a few minutes until everything is melded together. Stir in the wine (if using) and cook until it is evaporated. Pour in the can of tomatoes with their juices, fill the can with cold water, and add that to the pot, too. Stir well and let bubble away until the texture is more saucy than soupy.

• Bring a large pot of salted water to a boil for the pasta. Add the macaroni and cook for 1 minute less than the time indicated on the package.

• Now turn your attention back to the sauce, stir in the cream (if using), taste for seasonings, cover, and remove from the heat.

1 pound (450g) macaroni or other pasta

¼ to ⅓ cup (60 to 80ml) whipping cream (optional)

¼ cup chopped fresh parsley (optional)

Grated Parmesan cheese, for serving

Extra-virgin olive oil, for serving

- When the pasta is cooked, scoop out 1 cup (250ml) of the pasta cooking water and set aside, then drain the macaroni and add it to the pot of sauce. Place the pot over medium-high heat and cook, stirring well, until the sauce comes to a boil. If the mixture looks a bit dry, add enough of the reserved pasta water to loosen it so that when you draw your spoon across the pasta, some sauce pools at the bottom of the pot.

- Transfer to a serving platter and sprinkle with the parsley (if using), a handful of Parmesan, and a drizzle of extra-virgin olive oil. Serve immediately, with more cheese to pass at the table.

- **Vegetarian version:** Soak 1 cup (200g) dried brown lentils in cold water for about 4 hours, then drain and pulse-chop in your food processor for about 30 seconds (this will give the sauce a more Bolognese-like texture). Substitute the lentils for the beef in the Bolognese instructions and stir in a generous tablespoon of miso paste (any kind is fine). After you add the chopped tomatoes, stir in 4 cups (900ml) water and simmer for about 45 minutes, until the sauce has a porridgelike texture and just begins to stick to the bottom of the pot. Be careful about amounts: this makes more sauce than the meat version, so you'll end up with too much sauce for 1 pound (450g) of dry pasta. I suggest removing about a third of the sauce from the pot before adding the pasta and keeping it for a future meal.

RIGATONI WITH RAPINI AND SAUSAGE

SERVES 6

I first tasted a version of this pasta at the Italian restaurant Lucca, located in Montreal's Little Italy. I don't think the original recipe contained tomatoes, and I'm almost certain there was no cream. But I find these added elements make it even better. If serving this pasta to children, you might want to opt for mild Italian sausage.

1 bunch rapini

Fine sea salt

1 pound (450g) spicy Italian sausage, removed from the casings and pinched into walnut-size pieces

2 tablespoons olive oil

1 medium yellow onion, finely chopped

1 (14-ounce/398ml) can chopped tomatoes, or 1¾ cups (430ml) Basic Tomato Sauce (page 156)

1 pound (450g) rigatoni

¼ cup (60ml) whipping cream (optional)

Freshly ground black pepper

1 cup (about 20g) grated Parmesan cheese

Extra-virgin olive oil, for serving

• Wash the rapini and trim off the dry ends. Slice in half, separating the stems from the leaves, then slice the stems in half again. Set aside.

• Bring two large pots of salted water to a boil. At the same time, in a large, thick-bottomed skillet, sauté the sausage bits in the olive oil over medium-high heat until the meat begins to brown, then stir in the onion. Cook until the onion is softened, about 5 minutes. If there is a lot of fat accumulated in the pan, pour out most of it. Stir in the tomatoes along with ½ cup (125ml) water. Stir well, reduce the heat to medium, and simmer.

• When the water is boiling, stir the pasta into one pot of water and the rapini stems into the other. When the rapini water comes back to a boil, cook for 1 minute, then add the leaves and cook for about 3 minutes more, or until the stems are soft. Drain the greens immediately, rinse with cold water, and transfer to a plate lined with paper towels. Pat dry, then coarsely chop into 2-inch (5cm) pieces and place in a large salad bowl.

→

- When the pasta is cooked, reserve 1 cup (250ml) of the pasta cooking water, then drain.

- Stir the cream into the sausage sauce, then add the pasta. Sauté to coat the pasta well with the sauce, adding enough reserved pasta water to thin out the sauce if needed. Season with salt and pepper.

- Pour the hot pasta into the salad bowl with the rapini, sprinkle over half the cheese, then toss as you would a salad until everything is well combined. Drizzle over a few spoonfuls of your best extra-virgin olive oil and serve immediately, passing the remaining cheese at the table.

GARNISH IDEAS

- For stewed cherry tomatoes: Halve 2 cups (300g) cherry tomatoes and sauté them in 2 tablespoons olive oil until they begin to soften. Add ½ cup (125ml) water, stir, and simmer until most of the water is evaporated. Add some torn fresh basil leaves, season with salt and pepper, and toss into the pasta or serve alongside.

- For oven-roasted tomatoes: Preheat the oven to 250°F (120°C). Slice 6 to 8 large tomatoes horizontally into ½-inch-thick (1cm) rounds, or slice 2 cups (300g) cherry tomatoes in half. Place in rows on a parchment-lined baking sheet. Sprinkle with salt, pepper, some fresh thyme, and just a little sugar if your tomatoes are acidic. Add a drizzle of olive oil and a sprinkling of chopped fresh garlic or garlic powder, if you like. Bake for 2 to 2½ hours, until the tomatoes have dried out visibly but are still tender. Chop coarsely and toss into the spaghetti or pass at the table.

PICK-ME-UP SPAGHETTI

SERVES 6

I make this spaghetti when I need cheering up, and boy, does it ever work. Over the years, I've served additional toppings separately so that everyone can customize their pasta. These include stewed cherry tomatoes, oven-roasted tomatoes, diced fresh mozzarella, sautéed sausage, and grilled zucchini or peppers.

Fine sea salt

¼ cup (60ml) olive oil

2 garlic cloves, halved

1 (14-ounce/398ml) can diced tomatoes

Freshly ground black pepper

1 pound (454g) spaghetti

¼ cup (65g) Pesto (page 157)

¼ cup (60ml) whipping cream

2 large handfuls of arugula (preferably wild)

1 ball fresh mozzarella di bufala, drained and diced, for serving

- Bring a large pot of salted water to a boil.

- In a small saucepan, heat the olive oil over medium-high heat. Add the garlic and let it sizzle, turning once. Add the tomatoes, then fill the can halfway with water and add that as well. Stir, season generously with salt and pepper, and allow to reduce by one-third. Remove the garlic from the sauce, crush it to a paste with the back of a fork, and stir the garlic paste back into the sauce. Turn off the heat.

- When the water is boiling, add the spaghetti. While it's cooking, combine the pesto and cream in a small bowl. Place the arugula in a large serving bowl.

- When the spaghetti is ready, remove about ¼ cup (60ml) of the pasta cooking water and set aside. Drain the pasta, pour the pesto mixture and the reserved pasta water into the hot pot, and heat until it just begins to boil. Add the spaghetti, stir well, then quickly transfer the mixture to the serving bowl over the arugula. Toss until the greens are just wilted. Serve immediately, passing the hot tomato sauce and mozzarella cubes—as well as any other add-ins you want—at the table.

LINGUINE WITH PESTO, BEANS, AND POTATOES

SERVES 6

This traditional Italian dish hails from the picturesque Ligurian coast. Though the mix of potatoes and pasta may seem odd, it is absolutely authentic—and, especially in midsummer, utterly delicious! As this pasta is not reheated once the ingredients are mixed, it's important to work quickly after the pasta is drained and, if possible, to serve it in pre-warmed bowls.

12 ounces (340g) small new potatoes (preferably red-skinned; about 12)

Fine sea salt

1 pound (450g) linguine

⅓ cup (90g) Pesto (page 157)

8 ounces (225g) green beans and/or yellow beans (about 40)

Freshly grated Parmesan cheese, for serving

Extra-virgin olive oil, for serving

- Place the potatoes in a medium saucepan, add enough water to cover, and salt the water. Bring to a boil, then simmer until the potatoes are tender, about 10 minutes. Drain and then slice the potatoes in half (or quarters, if they are large) and set aside.

- Meanwhile, bring a large pot of salted water to a boil. Add the pasta and set your timer for the time indicated on the package. Put the pesto in a large saucepan and set aside.

- In the last 4 minutes of the pasta cooking time, add the beans to the pasta water to cook both together until they're just a little al dente. Right before draining, add the potatoes to the pot and scoop out 1 cup (250ml) of the pasta cooking water. Drain everything together in a colander. Quickly whisk three-quarters of the reserved pasta water into the pan with the pesto until blended, then add the drained pasta-vegetable mixture. Toss well to coat everything uniformly with the pesto. Do not reheat, or your pesto will lose its colour and become bitter. If the mix seems too dry, add the remaining pasta water.

- Divide among six bowls. Serve immediately, topped with a sprinkling of cheese and a drizzle of extra-virgin olive oil.

- * **Note:** Though frowned upon by Italian food purists, I sometimes gild the lily by adding ¼ cup (60ml) whipping cream with the pesto and pasta water, and I also sprinkle over ¼ cup (35g) toasted pine nuts.

NICE 'N' PIGGY PENNE ALLA VODKA

Serve this with a bottle of great Chianti and get ready to weep!
If you're counting calories, do not abstain. Just stretch this
recipe out to eight servings and serve a salad alongside.

Fine sea salt

3 tablespoons olive oil

3 garlic cloves, coarsely chopped

½ teaspoon red pepper flakes

1 (34-ounce/798ml) can plum tomatoes, with their juices

¼ cup (55ml) vodka

5 slices prosciutto

Handful of fresh parsley

Handful of fresh basil

1 pound (454g) penne rigate

½ cup (125ml) whipping cream

2 tablespoons unsalted butter

½ cup (30g) grated Parmesan cheese, plus more for serving

Freshly ground black pepper, for serving

- Bring a large pot of salted water to a boil.

- In a heavy-bottomed medium pot, heat the olive oil over medium heat. Add the garlic and stir until it just begins to colour. Add the red pepper flakes, stir for about 20 seconds, then pour in the tomatoes. Stir well, then, using a potato masher, press down on the tomatoes to break them up. Stir in the vodka, season with salt, stir, and let simmer.

- Meanwhile, cut the prosciutto slices into small squares and set aside. Chop the parsley and basil together and set aside also.

- Once the water is boiling, stir in the penne and cook until al dente, 10 to 11 minutes. At about the 6-minute mark, add the cream to the tomato sauce, stir well, and reduce the heat to maintain a low simmer.

- When the pasta is done, scoop out about ¼ cup (60ml) of the pasta cooking water and set aside, then drain the penne. Immediately add the pasta to the sauce, along with the prosciutto pieces, most of the chopped herbs, and the butter. Stir well, adding half the cheese and a few spoonfuls of the reserved pasta water if needed (the sauce should be just a bit drippy, not soupy or dry).

- Transfer to a serving platter, sprinkle over the rest of the herbs and cheese, crack over some black pepper, and serve.

- **For Penne Gigi:** Sauté 8 ounces (227g) sliced button mushrooms, then add to the pasta along with the sauce.

BREAD AND PIZZA:
YES, YOU CAN!

BREAD AND PIZZA:
YES, YOU CAN!

If you're lucky enough to live in a city with great bakeries, chances are, you buy your bread. Of course, there are terrific home bakers out there, with sourdough starters on their counters, steam injection in their ovens, and proofing baskets lining their kitchen shelves. But the quality of bread for sale these days is at such a high level that it's tough to reproduce such loaves at home.

That said, there is a wonderful sense of accomplishment that comes with holding a warm loaf of bread you've made yourself. It's also a great baking project for kids. My grandmother often made a massive bowl of sweet dough, sliced it in half, made cinnamon buns with one half and handed the rest over to us kids to get creative—and we did, shaping dough into braids, birds, turtles, breadsticks, and more.

One dough I believe is best made at home is pizza dough. Homemade pizza may sound daunting, but with a few pieces of equipment and a bit of skill (that improves quickly with practice), you can turn out pizzas almost as impressive as the ones at your best local pizzeria.

Working with yeast and making dough is the easiest part of these recipes, and the results will improve with every attempt to make a pizza, tarte flambée, or everyday loaf. These are basic recipes to—as the French say, *mettre la main à la pâte*—get your hands in the dough.

Good to Know . . .

— Rising times stated here are approximate. In the summer, your dough will rise faster, and in the winter, it might take longer to double in volume. Adjust your times accordingly, but even if you don't have everything timed perfectly, these recipes are quite forgiving.

— Always let your dough rise in the warmest, least drafty part of your kitchen. I like to let it rise in a turned-off oven, and if the dough is sluggish, I sometimes use the "proof" setting. If you don't have that setting, a pan of warm water placed on the floor of the oven will also help speed up the process.

— Learn how to "flour" like a pro: Instead of sprinkling the flour over your counter, pizza peel, or dough, take a step back and throw a small handful of flour over the dough using a sideways pitch, as if you were throwing a skimming stone over water, which results in a more even coating.

— Regarding yeast: All these recipes call for quick-rise yeast, which is a cinch to work with and ideal for beginners. It can be purchased in small packets or, if you bake often, in glass jars. Once a package or jar is opened, store the yeast in an airtight container in the fridge for up to 4 months or in the freezer for up to 6 months. If you are using another kind of yeast, make sure to read the instructions on the package first. And always check that best-before date!

— When deflating the dough, do not punch it down, but instead fold it over on itself to redistribute the yeast.

— Let it cool! Yes, it's tempting to rip that gorgeous, freshly baked loaf apart, but give it a chance to firm up a bit and for the crackly crust to set. And try to avoid wrapping your loaf in plastic. You worked hard to get that crisp crust—don't soften it by wrapping it up.

As for Equipment . . .

— First, a baking stone (also called a pizza stone) or baking steel ensures an even, hot temperature. You can bake pizza on a pan, but you'll get much better results if you bake directly on a baking stone or steel. These are readily available in kitchenware stores. I keep mine in my oven on a permanent basis and just scrape it clean instead of washing it.

— Second, a baker's peel is essential to help you get your pizza in and out of the oven with ease. These are sold in wood or metal versions; I recommend a wooden peel for beginners, as the dough tends to stick to metal peels. These are not expensive and should last a lifetime if treated with care.

— Third, though bread can certainly be baked directly on a baking stone or steel, my preferred method is baking one loaf at a time in a covered 10-inch (25cm) cast-iron pot. The advantage is that the pot traps the moisture that evaporates from the dough, which helps promote the final burst of rising in the first minutes of baking before the crust is formed (known as "oven spring"). This method also helps produce a uniformly crisp and golden crust without you having to create steam in your oven. You can use an enameled cast-iron pot (like a Le Creuset), but a regular cast-iron pot will hold up far better to the high heat.

PAIN DE CAMPAGNE

MAKES ONE 10-INCH (25CM) ROUND LOAF

This recipe was developed by legendary Montreal chef and baker James MacGuire. It's easy to make, though you will need a few hours to get the sponge going, which helps produce a white loaf with a more complex flavour. James does stipulate that it is essential to use unbleached flour that does not contain ascorbic acid as an additive, as it is not good for texture.

Sponge

1½ cups (210g) unbleached all-purpose flour

½ teaspoon quick-rise yeast

1 teaspoon fine sea salt

¾ cup (180ml) cool water

Dough

1¼ cups (175g) unbleached all-purpose flour

½ cup (70g) stone-ground whole wheat flour

1 teaspoon quick-rise yeast

½ teaspoon fine sea salt

¾ cup (180ml) cool water

Oil, for greasing

• **Make the sponge:** In a large bowl, combine the flour, yeast, and salt, then blend in the water and knead until smooth, about 1 minute. Cover with plastic wrap and a towel, set in a warm place, and let rise for at least 5 hours, or let rise for 2 hours on the counter and then overnight (10 to 14 hours) in the fridge, until the sponge has risen and bubbled up. (At this point, you can refrigerate the sponge for up to 3 days; bring it to room temperature before proceeding.)

• **Make the dough:** In a large bowl, combine the unbleached flour, the whole wheat flour, the yeast, salt, water, and sponge. Mix until a rough dough forms, scrape down the sides, cover, and let stand for 30 minutes. Turn the dough out onto a lightly floured counter and knead for a few minutes, until the dough springs back when pushed down with your finger. It should not be too sticky or too dry. Place in a lightly oiled bowl, cover with plastic wrap, and set in a warm place to rise for 1 hour.

• Fold the dough over on itself four times to deflate, turning the bowl a quarter turn as you go and stretching the dough lightly outwards before folding it over the top. Cover and let rise for another 30 minutes.

- **Shape the loaf:** Turn the dough out onto a lightly floured counter and flatten it into a rectangular shape. Pulling on the dough lightly (it should be quite elastic), fold it in quarters onto itself to make a little package, starting at the top, then the base, then right and left. Turn the dough over so that the folds are underneath, then, with your palms, hold the dough on either side and roll the base on the counter to help form a ball, making sure all the seams are underneath and the top is smooth. Place a clean kitchen towel in the bowl the dough was rising in and generously flour the towel. Place the dough on the towel, smooth-side down, and pinch together any seams (now on top) to seal. Cover loosely with another towel and let rise again until doubled in bulk, about 45 minutes. (Do not let the dough rise too long. It should still feel a little springy before baking to develop properly in the oven.)

- While the dough is rising, preheat the oven to 450°F (230°C). Place the oven rack in the lowest position, then place a covered 10-inch (25cm) cast-iron pot on the rack. The oven should be at the optimal temperature for a good 30 minutes before baking.

- When ready to bake, remove the towel covering the dough, place a square of parchment paper slightly larger than the base of the bowl over the dough and flip the bowl over so the base of the dough is on the paper. Carefully peel the towel off the smooth side of the dough and lightly flour the top. Using a baker's blade or serrated bread knife, cut two slashes in the top of the bread, cutting about ¾ inch (2cm) into the surface of the dough and forming a curved smile shape.

$\longrightarrow$

- Carefully remove the hot pot from the oven and remove the lid. Using the parchment, lift up the ball of dough and place it (still on the parchment) in the pot. Cover and place back in the oven.

- Bake for 20 minutes, then remove the lid and bake, uncovered, for a further 15 to 20 minutes, until the bread is deep golden and sounds hollow when you rap the base with your knuckles. Let cool completely on a wire rack before slicing.

MICHELE'S PIZZA DOUGH

MAKES ENOUGH FOR FOUR 8-INCH (20CM) PIZZAS

The Michele behind this recipe is Michele Forgione, the chef and co-owner of several of Montreal's best Italian restaurants and pizzerias. Forgione is passionate about his pizza, and most especially the dough. His recipe can be made several hours before you get going on the pizza, but is even better when made the day before.

3½ cups (500g) all-purpose flour

½ rounded teaspoon quick-rise yeast

1½ cups (330ml) cold water

1 tablespoon fine sea salt

1 tablespoon olive oil

- In the bowl of a stand mixer or in a large bowl, combine the flour, yeast, and water and mix with your hands to form a dough. Cover with plastic wrap and let rest for 5 minutes. Add the salt and oil and, using the dough hook on medium-low speed, knead the dough for 10 minutes (or about 15 minutes if kneading by hand) to develop the gluten. Transfer the dough to a lightly floured baking sheet, cover with a clean kitchen towel or sheet of plastic wrap, and leave at room temperature until doubled in volume, about 3 hours.

- Turn the dough out onto the counter, fold over into thirds, then cut into four equal portions (each should weigh about 8 ounces/220g). Roll each piece into a ball and place back on the floured baking sheet. Cover and let rise for another hour at room temperature, or wrap well and refrigerate for up to 24 hours. (At this point, you can also freeze the dough for longer storage; let it defrost in the fridge overnight before using.)

- If it has been chilled, let the dough come to room temperature for 30 minutes before shaping.

NO-KNEAD PIZZA DOUGH

MAKES ENOUGH DOUGH FOR FOUR 8-INCH (20CM) PIZZAS

Developed by James MacGuire, this is an incredibly simple pizza dough, ideal for those who don't have a stand mixer. It also makes an excellent basic loaf of bread, and can be used for the tarte flambée recipe on page 188. There's little work involved, but you will have to be nearby for 4 hours or so. Once completed, this dough can be kept refrigerated for up to 2 days; it also freezes well.

4 cups (560g) unbleached all-purpose flour

½ slightly heaped teaspoon instant yeast

1½ teaspoons fine sea salt

1¾ cups (435ml) room-temperature water

1 tablespoon olive oil

- In a large bowl, combine the flour, yeast, and salt and mix. Pour the water and olive oil into the center of the dry ingredients and gently mix for about a minute to form a coarse dough. Cover with a kitchen towel and let rest for 5 minutes.

- Uncover the dough and begin the folding process by holding the bowl with one hand, lifting up a side of the dough near the edge of the bowl and then plunging it into the center of the dough. While turning the bowl, repeat this movement about 20 times, going all the way around the bowl. This should only take a couple of minutes, but you will see the dough becoming more elastic and smooth, forming a ball even, as you go. Cover and let rise at room temperature for 1 hour.

- Uncover and repeat the lifting-and-folding operation, but only about four or five times. Cover and let rest for another hour, then repeat the operation, allowing the dough to rest for another hour. At the end of the third hour, turn the dough out onto a lightly floured surface and cut it into 4 equal pieces. Roll each piece firmly into a ball, place on the lightly floured counter, and cover with a clean dish towel while you preheat the oven and prepare your toppings.

- If you're not ready to make your pizzas right away, place the dough balls on a floured baking sheet, sprinkle lightly with flour, cover with plastic wrap, and refrigerate for up to 48 hours or freeze for up to three months.

Perfect Pizza

Making pizza isn't all that difficult, but it takes practice to make a pizzeria-level pie. The key is also to keep your toppings to a minimum, making the crust the key player in a pizza instead of a base to support a mound of ingredients.

Good to Know

— **To get going**, start off with a Margherita pizza, which consists simply of a swirl of tomato sauce, a few pieces of mozzarella di bufala, a sprinkling of grated Parmesan, and a couple of fresh basil leaves.

— **For the sauce:** The best sauce is made by simply placing the contents of a 28-ounce (798ml) can of Italian plum tomatoes (basil leaves removed but juice included) in a blender with 2 teaspoons of salt and puree just until smooth.

— **For the toppings:** Once you've mastered the Margherita, feel free to add spicy sausage, rapini, peppers, red onion . . . the works. Just keep the toppings on the light side or your pizza will turn into a soggy mess.

— **For the cheese:** When using fresh mozzarella, less is definitely more. One ball of fresh mozzarella (4.4 ounces/125g) is enough for about three pizzas. You can cut it or simply rip off small pieces from the ball. I like adding grated Parmesan, too, but a few large pinches is all you need. And I'll take grated caciocavallo or aged cheddar any day over commercial (and often tasteless) mozzarella.

What you are aiming for:

— The ideal pizza has a puffy crust, blistered back around the edges, pools of molten cheese, and a good balance of flavours and textures between the crust and toppings. The crust should have a good chewiness to it and, like all bread products, should taste like wheat. Chances are, your first pies will be misshapen, over- or undercooked and overly loaded down with toppings. Don't be discouraged. They'll still taste great and you'll quickly get the hang of it.

TO MAKE THE PIZZA:

Preheat the oven to 550°F (275°C) or the highest temperature it will go and place a pizza stone (or pizza steel) in the middle of the oven. Do this at least 30 minutes in advance, as your oven must be as hot as possible when you start making the pizza. Don't even think of baking your pizza until your oven is at maximum heat.

Flour your counter, then take a ball of dough (from page 181 or 182) and flip it over so that the smooth surface is down. Hand-shape each dough ball into a 10- to 12-inch (25 to 30cm) round. To do this, press the round of dough with your fingertips as much as you can to make an even round with a perimeter slightly thicker than the rest of the pie. If you accidentally tear the dough, just pinch the tear shut and carry on. You are aiming for a 10-inch (25cm) circle. You can lift the dough off the surface and expand it with the back of your hands or turn it in circles on the counter while stretching it out gently with your palms, even letting it hang over the side of the counter. Try to avoid rolling the dough with a rolling pin, which can result in a compact and lifeless crust.

Transfer the round of dough onto a lightly floured baker's peel, spread over about ¼ cup (60ml) of sauce (resist adding too much sauce!), and then quickly cover with toppings (see Perfect Pizza, page 185, for tips). Pick up the peel and slide the pizza onto the hot pizza stone.* Bake until the crust and cheese are golden brown (check the underside of the crust to be sure it's a deep golden brown). This shouldn't take long if your oven is hot enough (count on 7 to 10 minutes). Once out of the oven, you can drizzle with a bit of extra-virgin olive oil or spicy oil, top with a few spoonfuls of pesto, or scatter over a handful of arugula. Have fun with it!

*Once you've mastered this technique, try assembling the entire pizza on the counter, then slide under the peel and transfer it to the oven. This is the way skilled pizzaiolos do it, but it takes some practice.

FLAMMEKUECHE

MAKES ONE 10-INCH (25CM) PIE

*I developed this recipe, also known as tarte flambée, for the TV show
Curieux Bégin after having tasted these flatbread pies in Eguisheim, in
the heart of the Alsace wine region in France. You can serve these as a
main meal or cut them up for a predinner snack, preferably with a glass
of riesling or pinot blanc. Unlike with pizza, the aim here is to get your
dough as thin as possible, so feel free to use a rolling pin to help.*

1 cup (about 7 ounces/
200g) thick-cut smoked
bacon, chopped into
a large dice

1 medium yellow onion,
finely chopped

2 tablespoons white wine

⅓ cup (75g) crème fraîche,
mascarpone cheese, or
sour cream

⅓ cup (75g) quark cheese,
or Greek yogurt

1 tablespoon cornstarch

Grated nutmeg

Freshly ground black
pepper

1 (8-ounce/250g) ball pizza
dough (see pages 181 or
182)

- Preheat the oven to 550°F (275°C). Place a pizza stone on the middle rack.

- In a medium skillet, cook the bacon over medium-high heat until it begins to release its fat, then add the onion and fry until the onion is soft and the bacon begins to crisp. Add the wine, stir, and set aside.

- In a small bowl, combine the crème fraîche, cheese, cornstarch, and a good pinch each of nutmeg and pepper. Set aside.

- On a floured surface, press the dough into a thin round using your fingertips until you reach about 10 inches (25cm). A rolling pin can come in handy here to even out the dough if you're having trouble, but don't fret about keeping it round the first few times you make it. Leaving a slight border exposed, spread the cream mixture over the dough, then sprinkle over the bacon and onion. Slide the pie onto a floured baker's peel and then slide it directly onto your pizza stone. Bake until the dough is golden and the cream mixture is bubbling, 7 to 10 minutes. Remove from the stone using your pizza peel and let cool a bit before slicing and serving.

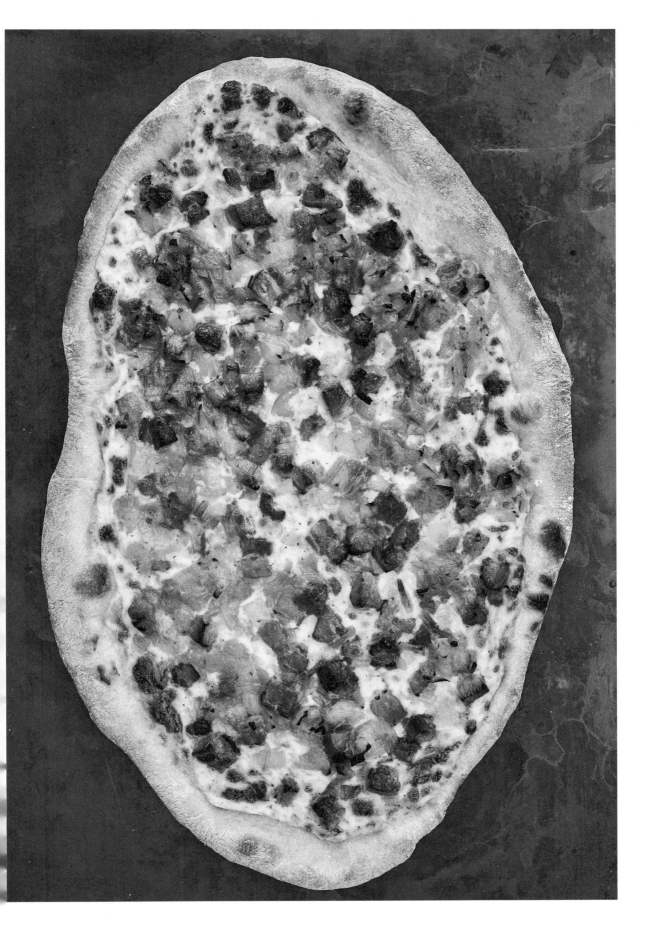

FISH AND SEAFOOD:
A WORLD OF POSSIBILITY

FISH AND SEAFOOD:
A WORLD OF POSSIBILITY

I was a latecomer to the world of fish. Part of me blames my parents, because we rarely ate fish at home. In their defense, there wasn't much to work with back in the '80s. Occasionally, a rainbow trout would emerge from the freezer in a blue plastic wrapper, frosted tail jutting out the side, and I recall visits to the fishmonger where both the crowds and the smell overwhelmed. Otherwise, save for canned tuna fish, nothing. As is the case with many people these days, my parents preferred to eat fish "out." Fish is a notorious house smeller-upper, and why even bother when chefs acquire the best specimens and cook it better than you can?

We fish-challenged were let off the hook, somewhat, a decade ago when the topic of sustainable seafood became a huge concern for consumers. Seemingly overnight, bluefin tuna, skate, red snapper, Chilean sea bass, and Atlantic cod were off-limits. And caviar? Fuhgeddaboudit! As for all that farmed salmon and shrimp, when you read about the dodgy fish-farming practices, you tend to think twice. That leaves wild fish and seafood, which have become increasingly rare and luxurious options.

There is no doubt that buying and preparing fish can be intimidating. And as good fish doesn't come cheap, we better know what we're doing. But fish is also incredibly rewarding to cook. I stick to five rules: always shop for the day you are cooking; always work with a solid recipe; try to go beyond the usual fried or deep-fried fillets (fish works beautifully in Indian- and Asian-inspired recipes); always head to a reputable fishmonger; and finally, never forget that when it comes to fish, the less you tamper with it, the more its delicate flavour will sing.

Good to Know . . .

— I have such a fear of overcooking fish that I have become a perennial under-cooker, the lesser of two evils, perhaps, yet still not a good thing when your guests are staring down at a plate of mush. A good test to check for doneness is to use a thermometer (you're looking for an internal temperature of 125°F/52°C for a salmon fillet). Or try inserting a metal skewer into the thickest part of the fish, pulling it out, and then placing the end of the skewer against your lip. If it is hot, the fish is cooked.

— My favourite fishmongers are the ones where the fish are displayed on ice and the whole display area is hosed down often and, even better, is kept refrigerated. It's a good sign when your fish shop is crowded and the staff can answer questions you have about the fish, from preparation to provenance. A wide selection is not as important to me as a regular rotation of stock. Also, don't count out your supermarket, as many have made a huge effort to improve their seafood offerings, even labeling specimens that are sustainable.

— Check out the apps: For definitive answers on sustainability, visit the Monterey Bay Aquarium Seafood Watch app. When looking for certification on packaging in Canada, the prominent ones include the Marine Stewardship Council (MSC), the Aquaculture Stewardship Council (ASC), and Ocean Wise, which labels products as recommended or not. An MSC blue fish label means the product has met the global gold standard for sustainability.

— Lean in: Smell the fish (it should smell fresh, not "fishy"), look at the gills (they should be bright red, not brown), then the eyes (they should be clear and bulging). Fillets should be firm. Avoid those sold on trays with liquid pooled at the bottom.

— Frozen fish and seafood is fine—in fact, it's usually flash frozen at sea right after being caught, making it preferable to most "fresh" fishmonger fare. Just make sure the expiry dates are far away and that there's no freezer burn on the fish or an excess of ice inside the packaging.

— When cooking fish, let the ingredient dictate the recipe. Buy the freshest fish of the day at your fishmonger's first, then find a recipe for it afterwards.

— Start small. If fish cookery is new to you, don't walk away with a whole salmon that won't fit in your oven. Start with fillets or smaller whole fish, and if the head and tail give you the heebie-jeebies, request that they be removed. Any good fishmonger will prepare the fish to your specifications.

— As for shellfish, I recommend beginning with mussels. They are cheap, easy to prepare, and delicious. Clams, too. Yes, scallops are lovely, but they're also expensive. Oysters are amazing, but if you are not experienced at opening them, ask the fishmonger to shuck them. Or, better yet, eat them at a restaurant.

FILLETS MEUNIÈRE

SERVES 1

I thought it was essential to begin this chapter with a recipe for beginners, so I asked my friend Chef James MacGuire for a recipe of his for a simple fish fillet cooked meunière-style. He happily accepted, and added these words of advice:

"This basic recipe is just a simple sauté, but the brown, roasty flavours on the outside go beautifully with the delicate, nutty flavour of a number of white-fleshed fish. Start small. Fish fillets or individual boneless portions are the least scary to try the method out. Sole and halibut work well; turbot is another good choice. Cod and haddock, though, can be too watery to brown well. Dredge only one side of the fillets: because most are thin, they're pretty much cooked by the time they're browned on one side, which means the flour on the second side only becomes gummy. The cooking process will be quick. Because there are so many variables (heat, size of pan, thickness of fillets), more specific guidelines are almost useless. The challenge will be to get the pan hot enough to brown the fish evenly without overcooking. As for accompaniments, steamed potatoes and, if you're feeling flush, a good Chablis."

1 (6- to 7-ounce/170 to 200g) fillet of halibut, fluke, turbot, grey sole, or lemon sole, skinned

Fine sea salt and freshly ground black pepper

¼ cup (35g) all-purpose flour

About 2 tablespoons vegetable oil or light olive oil

2 tablespoons unsalted butter

1 tablespoon finely chopped fresh parsley

Juice of ½ lemon

• Season the fish fillet on both sides with salt and pepper. Sprinkle the flour in an even layer on a plate and dredge the rounded bone side (as opposed to the flatter, more silvery-looking skin side) of the fish in the flour. If necessary, fold the tail end of the fillet under to even out the thickness.

• Heat a medium skillet over medium-high heat and add a shallow slick of oil. When things are just right, the oil should look quite hot but not be smoking. Add half the butter. If ever the oil-butter mixture begins to burn, it's best to start over.

• As the butter starts to foam and change colour, pick up the fillet by the folded end with kitchen tongs and carefully add it—floured-side down—to the hot pan, being careful that the end that goes flopping into the pan falls away from you so that you don't spatter yourself. The tail should remain folded under in the pan.

- Don't touch the fillet during the first moments of cooking; this will only cool things down and slow the browning process. The fish is almost done when you see a loss of translucency of the flesh around the edges; check brownness underneath by using a spatula to peek without moving the fish too much. The entire process can take 2 to 5 minutes. If the fillet appears to be cooked through, don't bother cooking it on the second side. Simply turn it over onto a warmed plate. (If the fillet is thick, give it a minute or two on the unfloured side.) To finish in the true meunière fashion, sprinkle the hot fillet with the parsley.

- Discard the oil-butter mixture from the pan and add the remaining butter. Cook until it turns very light brown, squeeze in the lemon juice, swirl, and pour over the fish.

→

- **Classic variations:** Try adding drained capers, and/or sliced blanched almonds (as in sole amandine), very slowly cooked in the butter until both are light brown. Omit the parsley garnish for the amandine.

- **Bone-in variations for whole fish or skate:** After experimenting with fillets, try a whole fish: portion-size grey or lemon sole, or for two or more, fluke or baby halibut. If you're lucky enough to have a fresh-caught trout, this recipe is the only way to go. MacGuire also recommends skate, saying: "Fan-shaped slices of skate (wing) have a delicious nutty flavour and great texture. When perfectly cooked, skate is fun to eat because the fillets come popping right off the bone. When buying skate or whole fish, have the fishmonger remove the skin from both sides, as well as the entrails, and cut away the pinlike bones that line the edges using sturdy scissors. Because a skate wing generally serves two to three, it should be cut into portions, and can always be filleted in the kitchen before being served."

- **To cook bone-in whole fish or skate:** The cooking process is the same as above, except your bone-in fish has to be cooked (and dredged) on both sides. For skate, brown the fish well on both sides, and finish it (on a baking sheet or a pie plate) in a 350°F (180°C) oven for a few minutes. Check for doneness by making an incision into the thickest part along the backbone near the spine, where the flesh cooks last. Generally, it's done once nicely browned on both sides.

SALMON WITH HERBED CREAM

This recipe is from my mother's small repertoire of fish recipes, and it's a no-fail family favourite. To make it even better (sorry, Mom!), I looked to the famous Troisgros recipe for saumon à l'oseille, *and used some of their techniques and flavour combinations. As for the herbs, I chose sorrel, but tarragon and dill work very well and are easier to find year-round.*

2 (6-ounce/about 180g) skin-on salmon fillets

Fine sea salt and freshly ground black pepper

2 teaspoons canola, sunflower, or grapeseed oil

½ cup (125ml) white wine or fish stock

1 large French shallot, finely chopped

½ cup (125ml) whipping cream, or ¼ cup (60ml) whipping cream and ¼ cup (60ml) crème fraîche

Leaves from 1 bunch sorrel (about ½ cup packed/15g), ripped into smaller pieces, or 2 tablespoons chopped fresh tarragon or dill

1 tablespoon unsalted butter

Squeeze of fresh lemon juice (optional)

- Preheat the oven to 350°F (175°C).

- Season the salmon fillets on both sides with salt and pepper. In a medium skillet (preferably nonstick), heat the canola oil over medium-high heat. Add the salmon, flesh-side down, and fry, undisturbed, for about 3 minutes, until lightly browned. Turn over and fry on the skin side for 2 minutes. Carefully transfer the fillets flesh-side up to a shallow ovenproof dish and set aside while you make the sauce.

- In a small pot, combine the wine and shallot. Bring to a boil and cook until almost all the liquid is evaporated, about 5 minutes. Add the cream and bring just to a boil (purists at this point will strain out the shallots, but it's fine to leave them in). Add the sorrel and cook until just wilted. Remove from the heat and whisk in the butter. Season with salt and pepper.

- Spoon the sauce over the fish, sprinkle over a bit of salt, and bake for 10 minutes (12 minutes for thicker fillets), until the salmon is cooked through but still moist in the middle. Transfer to warm plates and serve with the sauce spooned over the top and a squeeze of lemon, if you like.

SALT-BAKED BASS

SERVES 6 (OR 4 GENEROUSLY)

The idea of baking anything in a salt crust may seem odd, yet it's one of the easiest ways to cook a whole fish. The key is to be sure the fish is cooked through, or all that salt packing is a waste of time. For this recipe, purchase a fish between 3½ to 4 pounds (1.6 to 1.8kg), and if it's larger, increase the cooking time by 5 to 10 minutes. This is an impressive dish for a dinner party, as long as someone at the end of it all knows how to filet a fish. As an accompaniment, I like to serve Grilled Ratatouille Salad (page 112).

1 whole sea bass or striped bass, about 3½ pounds (1.6kg) in weight

4½ pounds (2kg) coarse sea salt

⅔ cup (150ml) water

Fine sea salt and freshly ground black pepper

1 large lemon

Enough rosemary or dill sprigs to generously fill the fish cavity

Best-quality extra-virgin olive oil

- Ask your fishmonger to gut and remove the gills of the fish and to clean out and open the cavity, but not to scale it (the scales prevent the salt from leaching into the fish flesh). If the fish is large, ask that they slice off the tail.

- Preheat the oven to 450°F (230°C). Pull out a baking sheet or skillet large enough to hold the fish flat. Let your fish come to room temperature before proceeding.

- Place the coarse salt in a large bowl and add the water. Mix by hand until it has the consistency of damp sand.

- Season inside the cavity of the fish with fine sea salt and pepper. Slice the lemon in half, then cut one half into thin slices and the other into wedges; set the wedges aside for serving. Place the lemon slices and the rosemary into the cavity of the fish, filling it generously.

- Place about half the wet salt on your baking sheet or skillet in an even layer slightly larger than the fish and lay the fish on top. Cover evenly with the remaining wet salt (you don't have to cover the head or the tail), mounding it well and packing it over the top to form a tight dome of salt around the fish.

- Place into the oven and immediately reduce the oven temperature to 400°F (200°C). Bake for 30 minutes (35 to 40 minutes for a slightly larger fish). With this timing, your fish should be perfectly cooked, but a telltale sign will be that at about the 25-minute mark, the smell of roasting fish will come wafting through the kitchen. Remove the pan from the oven and let cool for 5 minutes.

- Break off the salt crust (it should come away in large pieces) from the top, lift the fish off the salt base, and remove the skin from the top side. Filet the fish on both sides and place the gorgeous steaming flesh on a serving platter. Sprinkle with a bit of fine sea salt, drizzle with olive oil, and serve with the lemon wedges.

* **Note:** You can preheat your serving platter to ensure the fish will stay warm, but even if you don't get it out onto the table piping hot, it will still be delicious.

TROUT EN PAPILLOTE WITH ONION BEURRE BLANC AND POTATOES

SERVES 4

This recipe from Montreal chef Danny St Pierre has become a favourite, especially for dinner parties, because it can be assembled in advance and the presentation is just so cool. St Pierre says several other fish fillets work well in this recipe, including haddock, cod, sablefish, and halibut. Serve this right in the paper packets, and watch your guests scrape out every last morsel.

8 small new potatoes, peeled

½ cup (1 stick/110g) unsalted butter, divided

16 pearl onions, peeled, or 2 medium leeks, washed (see Note)

4 small garlic cloves, minced

1 cup (250ml) good dry white wine

¼ cup (60ml) whipping cream

Fine sea salt and freshly ground black pepper

4 trout fillets, about 5 ounces (150g) each, skinned

4 scallions, chopped

• Preheat the oven to 500°F (250°C). Have ready a large baking sheet and cut four sheets of parchment paper, about 12 × 15 inches (30 × 38cm) each.

• Place the potatoes in a small pot, add cold water to cover, and salt the water. Bring to a boil, then cook until the potatoes can be easily pierced with the point of a knife. Drain and slice into ½-inch-thick (1cm) rounds. Set aside.

• Meanwhile, in a medium saucepan, melt 2 tablespoons of the butter over medium-high heat. Add the onions or leeks and garlic and sauté until softened. Stir in the wine and cook until the liquid is reduced by half. Add the cream and remove from the heat. Stir in all but 1 tablespoon of the remaining butter. Season with salt and pepper. Set aside.

• Lay the parchment sheets on your counter and spoon equal amounts of the onion sauce onto the center of each sheet. Lay the slices of cooked potatoes equally over each. Next, place a fish fillet atop the potatoes, season with salt and pepper, then place a quarter of the remaining 1 tablespoon butter over each. Finally, sprinkle over the scallions.

Fold the top left-hand corner of the parchment to meet the bottom right-hand corner and, starting at the left, crimp the edges of the paper from left to right to seal the packets, forming a half-moon. Place the packets in one layer on a large baking sheet. (At this point, the assembled packets can be refrigerated for several hours. Just let them come to room temperature for 20 minutes before baking.)

• Bake for 15 minutes, then immediately slide a packet right onto each guest's plate, instructing everyone to immediately rip open their packet (if they sit too long, the fish will keep cooking). You can add a pinch of salt or a squeeze of lemon, but really, it's not necessary.

* **Note**: If using the leeks, trim off the root end and slice off the dark green tops. Peel away any withered or damaged outer leaves, then halve the leeks lengthwise. Rinse under cold water, getting well between the layers to remove any grit. Lay the leeks down flat on a cutting board and thinly slice.

About Mussels

Mussels have a lot going for them. They're inexpensive—less than half the price of littleneck clams—and they're also one of the most sustainable types of fish or shellfish. They grow on rocky coastlines in the wild, but most of the ones sold in fish shops and supermarkets are farmed blue mussels from Newfoundland or Prince Edward Island. They're also low-cal and fast-cooking, and lend themselves to all sorts of flavour combinations. *Moules-frites* are a classic in Belgian and French cuisine, but mussels also star in Italian seafood pastas and Portuguese *cataplanas*. Spanish chefs place them atop paella, and Thai and Indian chefs bathe them in curry. Mussels are soft, velvety, and fun to eat with your fingers, while offering a subtle taste of the sea.

That said . . . mussels sometimes get a bad rap, primarily because people are under the impression that if the mussels aren't fresh, they will make you sick. Sure, but then again, a lot of foods can, especially if mishandled by a clueless cook. So what better reason to make mussels at home, where you can take the time to check them one by one or verify expiry dates on the bags in which the mussels are sold? (Also, be sure the tag has not been cut off the bag.) They keep for up to 10 days, but I don't go beyond 7. Any open mussels should be knocked against the counter; if the shell doesn't shut, toss it. They shouldn't smell—if they do at all, don't buy them. If possible, try to get ahold of mussels from the Îles de la Madeleine, which are especially plump, meaty, and tasty. Honey Mussels from British Columbia are another great Canadian mussel, though pricier than most.

In the old days, you'd have to pick through mussels one by one, then soak them in a bit of floured water to get them to disgorge any sand, scrub them lightly, and finally remove their beards (the tuft of coarse hair that connects the mussel to the surface on which it grows). Nowadays mussels are cleaned and beards are removed at the plant, and farmed mussels are grown on suspended ropes so they don't get sandy or muddy. You just need to toss them in the sink, give them a fast rinse, then sort them to remove any cracked or open ones. After a short cooking time (usually around 3 minutes, though some recipes call for up to 8 minutes), you have a brasserie-worthy supper. All you need is a chunk of baguette to soak up the mussel juices at the bottom of the bowl.

As for cooking, if possible, try to find the traditional single-serving mussel pots with deep round lids, perfect for depositing the shells as you eat. Sold on every street corner in Belgium, they're rare in North America, but try your local kitchen or restaurant supply store (ask for Demeyere Resto stainless-steel mussel pots, imported from Belgium).

Mussels can be prepared marinière-style by steaming them over a little dry white wine (like muscadet or Sancerre), mixed with lightly sautéed garlic and/or shallots and, to finish, a sprinkling of chopped fresh parsley. But East Coast varieties can sometimes lack flavour, which is why a sauce with a bit of pizzazz can really make mussels sing. Slide some into a pot of simmering tomato sauce, cover, steam for 5 minutes, and serve in bowls with garlic bread alongside. Or add some clams and shrimp to that pot, cook them all together with a shot of pastis, and then mix them into pasta along with some chopped fresh parsley and tarragon. Voilà! Your very own red sauce seafood pasta.

Mussels are easy; the only rules are to treat them with care (always keep them refrigerated until cooked), to not overcook them (or they'll be tough), and to always discard any unopened mussels after cooking. They're also a great choice for a crowd. Get the guests in the kitchen to customize the mussel recipe with different sauces or seasonings and to give the pot a shake or two while they steam. Then lift off the lid, give them a stir, soak up the vivid sea aromas, and dig in.

And finally . . . a word on mussel-eating etiquette: Forget the cutlery—mussels are finger food. The ideal method is to pinch each mussel out of its casing with the aid of an empty shell. And once you get to the bottom of the pot, slurping up the remaining juices and vegetables is encouraged.

CURRIED MUSSELS

SERVES 4 (OR 2 GENEROUSLY)

I first spotted this recipe in an article by the famous Vancouver chef Vikram Vij. The original recipe called for shrimp, but I figured it would work well with mussels. And wow, did it ever! The first time I made this, I ate two pounds of mussels myself before slurping back the tangy and spicy coconut curry.

4 pounds (1.8kg) fresh mussels

½ cup (110g) Clarified Butter (page 57) or cooking oil

1 tablespoon cumin seeds

3 cups (about 375g) finely chopped red onions

1 teaspoon ground turmeric

1 teaspoon fine sea salt

1 teaspoon cayenne pepper

1 teaspoon chopped jalapeño

1 tablespoon finely chopped fresh ginger

½ cup (125ml) tamarind juice (see Note)

1 cup (250ml) coconut milk

½ bunch cilantro, chopped

• Rinse the mussels, discarding any that are open or cracked. In a large skillet, heat the butter over medium to high heat for 1 minute. Sprinkle in the cumin seeds and allow them to sizzle for about 45 seconds. Add the onions and sauté until golden brown. Reduce the heat to medium and add the turmeric, salt, and cayenne. Sauté for 1 minute, then add the jalapeño and ginger. Sauté for 1 minute more. Add the tamarind juice and bring to a boil. Add the mussels, cover with a tight-fitting lid, and cook on high heat, shaking the pot every so often, for about 4 minutes, or until the mussels open. Stir in the coconut milk, cover, and cook for 2 minutes more. Stir in the cilantro, then pour into a large bowl and serve immediately.

* **Note:** To make tamarind juice, stir 1 tablespoon tamarind pulp or paste into ½ cup (125ml) hot water. With your fingers, swish the tamarind around to help it dissolve, resulting in a thick light brown liquid. Remove any undiluted pulp from the liquid, and the tamarind juice is ready to use.

MOULES CASSEROLE

SERVES 2

This recipe is written for two individual mussel pots, but it can easily be made in a single covered pot that isn't too heavy to shake with ease. It can also be doubled or tripled, and you can add ingredients like extra herbs, peppers, or cream, if desired. Just be sure to respect the cooking times and temperatures listed. Serve with frites (see page 145) and a Belgian beer, or a dry white wine like a muscadet.

4 pounds (1.8kg) fresh mussels

1 medium yellow onion

1 celery stalk

2 medium carrots

1 leek, white part only, washed

2 tablespoons unsalted butter

2 tablespoons vegetable oil

2 garlic cloves, minced

2 wineglasses (about 1½ cups/400ml) dry white wine

Handful of fresh parsley, chopped

Fine sea salt and freshly ground black pepper

- Rinse the mussels in cold water and discard any that are open or have cracked shells. Chop the onion, celery, carrots, and leek into large pieces (about 1 inch/2.5cm).

- Place 1 tablespoon of butter and 1 tablespoon of oil in each pot over medium heat. When the butter starts to foam, divide the vegetables into the two pots along with the garlic. Cook, stirring occasionally, until the vegetables begin to soften. Add half the mussels and half the wine to each pot, cover, and turn the heat to high. Cook, occasionally shaking the pots gently, for 5 to 7 minutes (depending on the size of the mussels), until all the mussel shells open. Just before the cooking time is up, pour in the remaining wine, sprinkle with the parsley, season with salt and pepper, cover, and toss one last time. Keep covered until ready to serve.

Tips for Buying Shrimp

Do not hesitate to buy frozen shrimp, as most shrimp you see sold on ice has already been frozen—sometimes twice. Fresh shrimp are a rare treat and difficult to find at your fishmonger (and at quite a hefty price), so go for frozen. If they are wild shrimp, be sure to rinse them well with tap water once defrosted, as they are frozen in salt water.

You can purchase wild shrimp or farmed shrimp, but the former are more sought-after and therefore more expensive. If it's possible in your area, purchase local wild shrimp in season. In Quebec, Matane shrimp are available fresh in mid-April. In Canada, there are several species of wild shrimp from the West Coast that are well worth exploring, including spot prawns, humpback shrimp, and sidestripe shrimp.

Learn about the count: Chances are that bag of shrimp you see marked "Extra Large" contains medium shrimp, because names like "Jumbo" are meaningless on the shrimp scene. Size standardization is done with a count that represents the number of shrimp per pound; the lower the numbers, the larger the shrimp. A 16/20 count means there are 16 to 20 shrimp per pound; that shrimp you saw marked as "Extra Large" is probably a 26/30 count, which are medium shrimp, whereas a 36/45 count is for small shrimp. For even larger shrimp, you'll see a count like U/10 or U/15, meaning there are "under 10" or "under 15" shrimp per pound.

It's important to know that all shrimp are treated with sulfites. As for specifics regarding other chemical treatment or any other concerns, talk to your fishmonger directly.

And finally, don't expect to pay a small price for top-quality shrimp. Demand is the reason the industry is flooded with dodgy products. Shrimp is a luxury food that we shouldn't expect to eat every day. Save it for special occasions.

RED CURRY SHRIMP STIR-FRY

SERVES 4

Truth be told, shrimp are not my thing. I have, however, developed a shrimp recipe that I love, based very loosely on the red curry chicken recipe from the famous book Hot Sour Salty Sweet *by Naomi Duguid and Jeffrey Alford. As I rarely have all the ingredients called for in that recipe, I contacted Naomi, a good friend, who talked me through an abridged version of her original recipe. Success! Feel free to play around with the add-ins and the garnish to make this recipe your own. I serve this with plain basmati rice. Make sure to set a spoon so that your friends can enjoy every last drop.*

1½ pounds (680g) jumbo or extra-jumbo black tiger shrimp (I use 16/20 count)

2 tablespoons peanut oil or canola oil

3 tablespoons Thai red curry paste

2 tablespoons finely chopped French shallot

2 tablespoons finely chopped fresh ginger

2 tablespoons finely chopped garlic

1 red bell pepper, thinly sliced

3 Thai hot chiles (these are the small, hot ones), sliced in half

1 (14-ounce/400ml) can coconut milk

→

- Peel and devein the shrimp. Place in a colander, give them a quick rinse, and refrigerate until ready to use.

- In a large wok or skillet, heat the peanut oil over high heat. Add the curry paste and fry it in the oil, stirring in circles (I use the back of a ladle for this). When the oil is absorbed, add the shallot, ginger, and garlic and fry for another minute. Add the bell pepper and fry until it softens, then add the chiles. Starting with the thicker paste, pour half the coconut milk into the mixture, stir well, then add the rest of the coconut milk along with half a can of water. Bring to a rapid boil and cook to reduce the liquid by about a third. (At this point, the broth can be refrigerated for up to 1 day; bring it back to a boil before proceeding, adding a bit of water if it's too thick.)

- Add the shrimp in one shot and stir to bathe them in the bubbling broth. After a minute, stir in the basil and fish sauce, then add the spinach, cover, and let steam/cook for a good minute, or until the spinach leaves are wilted into the sauce.

½ cup fresh Thai or sweet basil leaves

2 tablespoons Thai fish sauce

5 ounces (140g) fresh spinach, thick stems removed, coarsely chopped

2 scallions, sliced into thin rounds, for serving

Handful of fresh cilantro, coarsely chopped, for serving

Juice of ½ lime, plus lime wedges to pass at the table

- Transfer the curry to a large serving bowl and scatter over the scallions and cilantro. Squeeze the lime juice over the top and serve with the lime wedges alongside.

* **Note:** You can make the sauce a day in advance and add in the shrimp and flavour enhancers just before serving.

- **Variation with chicken:** Substitute equal amounts of thinly sliced chicken breast for the shrimp, but simmer for a good 10 minutes before adding the basil and fish sauce. You can also use boneless, skinless chicken thighs, but double the simmering time to about 20 minutes, adding a bit of water if the sauce gets too thick.

ROAST CHICKEN:
MY QUEST FOR THE BEST

ROAST CHICKEN:
MY QUEST FOR THE BEST

The quest for perfection is an arduous journey. But once you have tasted perfection, there is no turning back: the desire to recapture that moment of bliss becomes an obsession. Like many home cooks, I've spent years in search of a recipe for the perfect roast chicken. I'm talking moist, flavourful, golden, evenly cooked. It hasn't been easy.

At cooking school, the method we learned consisted of browning the chicken on the stovetop before roasting at 375°F (190°C) for an hour. The resulting bird was good, sometimes patchy-looking, and almost always with a soggy-skinned back. My mother cooked chicken by standing it upright in the oven, which produced a uniformly golden roast. Yet with the bird positioned in this manner, the pan juices ran downward, resulting in a cottony, dry breast.

Cookbooks provide a wealth of information, as almost every one includes a recipe for chicken that's buttered, placed in a roasting pan, sometimes atop a bed of onions, and roasted at high heat (usually about 400°F/200°C) for just over an hour. The method is fine, but the results are hardly exciting. More ambitious recipes recommend starting the chicken off upside down, then placing it on one side for 20 minutes, flipping it to its next side for 20 minutes, and then roasting it on its back for the last 20 minutes. Better, but the flavour is sometimes still lacking. Though many recipes call for smearing the raw bird with butter or stuffing a bunch of lemons and herbs into the cavity, in my experience, all those extras have a negligible effect on the taste. So I tried marinating the chicken, and instead of keeping its football shape, I spatchcocked it. Spatchcocking involves slicing the bird open so that the meat and skin lay flat. The chicken can be cut open along the backbone or sliced right down the middle of the breast, which keeps all the magnificent bits of back meat—including the succulent "oysters"—intact. Not only is this technique the ideal way to achieve a uniform layer of crisp skin, it's also faster, and the bird's a cinch to carve. This butterflied method became a favorite.

Two other techniques have also won me over: One calls for the chicken to be poached first and then roasted at high heat. The other consists of roasting the bird at a lower temperature in an olive oil bath filled with flavour enhancers. All three are very different, but with the same delicious results. Having devoted a lifetime in the kitchen to roasting the perfect chicken, I am delighted to share my holy grail of recipes with you.

Good to Know . . .

— **Buying the bird:** After testing recipes on several different chickens, the certified-organic and grain-fed chickens came out on top for texture and pronounced chicken flavour. However, I wouldn't go so far as to say the more costly the bird, the better. A lousy recipe can easily ruin a $25 chicken—or conversely, proper roasting can make a $12 chicken into an excellent meal. Trust your judgment here while respecting your budget.

— **Take off the plastic!** I prefer buying chicken at a butcher shop, where the birds are sold wrapped in brown paper instead of plastic. But when I do buy a chicken wrapped in plastic, I immediately unwrap it, place it on a rack over a plate, and refrigerate it for up to 2 days before roasting so that the skin dries out, which helps give it a crisper skin.

— **Size matters:** A small chicken, known as a fryer (about 3 to 3½ pounds/1.4 to 1.6kg) is my preference, for several reasons. When you slice it into eight pieces to serve (thigh removed from drumstick and each breast cut in half), the portions aren't too large, so people can enjoy both dark and white meat. The choice of rotisserie restaurants, smaller chickens roast more uniformly, with a higher skin-to-flesh ratio than larger birds. And they are less expensive, and often on sale. A larger bird, known as a "roaster" (5 to 6 pounds/2.3 to 2.7kg) is a good fit for butterflied chicken, because it roasts flat and therefore crisps up more evenly than when left whole. Always check the recommended size of the chicken before beginning a recipe to be sure the cooking times will be accurate.

— **To wash or not to wash?** Debates rage on regarding whether raw chicken should be washed. Fact is, roasting at high temperatures will kill off any bacteria. And speaking of bacteria, washing your chicken risks covering your sink with unwanted bacteria, so if you do prefer to wash it, make sure you clean your sink area well with an antibacterial cleaner afterwards. I usually just pat the bird dry, being sure to get inside the cavity where it's often quite wet, especially if the chicken has been frozen.

— **About internal temperatures:** Chicken is cooked when the thickest part of the leg reaches an internal temperature of at least 165°F (75°C). But keep in mind, the breast meat is done at 145°F (63°C), so if you are cooking your chicken cut into parts, you could remove the pieces of white meat before the dark. For a whole roast chicken, I tend to cook it to an internal temperature of 170°F (76°C) to be absolutely sure it's not pink at the joints.

— **Give it a rest:** Let your chicken rest for at least 15 minutes before carving to allow the residual heat finish off the cooking and to avoid all the juices running out, as they would if you cut into the bird while it's piping hot. Tenting it with foil will keep it warmer for longer, although this tends to reduce the crispiness of the skin.

BUTTERFLIED ROAST CHICKEN

SERVES 6

When it comes to evenly cooked, crisp-skinned birds, this recipe is hard to beat. It's best to begin marinating on the morning of the day you plan to do the roasting, but at the very least, try to marinate for an hour.

1 (5- to 6-pound/2 to 3kg) roasting chicken

Grated zest of 1 lemon (preferably organic)

3 tablespoons fresh lemon juice

¼ cup (60ml) olive oil

2 garlic cloves, finely chopped

1 tablespoon chopped fresh rosemary

1 tablespoon chopped fresh thyme

Fine sea salt and freshly ground black pepper

• Prepare the bird (you could ask your butcher to do this for you): Trim off any excess neck skin and remove any large chunks of fat from the cavity. Turn the chicken upside down on a cutting board and, using a heavy pair of scissors or kitchen shears, cut along both sides of the backbone—from the neck to the tail end—and remove it, as well as the wishbone along the way. Turn the chicken over and press down firmly on both ends of the breastbone to flatten it out. (Alternatively, place the bird on its back and slice right down the middle of the breast, then open it up, which keeps all the tender nuggets of back meat intact.) Then, using a heavy knife, cut off the wing tips and fold them under the shoulder. For a larger bird, cut partway through the flesh at the two leg joints and where the wing joins the body, which will help even out the cooking time. Place the chicken in a large, flat dish.

• In a small bowl, whisk together the lemon zest, lemon juice, oil, garlic, rosemary, and thyme and rub the mixture over the chicken, front and back. Season generously on both sides with salt and pepper. Cover and refrigerate until ready to roast.

- Preheat the oven to 400°F (200°C). Place the oven rack so the chicken will be about 6 inches (15cm) from the broiler heat element. Line a baking sheet with aluminum foil and set a flat wire rack on top. Remove the chicken from the refrigerator while the oven comes up to temperature.

- Transfer the bird, skin-side down, to the rack on the baking sheet. Do not discard any excess marinade. Slide the chicken into the oven and switch the oven to broil.

- Broil the chicken for 10 minutes. Remove from the oven, set the oven temperature back to 400°F (200°C) and place the oven rack in the middle position for roasting. Turn the chicken over (skin-side up), brush with any remaining marinade, and season with salt again. Return the chicken to the oven and roast for about 40 minutes more (30 minutes for a smaller chicken, 3½ to 4 pounds/1.6 to 1.8kg), until the thickest part of the chicken leg reaches an internal temperature of at least 165°F (75°C). Let the bird rest, loosely covered with foil, for about 15 minutes before carving.

ANTOINE'S CHICKEN

SERVES 4 TO 6

This recipe is inspired by the chicken served at Le Coq Rico, the great chicken restaurant of French chef Antoine Westermann. The chicken I enjoyed there was the best I've ever tasted. The secret, I was told, was that he begins by poaching the bird and then roasting it on a rotisserie. Intrigued, I gave it a try, and the results were simply amazing. This recipe is a bit more trouble than your standard roast chicken, but the cooking time is just 1 hour and yields 6 cups of excellent chicken stock for your next recipe. It's important to use a small but meaty chicken for this recipe so that it doesn't fall apart when you poach it.

1 (3- to 3½-pound/1.4 to 1.6kg) chicken

8 cups (1.8L) Chicken Stock (page 82) or store-bought, or 1 (30.4-ounce/900ml) carton chicken stock plus 4 cups (900ml) water and 1 chicken bouillon cube

1 large carrot, cut into large pieces

1 large celery stalk, cut into pieces

1 medium onion, cut into 8 wedges, divided

4 garlic cloves, peeled

About 12 sprigs thyme, divided

2 tablespoons unsalted butter

2 tablespoons olive oil

Fine sea salt and freshly ground black pepper

→

- Rinse your chicken thoroughly inside and out with cold water and pat dry. Truss the chicken with kitchen string, or at least tie the legs together.

- Fill a medium stockpot (mine is 9 × 5 inches /23 × 12cm) with the stock (or the stock, water, and bouillon cube). Add the carrot, celery, half the onion wedges, the garlic, and half the thyme. Add a large pinch of salt and bring to a boil. Lower the chicken into the stock, breast-side up, bring back to a boil, and immediately reduce the heat to maintain a simmer. The chicken should be submerged save for the top part of the breast, and the stock around it should be bubbling ever so slightly. Poach for 30 minutes, keeping the pot partially covered throughout, uncovering only to ladle some hot stock over the breast every once in a while.

- Ten minutes before the chicken is done, preheat the oven to 450°F (225°C). Set a roasting rack in a roasting pan.

- In a small pot, melt together the butter and olive oil. Keep warm.

1 tablespoon all-purpose flour

½ cup white wine (optional)

- When the chicken is done, carefully lift it out of the stock and place it breast-side down on the roasting rack. With a slotted spoon, lift out all the aromatics from the stock and scatter them over the bottom of the roasting pan, along with the remaining onion. Save 1 cup (250ml) of the stock for the sauce and keep the rest for another recipe.

- Place the remaining thyme sprigs inside the cavity of the chicken, brush the skin with a good layer of the butter-oil mixture, and season all over with salt and pepper.

- Roast the chicken for 15 minutes. Remove from the oven and carefully turn it over (breast-side up), brush again with the butter-oil mix, and roast for another 15 minutes. At this point, the bird should be a nice golden colour and the inner temperature in the leg joint should read at least 170°F (77°C).

- Remove from the oven and transfer to your cutting board. Let rest for 15 minutes before carving while you make the sauce.

- Place the roasting pan over medium-high heat. Sprinkle over the flour and stir it all together until the flour disappears. Deglaze with the wine, if using, and stir for about a minute, until the wine is almost all evaporated. Ladle in the reserved stock, stir well, and cook for about a minute, until the sauce takes on a caramel brown colour.

- Meanwhile, cut the chicken into 8 pieces (see Note), place on a serving platter, and sprinkle over a bit of salt. Strain the sauce into a sauce boat and serve alongside the chicken.

- * **Note:** If the chicken legs are still pink in the joints, place them on a baking sheet, skin-side up, and return them to the warm oven for a few minutes to cook through. This can sometimes happen if you use a large chicken.

ROAST CHICKEN CONFIT WITH NEW POTATOES AND CHERRY TOMATOES

SERVES 4 TO 6

This recipe was inspired by cookbook author Alison Roman, though I couldn't resist changing the flavour combinations and part of her technique. She goes heavy on the carrots, but I prefer potatoes and tomatoes, especially in summer when new potatoes and tomatoes are irresistible. I like using a whole chicken, browning it first and roasting it at a higher temperature to help it achieve that ideal glowing golden skin. This recipe calls for quite a bit of oil, but you can strain any you have left over and refrigerate it to use the next time you make this recipe.

1 small (3- to 3½-pound/ 1.4 to 1.6kg) chicken

Fine sea salt and freshly ground black pepper

1¼ cups (285ml) good-quality olive oil, divided

4 to 6 garlic cloves, smashed with the back of your knife, peeled, and coarsely chopped

1¼ pounds (600g) small new potatoes (about 12), scrubbed clean and cut in half (larger ones could be cut in thirds—you want them all about the same size)

14 ounces (400g) cherry tomatoes (about 25)

½ lemon, sliced into thin rounds

Handful of fresh thyme, soft-stemmed, if possible

- Preheat the oven to 375°F (180°C). Have ready a shallow casserole about 12 inches (30cm) across. A 3-inch-deep (7.5cm) skillet that size will also work well. Just don't go bigger.

- Using kitchen shears or a chef's knife, cut your chicken in half straight down the breast and along the back (you can remove the backbone or keep it). Pat dry with paper towels and season generously with salt and pepper.

- In a large skillet, heat 2 tablespoons of the olive oil over medium-high heat until quite hot and then add one chicken half, skin-side down, swirling it around the pan to coat it well with oil (this will help keep it from sticking). Repeat the operation with the second chicken half and sear, without moving them anymore, for a good 3 minutes, or until they are golden and turn over easily without sticking. Turn them over and sear for 3 minutes on the second side, then remove the pan from the heat. Transfer the chicken pieces skin-side up to your casserole in a head-to-toe configuration. If the oil remaining in the skillet is burnt, discard it and wipe the skillet clean.

If not, just leave it. Pour 1 cup (25ml) of the remaining oil into the warm skillet and add the garlic pieces. Heat over low heat until they just begin to sizzle, then turn off the heat and let them steep in the oil.

- Arrange the potato sections around the base of the chicken. With the tip of a sharp knife, pierce a hole in each tomato and arrange them around the chicken as well. Tuck the lemon slices in and around everything and add the thyme sprigs as well, pushing them into the crevices of the meat and vegetables.

- Pour over the hot garlic oil, scraping up any bits left in the pan and distributing them evenly around the dish. If the oil does not come halfway to the top of the chicken halves, drizzle the remaining 2 tablespoons of the oil over the top.

- Place the casserole into the oven, reduce the oven temperature to 350°F (175°C), and roast for about 70 minutes. At the 30-minute mark, you can baste the chicken and vegetables with the oil; at the 1-hour mark, baste again and push any potatoes that still aren't cooked through right down into the oil.

- Remove from the oven and let rest for 10 minutes before serving. Be sure to spoon some of the delicious cooking juices over the chicken, potatoes, and tomatoes when serving.

BIG BEEF: A RARE TREAT

BIG BEEF: A RARE TREAT

Few ingredients offer such an intense flavour experience as a gorgeous slice of marbled, aged beef. I'd go so far as to say Montreal butcher Marc Bourg's 350-day aged steak ranks as one of the most delicious things I've ever eaten. That said, beef has played a decreasing role in my home-cooking repertoire over the years. Given environmental and health factors, many people are cutting back. And given the increasingly prohibitive price of quality beef, it's now squarely in the luxury category.

For an extra-special occasion, I often blow my budget on a luxurious cut. Filet mignon, you're thinking? No thanks. I'm talking côte de boeuf and standing rib roast, custom-cut, meticulously cooked, and eaten with just the right accompaniments, as well as a serious bottle of red wine. Yes! For weeknights, though, I'll opt for braising pieces in the winter, and bavette or hamburgers to grill in the summer. With lots of vegetables on the side, they make for a serious treat once in a while.

A Big Steak for Sharing

For two to four diners, I recommend a single steak, cut thick—2¼ inches (6cm), to be specific. The initial searing adds flavour without drying out the meat—which is a risk when grilling thin steaks—and the meat cooks to a uniform medium-rare. Ask your butcher to cut the steak to order.

As for size, count 8 ounces per person (225g) for boneless meat, or 12 ounces (340g) per person for bone-in meat.

What to buy

A côte de boeuf, cut 2¼ inches (6cm) thick, weighing in at about 2¼ pounds (1kg), which should serve three or four. In France, any supermarket butcher will slice you a côte de boeuf straight off the rib. In North America, while you'll increasingly see these babies featured on restaurant menus—for two or more diners—they are rarely sold in your standard supermarket, so your best bet is to head to a butcher shop, where those offering French cuts will usually stock 1½-inch (4cm) rib steaks, as well as the uncut train de côtes (seven-bone rib) for people who want thicker cuts.

A porterhouse, cut 2¼ inches (6cm) thick, weighing in at about 3 pounds (1.5kg), serves four or five. Almost identical to a thick T-bone (as both steaks are cut from two muscles, the top loin and the tenderloin), the porterhouse contains a larger portion of the tenderloin than the T-bone. Because of its thickness, you will want to finish the cooking in the oven or on the cool side of the grill. A porterhouse isn't as easy to find as a côte de boeuf, but it's worth seeking out or custom-ordering from your butcher.

Good to know . . .

— Should steaks be left at room temperature for several hours before cooking? The jury is still out on this question, but I prefer to take them out a good hour (or two, for especially thick steaks) before grilling.

— Inexperienced grillers might want to get ahold of a meat thermometer to best judge doneness. And for increased accuracy, spring for a digital one. At about $50 a steak, it would be miserable to mess up such magnificent meat.

— When purchasing steak, keep in mind that the most flavourful meat is aged a minimum of 40 days (see page 242).

— The steak must be seared first, then roasted in the oven or finished on the cooler side of the grill. A large grill pan does the job nicely, but in the summer, it would be a shame not to grill it outside on a wood-fired grill, which not only imparts more flavour, but can char the meat faster than a stovetop grill pan.

— If you're up for a little fun, try reverse-searing your steak. Start off in a 275°F (135°C) oven and roast your steak to 10°F (6°C) below the desired internal temperature, then finish it off with a good sear in a hot pan (or grill) on each side. It is imperative, though, to use a thermometer when applying this technique.

— The secret to a deeply caramelized crust is to keep your steak dry. Pat it dry and, if you have a day to spare, place it on a rack, uncovered, in your fridge overnight. For dry-aged steak, you won't have to bother.

— A simple way to test for doneness is to press your finger down on the thickest part of the steak. If the meat is raw, it will be soft and squishy. As it goes from rare to medium to well-done, it toughens and becomes progressively firmer. When well-done, the meat is unyielding.

— A guide to steak internal temperatures:
- Rare = 125°F (52°C)
- Medium-rare = 135°F (57°C)
- Medium = 145°F (63°C)
- Medium-well = 150°F (66°C)
- Well-done = 160°F (71°C)

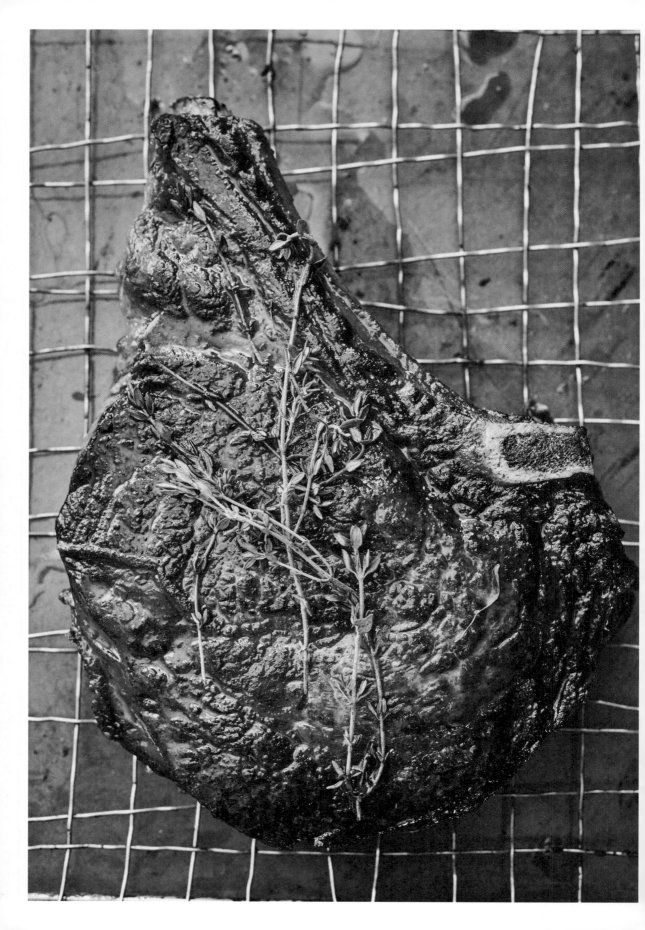

GRILLED CÔTE DE BOEUF OR T-BONE

SERVES 3 TO 5

I suggest this steak be cooked rare or medium-rare. For anything else, consult the temperatures on page 237. And what to serve with this? Potatoes in any form, a garlicky Caesar salad (page 108), a plate of steaming buttered asparagus, and a sauce boat filled with béarnaise (see page 65).

1 (2¼-inch-thick/6cm) côte de boeuf or T-bone steak, about 2¼ pounds (1kg) for a côte de boeuf, 3 pounds (1.5kg) for a T-bone

Fine sea salt and freshly ground black pepper

1 tablespoon cold unsalted butter

A few sprigs fresh thyme

Fleur de sel, for serving

- Let your steak sit at room temperature for an hour before cooking.

- Preheat the oven to 450°F (220°C). Line a baking sheet with aluminum foil and set a flat wire rack on top, then place in the oven.

- **For stovetop cooking:** Heat a cast-iron skillet or grill pan over high heat until it just begins to smoke. Be sure your ventilation system is turned on once the pan begins to smoke.

- **For outdoor grilling:** Heat the grill so that the coals are quite hot (you should only be able to hold your hand over them at grill height for about 4 seconds), then set the grill grate about 4 inches (10cm) above the coals and let it heat for a few minutes.

- Just before cooking, generously season your steak on both sides with salt, then place the steak on the pan or grill. Let it sear for 3 minutes without touching it— being sure it is browning, not burning—then turn the steak over and sear for 3 minutes on the second side. What you want is a deep, caramelized crust.

- As soon as the steak comes off the pan or grill, place it on the rack in the oven and roast for 8 to 10 minutes for rare, depending on the cut, the size of the bone(s) in the meat, and the heat of the initial searing process.

(If you're grilling outdoors, you could skip the oven and just move your steak to a cooler part of the grill and cover to roast.) Place a meat thermometer into the steak and check the internal temperature (see the chart on page 237) to ensure it's cooked to the desired doneness.

- When the steak is done, transfer it to a cutting board, season with pepper, rub the butter over the surface, top with a few sprigs of thyme, and wrap the board in foil. Let the steak rest for a good 15 minutes before slicing (do not omit this step, which allows the juices to redistribute evenly throughout the steak and the colour of the meat to even out).

- To serve, take the whole cutting board to the table and slice the steak in front of your guests with your sharpest chef's knife, first removing the meat from the bone(s) and then cutting the meat against the grain into thick slices. While everyone "oohs!" and "ahhs!" sprinkle over a large pinch of fleur de sel and serve.

* **Note:** For a Tuscan-style steak made with the T-bone, marinate the meat for a few hours in 3 parts olive oil to 1 part lemon juice and chopped fresh rosemary before grilling. Sponge off the oil before grilling, and really, an outdoor grill over live fire is de rigueur for getting this one right.

Regarding Aged Meat

Aged beef is one of the biggest trends on the restaurant scene today. There is wet-aged meat, a process where racks of ribs are aged in vacuum-sealed bags for about 14 days. But for the more interesting taste sensation, dry-aged meat is the way to go.

Aging involves the ribs being hung in a temperature-controlled refrigerated meat locker with a specific humidity setting for the process to evolve slowly. Good ventilation is key, as a constant flow of air around the meat is required to keep bacteria growth at bay. Steak benefits from aging, becoming more tender and flavourful after some 11 days in such an environment. A crucial element to the dry-aging process is to begin with carcasses that have never been vacuum-packed in plastic bags, where the meat stews in its own juices. Even a brief period in plastic compromises the outcome of aged meat.

You will see steaks aged 20 to 30 days in many restaurants, but ribs aged for twice that long—even up to a year!—are becoming more mainstream. Of course, dry-aged meat is not for everyone, taste-wise, but also cost-wise, with top-quality steaks sold at about $60 per kilogram. Yet when watching the butchering process of an aged side of beef, you quickly understand why they are so expensive. As the meat ages, the carcass shrinks, and its outer crust rots. When that outer crust is removed, the most inner part of the carcass is unveiled, offering meat that is stronger in flavour and firmer in texture due to evaporation. But the magic of the process is not only that aging concentrates the flavour, it also tenderizes the flesh and breaks down proteins into amino acids, which break down further into sugars, which gives aged meat that little sweetness.

At first bite, aged meat wows with its tenderness and buttery texture. As all the moisture has evaporated, the fat provides the softness in the flesh. As for the flavour, we're far from your usual steak here, especially with specimens aged beyond the 120-day mark. Expect hints of liver and Gorgonzola cheese, with increasing minerality near the bone. Aged Ibérico ham, hazelnuts, resin, even a sort of petrol taste in the connective tissues are typical with dry-aged steaks. The beauty is that each bite tastes different—some odd, some intriguing, and still others pleasantly pungent.

The King of Roasts

A honking roast beef always seemed to me like something my mother served for Saturday-night dinner parties rather than a dish I would ever consider offering my hip foodie friends. But with food trends swaying towards first-class ingredients, simply prepared, the time is ripe for a roast beef comeback.

A standing rib roast or prime rib is a cut of beef from the ribs, comprising anywhere from two to seven of them. If sliced raw, a roast beef yields rib-eye steaks, or rib steaks if the bone is left intact. This is a seriously luxurious dish, and I probably only eat it once a year, or even every two years. But there's nothing quite like a gorgeous roast beef . . . with mashed potatoes . . . horseradish sauce . . . some roasted carrots . . . a crisp puff of Yorkshire pudding . . .

Good to know . . .

— Cooking methods may be diverse, but the goal is the same: a roast with a well-crusted exterior and a solid pink interior. It must also be tender. The sign of a perfect prime rib is that it can be sliced easily with a butter knife. But texture has more to do with the quality of the meat than the cooking method. If you want tender, look for a well-marbled roast, preferably aged 6 to 8 weeks, graded at least AA or, better yet, AAA or Prime. And a word of warning, the price rises every time you add an "A" to that grading.

— Roasting techniques seem to fall into two categories: low-and-slow methods and high-heat methods, with several variations in between. Mine is a cross between the two, with a long resting time: 20 minutes in the oven at 500°F (260°C), then reduce the temperature to 300°F (150°C) and roast to an internal temperature of 120°F (49°C) for medium-rare and rest for 45 minutes. Always consider that the internal temperature of your roast will increase by up to 10°F (6°C) as it rests.

— Other helpful hints when roasting: Laying the bones facedown eliminates the need for a roasting rack; a convection oven is ideal for producing a good crust, even heat, and shortened cooking times; when seasoning, the recommended technique is to rub the roast and bones with oil and then sprinkle generously with salt and pepper; a little chopped garlic is deemed acceptable, but nothing else.

— To help your roast form a better crust, let it sit, unwrapped, in the refrigerator for a day before you roast it.

— To gauge temperatures, a meat thermometer is essential; so is a long resting period after roasting (a half hour is the minimum) to allow the juices to redistribute themselves evenly and for the heat to penetrate to the core of the meat. If you see blood pooling under your roast as you slice it, you didn't rest it long enough.

— If possible, ask your butcher to remove the bones and then reattach them to the roast; that way, you get the rib bones for flavour and can eat without the hassle of cutting around or through them, because they easily detach when you're ready to slice. And when you're ready to eat the bones, try spreading them with mustard/horseradish/garlic, coating them with crumbs, and baking until browned. Major yum.

— Small guide to internal temperatures for your roast:
  • Rare = 120°F (49°C); 130°F (54°C) after resting
  • Medium-rare = 130°F (54°C); 140°F (60°C) after resting
  • Medium = 140°F (60°C); 150°F (66°C) after resting
  • Well-done = 160°F (70°C); 170°F (77°C) after resting

STANDING RIB ROAST

SERVES 6 TO 8

*For best results, try to purchase your roast from a reputable butcher.
Because times vary according to size, it is best to use a thermometer and
be guided by the internal temperature rather than cooking times (see the
guide on page 245). To be on the safe side, plan to begin this recipe about
5 hours before you'd like the sliced roast to hit the table. If you are using
a convection oven, reduce all the oven temperatures by 25°F (15°C).*

1 (8-pound/about 3.6kg)
prime rib of beef

¼ cup (60ml) vegetable oil

Fine sea salt and freshly
ground black pepper

2 garlic cloves, finely
chopped (optional)

1 cup (250ml) red wine

2 cups (500ml) beef stock

- The night before roasting, unwrap your roast and place it on a rack over a large plate or pan. Leave, uncovered, in the refrigerator overnight.

- One hour before roasting, place the roast on the kitchen counter to come to room temperature. Preheat the oven to 500°F (260°C). If you have two ovens, preheat the other to 300°F (150°C).

- When ready to roast, drizzle the oil over the entire roast and massage it well into the meat, fat, and bones. Season generously with salt and pepper and rub with the garlic (if using). Place in the hot oven for 20 minutes to brown, then remove from the oven and either place the roast in the cooler oven or leave your oven door open long enough for the oven to cool to 300°F (150°C).

- Cook the roast until it reaches an internal temperature of 120°F (49°C) for rare. This should take from 2 to 2½ hours, depending on the size of your roast. Add about 30 minutes for medium-rare, and 1 hour for well-done.

- Remove the roast from the oven, transfer to a large plate, and let it rest for 45 minutes (or at least 30 minutes) in a warm place near the stove until the internal temperature rises to about 130°F (54°C). For a longer rest period, tent the roast lightly with aluminum foil.

- Meanwhile, pour off all the fat from the roasting pan (reserve it if making Yorkshire pudding), then place the roasting pan on the stovetop over medium-high heat. Pour in the wine and scrape up any browned bits stuck to the pan with a wooden spoon. After a few minutes at a rolling boil, pour in the stock. Bring back to a boil, then reduce the heat to maintain a simmer and let it bubble for about 5 minutes more, until the juices are reduced by half. Strain the sauce into a heated gravy boat.

- When the roast has rested, cut the strings, remove the bones, slice, and serve with the sauce alongside.

HORSERADISH SAUCE

MAKES 1 GENEROUS CUP (250ML)

Some prefer hot mustard as an accompaniment to roast beef or horseradish straight from the jar. For something a bit more elegant, try this simple sauce. Avoid overwhipping the cream so the sauce will not be cloying.

1 cup (250ml) whipping cream

2 heaping tablespoons grated fresh or bottled horseradish

1 tablespoon fresh lemon juice

Fine sea salt and freshly ground black pepper

- Whip the cream until it just begins to hold soft peaks, then whisk in the horseradish and lemon juice and season to taste with salt and pepper. Keep chilled until ready to serve.

FAUSSO BUCO WITH GREMOLATA

SERVES 4

I went through a period of making osso buco whenever I had people over for dinner. But as my bank balance diminished, I became a bit weary of handing over big bucks for top-quality veal shanks, so I started making the recipe with blade roast sold for half the price. Yes, I miss the gorgeous marrow, but sometimes in life you have to make sacrifices—and it's a pretty small sacrifice, because this version is terrific. Best of all, any leftovers make a luscious pasta sauce the next day. I serve this with a sprinkling of gremolata over a bed of mashed potatoes (see page 139) or risotto à la Milanese.

About 2¼ pounds (1kg) veal blade roast

Fine sea salt and freshly ground black pepper

About ¼ cup (35g) all-purpose flour

¼ cup (60ml) vegetable oil, divided

2 carrots, diced

1 large celery stalk, diced

1 medium red onion, diced

3 garlic cloves, smashed and peeled

2 tablespoons tomato paste

A few sprigs thyme and/or sage, torn

1 teaspoon dried oregano

2 strips lemon zest

1 (14-ounce/398ml) can diced Italian plum tomatoes

→

- Preheat the oven to 325°F (160°C). Blot the veal well with paper towels, season with salt and pepper, and sprinkle a few spoonfuls of flour over each side, rubbing it into the meat to coat all surfaces.

- In a Dutch oven or deep skillet with a lid, heat half the oil over medium-high heat. When it's hot, add the veal, sear for 3 minutes, turn over, and repeat the operation. Transfer the meat to a plate and, if the oil is at all blackened, wipe out the pot with paper towels, being careful not to touch the hot oil. Add the remaining oil, along with the carrots, celery, onion, and garlic. Sauté over medium-high heat for a few minutes to soften, then stir in the tomato paste. Keep frying and stirring to cook the paste a bit, then add the thyme and/or sage, oregano, lemon zest, and tomatoes. Stir in the wine and veal stock and allow the liquid to come to a boil. Place the browned veal over the top, then cover and place in the oven. Braise for about 2 hours, until the veal is tender, then remove from the oven.

2 cups (500ml) dry red wine

2 cups (500ml) Veal Stock or Chicken Stock (page 82)

Gremolata (recipe follows), for serving

- Carefully transfer the meat to a plate or cutting board and shred it into large pieces. Taste the sauce and season with salt and pepper. If it seems very thin, bring it to a boil to reduce a bit. Place the shredded meat in a serving dish, pour over the sauce, and serve immediately, with the gremolata passed alongside.

VARIATIONS

- For traditional osso buco: Substitute 4 large (or 6 small) veal shanks, about 1½ inches (4cm) thick, for the blade roast.

- With lamb shanks: Substitute 4 lamb shanks for the veal, and for the herbs, use 2 sprigs each of rosemary and thyme. I also like to substitute orange zest for the lemon, and for the stock, I use vegetable stock, chicken stock, or water. For large shanks, up the braising time to 2½ hours.

GREMOLATA

SERVES 4 TO 6

Gremolata is a bitter garnish for braised meats and works brilliantly at brightening the flavour of a dish. I make mine as simple as possible, with just three ingredients chopped together. You don't have to be all that precise with measures here, but use a vegetable peeler for removing the zest from the lemon, avoiding the white pith as much as possible.

1 cup fresh parsley leaves (flat-leaf or curly), washed and dried

2 garlic cloves, peeled

3 fat strips lemon zest

- On a clean cutting board, chop the parsley, garlic, and lemon zest together until quite fine and transfer to a ramekin to pass around at the table with the veal.

Hamburgers

When well made, a good hamburger is as satisfying as a fat steak. It doesn't take much to make a great burger: ground beef, salt, and pepper . . . If you're looking for recipes, there are hundreds of ways to make an awesome hamburger. Chop the meat yourself, add some bison meat, stir in a packet of Lipton's powdered onion soup mix, or steak spice, or blue cheese, or barbecue chip bits . . . Why not? But before thinking of mix-ins, let's cover a few basics that separate the merely good burgers from the great.

Good to know . . .

— **The meat is key:** There are several options when it comes to patty makeup. Burger snobs insist on patties with a high-fat content, about 25 percent for prime juiciness, but 20 percent fat is a minimum. For weight, about 150 to 180g per burger, and for thickness, a thick burger would always be juicier.

— **Seasoning** is a topic up for debate as well. Is the meat salted at the mixing stage, or just before hitting the griddle? And what about add-ins? Bread crumbs lighten the texture of the patty, but too many spices distract from the beef flavour. Recently I've kept my mix-ins to salt, a bit of steak sauce (HP Sauce especially), and steak spice. And when I shape the burgers, I toss each ball of meat from hand to hand several times with force and then shape it into a patty.

— **What's your burger ideal?** Mine is charcoal-grilled and juicy, with a blackened crust, a slight pink center, and a slight smoky aftertaste. But we can't always cook outside, so in the winter I start with a very hot pan or grill pan and sear for about 3 minutes per side. And avoid crushing the burger with a spatula while it's cooking, or you'll lose all the juices.

— **Don't neglect your buns:** A big bun overwhelms a burger. The bun is basically just the handles of the burger, with its ideal size about the same thickness as the patty. If the bun is too sweet, the burger can be cloying. The best buns play a supporting role. And for the best soft texture, a potato bun cannot be beat. Even better, make them yourself. A hamburger assembled on a homemade bun is next level.

— **Condiments, the burger maker or breaker:** A great burger can be ruined by an excess of mustard, and an overdose of mayonnaise makes the whole thing gloopy. The best-case scenario is the use of a special sauce that combines many condiments into one. Try a mixture of mayonnaise, ketchup, and spicy sauce (like sriracha). Add some chopped pickle, and you're on your way.

— **And about all those fixin's:** The classic garnish of lettuce (iceberg is crunchiest), a slice of tomato, and a few rounds of red onion is plenty. Caramelized onion brings an unwanted sweetness to the mix; mushrooms tend to slide out when eating. Arugula adds a welcome bitterness to an overly sweet burger. As for bacon, not for me, thanks, but I'm all for a few slices of pickle.

— **It's all about how you stack it:** The combination of soft bun, chewy meat, and crisp and juicy condiments must be kept in proportion. A towering burger is a mess to manage and even harder to bite into.

— **What about cheese?** Yes! It makes all the difference. Opt for a cheeseburger when you can—the cheese adds an extra hit of richness and creaminess that saves many a burger from boredom. And as for the cheese itself, a simple slice of commercial cheddar is hard to beat.

— **Regarding temperature:** Burgers must be piping hot, because a lukewarm burger is a sludgy mess. And if your burger isn't juicy, you've failed. It's either overcooked, or the fat count on the meat wasn't high enough.

— **And finally** . . . don't make a burger into something it's not. When you start loading on the toppings and outlandish condiments, you're turning your burger into a sort of fancy gourmet sandwich. Remember, it's a hamburger, not the *Mona Lisa*.

PART 4

SWEET!

FROM THE BREAKFAST BAKERY

FROM THE BREAKFAST BAKERY

There are few routines more entrenched than the weekday drill. The same gestures, repeated robotically, day after day, until one morning, we wake up and realize that the weekend has arrived. The most sacred weekend ritual that banishes the monotony for me is a long, leisurely breakfast. Pancakes are a guilty pleasure, French toast, too. But what I really like to do is bake. We're talking scones, muffins . . . the works. If I'm having people over for brunch, I'll take it a step further and add something special like a coffee cake or cinnamon buns. Breakfast often divides people into two camps, the sweet and the savoury, and though I'm big on both, I lean sweet. Maybe after trying these baked goods, you will, too.

Good to know . . .

— I always keep a container of buttermilk in my fridge especially for pancakes, which are good without it but great with. It keeps for a long time and can be used in muffins, cakes, and salad dressings as well.

— Weighing out ingredients the night before speeds up morning baking. No one wants to wait an hour in the morning for a muffin. Weigh all the dry ingredients together, put the muffin liners in the pan, set the eggs and butter aside in the fridge . . . do as much as you can.

— When it comes to heavy mixes like muffin batter or scone dough, the less mixing at the end of the process, the better. This goes for pancake batter, too, which ideally should remain a bit lumpy when made correctly.

— Coffee cake also works well served as dessert. Just add a little whipped cream and some berries, and you're set.

BUTTERMILK PANCAKES

MAKES ABOUT 16 PANCAKES

I've eaten my weight in pancakes over the years, and these are my favourite. The addition of buckwheat flour gives them a slight bitterness that contrasts well with the sweet syrup. I fry my pancakes in a bit of vegetable shortening, but you could use clarified butter or vegetable oil instead. If you prefer not to use buckwheat flour, omit it and increase the all-purpose flour to 1½ cups (210g).

1¼ cups (175g) all-purpose flour

¼ cup (35g) buckwheat flour

2 teaspoons baking soda

1 teaspoon fine sea salt

2 cups (500ml) buttermilk

1 tablespoon sugar or maple sugar

2 large eggs, separated

5 tablespoons unsalted butter, melted, plus more for serving

Vegetable shortening, for frying

Pure maple syrup, for serving

- Into a medium bowl, sift together the all-purpose flour, buckwheat flour, baking soda, and salt. In a separate medium bowl, whisk together the buttermilk, sugar, and egg yolks. In a small bowl, beat the egg whites until they hold soft peaks. Pour the buttermilk mixture and melted butter into the flour mixture and whisk lightly until just combined (you don't want to overwork the batter or the pancakes will be tough), then fold in the beaten egg whites. Don't worry if the batter is a bit lumpy.

- Heat your griddle over medium-high heat and grease the surface with shortening so there is a thin film all over (I use a silicone brush for this). With a ladle or spoon, drop about ¼ cup (60ml) of the batter onto the hot griddle for each pancake. The batter should sizzle when it hits the surface. Fry for about 45 seconds on each side, until golden brown and cooked through. Serve immediately, with more butter and plenty of maple syrup. Any leftover batter can be covered and refrigerated for a day.

PUMPKIN SPICE MUFFINS

MAKES 12 MUFFINS

I like to make these muffins for Thanksgiving breakfast to use up the excess puree left over after baking Pumpkin Pie (page 369). These muffins have a great gingerbread flavour, which makes them ideal for Christmas morning as well. They're also delicious made with gluten-free flour.

¾ cup (70g) pecans

1½ cups (210g) all-purpose flour or all-purpose gluten-free flour

1 teaspoon fine sea salt

1 teaspoon baking powder

1 teaspoon baking soda

1½ teaspoons ground cinnamon, divided

1 teaspoon ground ginger

¼ teaspoon ground cloves

¼ teaspoon ground mace

½ cup (1 stick/110g) unsalted butter

1 cup (200g) firmly packed brown sugar

2 large eggs

¼ cup (35g) chopped candied ginger

1 cup (250g) pure pumpkin puree

1 tablespoon granulated sugar, for topping

- Preheat the oven to 350°F (180°C). Line a 12-cup muffin tin with paper liners.

- Spread the pecans over a baking sheet and toast in the oven for 7 minutes. Let cool, then chop them into rough pieces.

- Into a medium bowl, sift together the flour, salt, baking powder, baking soda, 1 teaspoon of the cinnamon, the ginger, cloves, and mace.

- In a large bowl using a handheld mixer, cream together the butter and brown sugar until light and fluffy. Beat in the eggs one at a time, followed by the candied ginger. Alternate stirring in the dry ingredients and the pumpkin puree. Gently fold in the pecans. Do not overmix the batter or the muffins will be tough.

- Spoon the mixture into the prepared muffin tin. Combine the granulated sugar and remaining ½ teaspoon cinnamon in a small bowl, then sprinkle the mix over the top.

- Bake for 30 minutes, or until the tops spring back when lightly pressed. These are nice warm, but perhaps even better the next day.

BANANA COCONUT MUFFINS

MAKES 12 MUFFINS

These terrific little muffins are great for using up that last bit of cereal or granola in the back of the pantry. If you prefer a less sweet muffin, use unsweetened flaked coconut. And if you don't have coconut oil on hand, use butter instead.

¾ cup (160g) coconut oil (or butter), melted

1 large egg

1 large egg yolk

3 very ripe medium bananas

¾ cup (150g) sugar

1 teaspoon vanilla extract

1¾ cups (260g) all-purpose flour

½ teaspoon fine sea salt

1½ teaspoons baking powder

1 cup (about 100g) granola or oatmeal

½ cup (45g) flaked coconut, sweetened or unsweetened

- Preheat the oven to 375°F (190°C). Place the oven rack in the middle position. Line a 12-cup muffin tin with paper liners.

- In a blender or food processor, combine the coconut oil, egg, egg yolk, bananas, sugar, and vanilla. Puree until smooth.

- In a large bowl, whisk together the flour, salt, and baking powder, followed by the granola and two large pinches of the coconut flakes. Pour the liquid mixture over the dry mixture and then fold them together until just combined. Do not overmix or the muffins will be tough.

- Divide the batter evenly among the prepared muffin cups and sprinkle the tops with the remaining coconut flakes. Bake until the muffins are puffed and golden, and spring back when pressed, about 30 minutes. Rotate the pan halfway through the baking time. Transfer to a wire rack and let cool slightly before eating.

SATURDAY SCONES

MAKES 12 SCONES

For best results, treat scone dough like pie dough; that is, keep all the ingredients cold and use as light a touch as possible to avoid making them tough. It's essential that scone dough be neither sticky nor dry and crumbly. You're after a texture in between. Using a straight-sided cookie cutter to cut out your scones will help them rise up straight. It's important when making scones to always keep a spoonful of cream nearby to add to the dough in case it is too dry, especially in winter.

3 cups (420g) all-purpose flour

1½ tablespoons baking powder

1 tablespoon sugar, plus more for finishing

¾ teaspoon fine sea salt

½ cup (1 stick/110g) cold unsalted butter, cut into very small pieces

1¼ cups (300ml) whipping cream, plus extra for glazing

2 large eggs

- Preheat the oven to 400°F (200°C). Line a baking sheet with parchment paper. Have a straight-sided 2½-inch (6cm) round cookie cutter ready for cutting out the scones (you can also use the rim of a sturdy glass).

- In a large bowl, whisk together the flour, baking powder, sugar, and salt to combine. Add the butter and work it into the flour mixture by either rubbing together with your fingers or mixing in the bowl of a stand mixer fitted with the paddle attachment on low speed. Mix just until the largest butter pieces are the size of peas.

- In a large measuring cup, whisk together the cream and eggs, then pour this mixture into the flour mixture and, by hand, combine just until the dough is moistened. Turn out onto your work surface and knead a few times to make a smooth but still slightly rough dough.

- Lightly flour the counter and pat the dough to an even thickness, then roll the dough lightly to 1-inch (2.5cm) thickness. It's worth pulling out a ruler here, because if the dough is rolled too thin, the scones will not rise adequately.

- Cut out rounds as close together as possible and place them on the prepared baking sheet. Gather any scraps, knead lightly together, roll out again to 1-inch (2.5cm) thickness, and keep cutting until all the dough is shaped.

- Brush the tops of the scones with cream (I use what's left in the measuring cup mixed with a bit extra) and sprinkle with sugar, if you like a crunchy topping. Place in the oven, reduce the oven temperature to 375°F (190°C), and bake until deep golden, about 30 minutes.

* **Note:** Most often eaten with butter and jam for breakfast in North America, scones are traditionally served with jam and clotted cream for tea in the UK. Another idea: Split them in half, mound with Crème Chantilly (page 308), scatter over a few strawberries, pour over some Strawberry Coulis (page 308), and you're looking at the perfect strawberry shortcake.

THE BIG COFFEE CAKE

SERVES 16

I remember my mother making this cake the morning of Charles and Diana's Royal Wedding back in 1981. While everyone was swooning over Lady Di's dress, I was swooning over this cake. It's a great choice for a brunch table and is best made the day before you serve it, as the flavour and texture improve overnight.

Topping

1 cup (90g) walnuts or pecans, chopped

⅓ cup (75g) brown sugar

1 tablespoon all-purpose flour

1½ teaspoons ground cinnamon

¼ teaspoon grated nutmeg

Pinch of fine sea salt

Batter

3 cups (420g) all-purpose flour

1½ teaspoons baking powder

¾ teaspoon baking soda

1 teaspoon fine sea salt

1 cup (2 sticks/220g) unsalted butter, at room temperature

2 cups (400g) sugar

3 large eggs

→

- **Make the topping:** In a small bowl, combine the walnuts, brown sugar, flour, cinnamon, nutmeg, and salt. Set aside.

- **Make the cake:** Preheat the oven to 350°F (180°C). Generously butter a 9-inch (23cm) angel food cake (tube) pan.

- Into a medium bowl, sift together the flour, baking powder, baking soda, and salt. Set aside.

- In the bowl of a stand mixer fitted with the paddle attachment, or in a large bowl using a handheld mixer, beat together the butter and sugar at high speed until very light and creamy, about 5 minutes. Blend the eggs in one by one, followed by the egg yolk and vanilla, scraping down the sides as needed.

- Reduce the mixer speed to low and add half the dry ingredients, followed by the sour cream, then the rest of the dry ingredients. Mix until just combined, then finish folding with a spatula, scraping well to the bottom of the bowl to be sure everything is completely blended. Resist the temptation to overmix.

1 large egg yolk

1 tablespoon vanilla extract

1½ cups (375ml) sour cream

- Spoon half the batter into the prepared cake pan and spread it out evenly. Sprinkle on a third of the nut topping, then add the rest of the batter and spread it out evenly. Sprinkle the remaining topping evenly over the top.

- Bake for about 70 minutes, until a cake tester inserted into the center comes out clean. Let cool completely in the pan before unmoulding and slicing.

* **Note:** If you have any blueberries, preferably the small ones, consider adding ¾ cup (140g) to the batter.

CINNAMON BUNS

MAKES 15 BUNS

*The challenge when making cinnamon buns is to find the right
balance between ho-hum and sugar bomb, and I think these hit the
mark. This recipe is quite simple, but to make it even easier, you can
leave out the turn (incorporating extra butter) in the dough and roll
it out straight after the first rise. They won't have the same flaky
texture, but I assure you they will be devoured just as quickly.*

Dough

1 cup (250ml) milk

1 cup (2 sticks/220g)
unsalted butter, at room
temperature, divided

3½ cups (500g) all-purpose
flour

1½ teaspoons fine sea salt

1 (¼-ounce/7g)
packet quick-rise yeast
(2¼ teaspoons)

⅓ cup (65g) granulated
sugar

1 large egg

2 large egg yolks

Filling

6 tablespoons
(¾ stick/80g) unsalted
butter, at room temperature

⅔ cup (140g) brown sugar

→

- **Prepare the dough:** In a small saucepan, heat the milk
  until it is hot to the touch, then remove from the heat
  and add ½ cup (1 stick/110g) of the butter. Let it melt,
  and when the mixture is lukewarm (about 104°F/40°C),
  proceed with the recipe.

- In a large bowl, whisk together the flour, salt, yeast, and
  granulated sugar. Make a well in the center and pour in
  the buttery milk, the egg, and the egg yolks. Mix it all
  together with your hands until you have a sticky dough.
  Cover and let stand for 15 minutes.

- Turn the dough out onto a lightly floured surface and
  knead vigorously (add a few extra spoonfuls of flour
  if it's sticky) until it's smooth and bounces back when
  pressed down, a good 5 minutes. Place the ball back in
  the bowl, cover, and let rise in a draft-free spot in your
  kitchen until doubled in volume, 1 to 1½ hours.

- Turn the dough out onto a lightly floured surface,
  flatten it into a rectangular shape, and then, with
  a rolling pin, roll it into a rectangle about 12 ×
  16 inches (30 × 40cm). Take the remaining ½ cup
  (1 stick/110g) butter in your hands, break off walnut-
  size pieces, and, starting on your left, dot them
  evenly over two-thirds of the surface of the dough.

1½ tablespoons ground cinnamon

1 tablespoon all-purpose flour

1 egg, beaten, for glazing

Icing (page 275)

Fold the dough into thirds, placing the flap on the right with no butter over the center of the dough and then flipping the buttered left-hand flap over the center section, the idea being to fold the layers of dough with butter between those that do not. Now turn the dough a quarter turn so that it is seam-side up, and roll it out again into a rectangle about the same size as before, then fold into thirds again. Give it a final roll just to even it out and then transfer the dough to a lightly floured baking sheet. Cover with a plastic bag and refrigerate for at least 30 minutes or up to a day for the butter to firm up and the dough to relax.

- **Prepare the filling:** In a medium bowl, beat together the butter, brown sugar, cinnamon, and flour until creamy. Set aside at room temperature.

- To shape the buns, line a 12 × 16-inch (30 × 40cm) baking sheet or a 12 × 14-inch (30 × 35cm) roasting pan with aluminum foil or parchment paper.

- On a lightly floured surface, roll out the chilled dough into a slightly smaller rectangle this time, about 12 × 15 inches (30 × 38cm), with a thickness of about ½ inch (1cm), making it as even as possible. Spread the cinnamon-sugar filling over the entire surface of the dough, save for a thin strip at the bottom, then brush that strip with water (this is where you will seal the rolled dough). Working from top to bottom, roll the dough towards you, keeping it snug but not too tight. You will end up with a fat roll about 15 inches (38cm) long. Roll the log a bit to even it out and place the seam at the bottom. Cut the roll crosswise into 15 equal-size pieces. It's not the end of the world if they aren't perfect, but a ruler comes in handy to help guide you. Place the rounds cut-side down on your baking sheet (or pan), in rows of 3 across and 5 down.

→

- Cover the entire pan with a large plastic bag and set aside in a warm part of the kitchen to rise for about an hour, or until the buns fill up most of the empty spaces in the pan.

- After an hour, preheat the oven to 350°F (180°C). Place the oven rack in the middle position. If the buns have risen enough that the dough doesn't bounce back when you press it, proceed; if not, give them a bit more time to rise.

- When you're ready to bake, brush the tops of the buns with the beaten egg and bake until golden, about 30 minutes. Remove from the oven (keep the oven on) and let cool, then spread the icing generously over the top of the buns. Raise the oven temperature to 375°F (190°C), then return the pan to the oven for about 3 minutes, until the icing is crusted over. Let cool. Wrap the buns well if not eating the same day—as if that were possible!

ICING

2 tablespoons cream
cheese, at room
temperature

2 tablespoons unsalted
butter, at room temperature

½ teaspoon vanilla extract

1 cup (120g) icing sugar

3 tablespoons heavy cream

- In a small bowl using a hand mixer, beat the cream cheese, butter, and vanilla until very smooth and creamy. Add half the sugar, blend, then add the remaining sugar and blend thoroughly. Add the cream and beat until smooth and of spreadable consistency.

CHOCOLATE:
DELICIOUS BUT CAPRICIOUS

Why Homemade Desserts?

I love the way some people say they don't have a sweet tooth. "I don't do dessert" has become a sort of code for "I take care of myself. I count calories. I drink green juice. I'm more disciplined than you are." Oy.

Well, I like desserts, but mainly just the good ones. I'm not talking about Oreo cheesecake or triple-chocolate-chunk ice cream. But how about an apple galette glazed with crab apple jelly? And let's add a slice of rich English cheddar to that. Or how about a few quenelles of bitter cocoa sorbet served with a glass of Pedro Ximénez sherry? Or even a ripe white peach paired with pistachio biscotti? Yes! Nothing provides a direct hit to the brain, triggering our perception of pleasure, like the taste of something sweet.

Making desserts can be intimidating. Everyone hesitates before tackling French desserts with names like *clafoutis* and *soufflé glacé*, but even the least experienced cook can pull together bowls of fresh berries and ice cream. Many of us prefer to stick to reliable family recipes than to venture into the world of the unknown. But as much as we all love a good lemon meringue pie, I urge you to experiment. Once you've mastered one recipe, move on to something new and intriguing. Yes, homemade desserts can be time-consuming, but the results are worth it.

My first recommendation would be to let the seasons dictate your dessert choices. Summer desserts should be light and full of fruit. In the winter, think caramel, nuts, and chocolate. Beginners might want to try a plum crumble (see page 351), especially when stone fruits are in season, or a quick six-ingredient weekend cake (see page 296). And I promise that chocolate mousse (see page 282) won't let you down. More advanced bakers might want to try the Lemon Tart (page 335) or an apple tart (see page 341), and how about that Black Forest Cake (page 310)? Nothing here is all that difficult to make. And many of the simplest recipes I've given you—the brownies, the crisps, the shortcake—are also some of the best.

Desserts are more of a treat than a necessary part of a meal, but they're fun to make and much appreciated by friends and family, offering not only a pleasant pick-me-up but an opportunity to get creative in the kitchen as well.

Let's go!

Chocolate is one of the few ingredients that never falls out of fashion. Its unique flavour and sensual texture are the basis of some of the greatest desserts we happily devour. What has changed, though, are our chocolate taste preferences. If the '60s and '70s were the golden age of Swiss milk chocolate, the '80s were dominated by sweet-'n'-creamy, praline-filled Belgian bonbons. Today's taste veers towards dark chocolate. Semisweet and bittersweet chocolates are the pastry chef's first choices for making chocolate confections. Unlike milk and white chocolates, their flavour is strong enough to dominate in mousses, cakes, and icings.

Gourmets, flavour fanatics, and food snobs savour dark "Grand Cru" chocolate as they would fine wines. According to the French club of chocolate lovers Les Croqueurs de Chocolat, a true connoisseur seeks chocolate with a "warm, rich colour and a glossy finish, a velvety texture that melts smoothly, wrapping itself around your palate, a deep, strong flavour with a slight bitterness offset by a note of sweetness, and a finish that continues long after the last swallow." Yes! The best chocolate delivers all that and more, every time. From a simple chocolate brownie to a luscious chocolate mousse, chocolate needs little in the way of accompaniment. You can add some whipped cream or plump raspberries, but they will always play a supporting role to this magical ingredient. With chocolate, less is more. Like Greta Garbo, chocolate prefers to be left alone.

Good to Know . . .

— When purchasing chocolate (dark, milk, or white), look for a product that contains about 34 percent cocoa butter. This is "couverture-quality" chocolate. The taste of your dessert is based on the amount of cocoa mass and sugar, but the texture is based on the cocoa butter content. Never bake with chocolate that does not contain cocoa butter. Many makers of expensive imported chocolate prominently display large numbers on their packaging representing the percentage of cocoa mass. A standard eating chocolate has anywhere from 65 to 80 percent, but buyer, beware: higher isn't always better. Chocolate with a cocoa mass content above 70 percent is intense.

— Chocolate should be stored in a cool, dry place. Make sure it's well wrapped, since it will absorb surrounding smells. This is especially true of white chocolate, which will even absorb the smell of plastic wrap. Dark chocolate can be stored for many years under ideal conditions, whereas white and milk chocolates can be kept no more than 6 to 9 months before the milk solids turn rancid. Grey streaks on the surface of solid chocolate are the result of warm temperatures. This is the cocoa butter that has separated and risen to the surface. Despite its grainy appearance, chocolate in this state can still be used.

— Never store your chocolate in the refrigerator or freezer. When it warms to room temperature, the chocolate will "sweat" and the moisture will prevent it from melting smoothly. Even the smallest amount of water (a damp wooden spoon) can cause the chocolate to seize into a thick paste, which is impossible to melt. The solution to this problem is either to add enough liquid (about 1 tablespoon to every 2 ounces of chocolate) to smooth the paste into a sauce or icing (ganache), or to gradually blend in a few drops of vegetable oil.

— To facilitate the melting process, always chop your chocolate into small pieces. As chocolate will burn over a direct heat source, melt it over a pot of simmering, not boiling, water (a bain-marie or double boiler), and avoid heating it above 120°F (49°C). Be especially careful to melt milk and white chocolates over low heat since they burn easily. If you choose to use a microwave, melt the chocolate on a high heat setting for 30 seconds, stir, then continue in no more than 30-second increments at a time on a medium setting. Close attention and continuous stirring are important, or the intense heat will scorch the chocolate.

— Be careful when combining warm chocolate with cold ingredients, such as whipped cream. The cold will cause the cocoa butter in the chocolate to harden instantly. So, for example, when making chocolate mousse, do not refrigerate the heavy cream after it has been whipped.

— Substituting one type of chocolate for another can cause problems. Chocolate chips are good for cookies, but not ideal for melting. Best results are achieved with high-quality chocolate. The rule of thumb concerning cooking with chocolate is like that for cooking with wine: if you wouldn't drink it on its own, don't cook with it.

— When a recipe calls for unsweetened chocolate, I use Baker's brand. Otherwise, I use imported semisweet (known as *mi-amer* in French) chocolate such as Barry Callebaut, Lindt, and the pricey but excellent Valrhona.

— Supermarkets, coffee shops, and gourmet stores carry many different varieties of bittersweet and semisweet chocolate, but when purchasing high-quality chocolate in bulk, for best prices, check out your local restaurant supply stores. And always look for "couverture-quality" chocolate, often sold in chocolate "buttons" that eliminate the need for chopping and facilitate recipe preparation.

—

Bean-to-Bar, the Chocolate for Purists

The most recent trend is chefs, chocolatiers, and artisans taking chocolate-making a big step further by producing their own chocolate from bean to bar. The ultimate goal of these artisans is to produce chocolate in small batches to best exploit each bean's terroir, as is done with wine, coffee, and tea. The movement is taking hold in North America, where sought-after brands include Mast Brothers and Askinosie Chocolate in the States, Soma Chocolatemaker and Hummingbird Chocolate in Ontario, as well as Palette de Bine and État de Choc in Quebec, with new companies coming on to the scene often. In France there are several famous bean-to-bar confectioners such as Bonnat, Pralus, Morin, Lyon's renowned Bernachon, and Le Chocolat Alain Ducasse in Paris. Commercial producers like Valrhona, Michel Cluizel, Barry Callebaut, and Amedei in Italy often offer a line of terroir-driven chocolates. Bean-to-bar artisan chocolate can offer interesting taste experiences (at often eyebrow-raising prices). It is important to note, however, that such chocolate is not always ideal for cooking. Prohibitive prices are a factor, but the real issue is texture. Bean-to-bar philosophy dictates that no extra cocoa butter or lecithin is added during the chocolate-making process, ingredients that make chocolate more fluid and therefore easier to manipulate or even melt. Word to the wise: Save the bean-to-bar chocolate for tasting, not baking.

THE MEGAMOUSSE

SERVES 8 TO 10

This classic dessert is the perfect choice when having people over because a) it's gorgeous, b) everyone loves chocolate mousse, and c) it's even better when made in advance. The secret of its success lies in the quality of chocolate, so avoid the temptation to use up any old chocolate Easter bunnies crowding the back of the cupboard. For a smaller crowd, this recipe can easily be halved.

3 cups (750ml) whipping cream

12 ounces (340g) semisweet or bittersweet chocolate

6 large egg yolks

½ cup (100g) sugar

½ cup (125ml ml) water

Crème Chantilly (page 308), for serving (optional)

Chocolate shavings (see Notes page 312), for garnish (optional)

- In a medium bowl using a handheld mixer, beat the cream until it just begins to hold soft peaks. Set aside but do not refrigerate.

- Bring a medium pot of water to a simmer over low heat. Chop the chocolate into small pieces and place in a large stainless-steel bowl. Place the bowl over the pot of simmering water and raise the heat to medium. Heat the chocolate, stirring often, until melted, smooth, and very warm to the touch. Set aside in a warm place. Do not turn off the flame.

- In a medium stainless-steel bowl, whisk together the egg yolks and sugar, followed by the water, until well blended. Place this bowl over the pot of simmering water and whisk the mixture by hand until it turns from a liquid state to a thick mousse.

- Remove from the heat. With the handheld mixer, beat on high speed until cool. It should be creamy and doubled in volume.

- Pour one-third of the whipped cream into the warm chocolate and whisk until just blended. Gently fold in the yolk mixture with a rubber spatula, followed by the remaining cream. Fold until just combined. You should still see a few streaks of chocolate in the mix. Pour into a large decorative serving bowl and chill for about 6 hours. To serve, top with Crème Chantilly and chocolate shavings, if you like.

BRILLIANT BROWNIES

MAKES 24 BROWNIES

What I was after in this recipe was a brownie with a deep chocolate flavour, a moist texture, and a crackly, shiny top. After days of intense testing, I nailed it. Yay! This recipe can also be halved and baked in an 8-inch (20cm) square pan. They are also excellent when made with gluten-free flour, but will be more fragile.

4 ounces (115g) unsweetened chocolate (preferably Baker's brand)

1¼ cups (175g) all-purpose flour

¼ cup (25g) unsweetened cocoa powder

7 ounces (200g) semisweet chocolate

1 cup (2 sticks/220g) unsalted butter, at room temperature

2 cups (400g) superfine sugar (see Notes)

1 teaspoon fine sea salt

1 teaspoon instant espresso powder

1 tablespoon vanilla extract

4 large eggs

¾ cup walnuts, toasted and chopped (optional; see Notes)

Flaky sea salt (optional)

- Preheat the oven to 350°F (180°C). Grease a 9 × 13-inch (23 × 33cm) pan and line the base with parchment paper.

- Melt the unsweetened chocolate over a bain-marie (or in the microwave in 20-second increments, stirring well between each). In a small bowl, whisk together the flour and cocoa powder. Chop the semisweet chocolate into pieces about the size of chocolate chips. Set it all aside.

- In a large bowl, in a stand mixer or with a handheld mixer, beat together the butter, superfine sugar, and salt until very light and fluffy. Dissolve the espresso powder in the vanilla, then add it to the mix. Add the eggs one by one, then beat on high speed for about 4 minutes. Blend in the melted chocolate.

- Stir the flour mixture into the beaten butter mixture, blend to combine, then fold in the chopped chocolate and nuts (if using).

- Pour the batter into the prepared pan and smooth it out evenly, getting it right into the corners. For those who like a saltier brownie, sprinkle a little sea salt lightly all over the surface of the batter, but go easy.

- Bake for 25 minutes for fudgier brownies or 28 minutes for cakier brownies. It's okay if a few crumbs stick

$\longrightarrow$

to a toothpick when inserted, but it shouldn't be gooey. Remove from the oven and let cool completely before slicing. Wrap leftover brownies individually in aluminum foil or plastic wrap and keep at room temperature.

* **Notes:** If you don't have superfine sugar, grind regular granulated sugar in a food processor or blender for about 30 seconds.

• If you choose to add walnuts, I suggest starting out with whole nuts rather than nuts sold chopped, as they are often rancid.

MOLTEN CHOCOLATE CAKES

SERVES 8

Known in French as a moelleux, fondant, coulant, *or* mi-cuit, *molten chocolate cake is little more than a cooked chocolate mousse. It's so popular that for years it relegated other chocolate desserts to near obscurity. Like puff pastry and tarte tatin, the creation of the molten chocolate cake was originally a culinary faux pas: its liquid center is the result of undercooking. The late, great Nicolas Jongleux was one of the first chefs to serve this crusty, puddinglike cake in Montreal at La Cigale on rue Saint-Denis in the mid-1990s. This recipe, Jongleux's creation, is baked in a ramekin, so it can be prepared in advance and cooked just before serving.*

½ cup (1 stick/110g) unsalted butter, plus more for greasing

8½ ounces (240g) best-quality semisweet chocolate, chopped

4 large eggs

4 large egg yolks

½ cup (100g) sugar

¼ cup (35g) all-purpose flour

Ice cream, for serving

- Preheat the oven to 425°F (220°C). Lightly butter eight ⅔-cup (160ml) capacity soufflé ramekins or small ovenproof bowls.

- In a small saucepan, melt the butter and chocolate over low heat, stirring until smooth. Remove from the heat and let cool to room temperature.

- In a large bowl, whisk together the eggs, egg yolks, and sugar until light and fluffy, then whisk in the flour. Stir the chocolate-butter mixture into the egg mixture until well blended. Pour the mixture into the prepared ramekins and bake for 9 to 10 minutes, until a crust forms.

- Remove from the oven and serve immediately, preferably with a scoop of ice cream, either vanilla . . . or pistachio . . . or caramel . . . or chestnut . . . or . . .

- * **Note:** If the mixture is refrigerated before you place it in the oven, count on about 14 minutes baking time.

CAKES 101

CAKES 101

There's something about a magnificent cake that excites everyone from toddlers to seniors to blasé teenagers. Even before the first slice, we imagine it will be sweet, moist, melting and either buttery, chocolaty, fruity, creamy, fudgy, spicy, or just plain ol' vanilla. A cake symbolizes celebration, epitomized by the nostalgic image of the candle-spiked, frosting-swirled birthday cake. But why save cake for a party? I like cake for any occasion.

What makes a great cake? The texture must be light, but the crumb should be tight. Fluffy is preferable to dense, and a good cake is never too bouncy. A tough cake means the batter has been overworked or the wrong flour was used. Moistness is a must, but gummy = undercooked. And the flavour must be bold. A yellow cake must taste of butter and vanilla, while a chocolate cake must be rich but not cloying. And how about those boozy cakes! A shot of rum or Grand Marnier can work wonders on a lackluster gâteau. Then there's the cake's coating: glaze, buttercream, ganache, whipped cream, frosting, or just a sprinkling of icing sugar . . .

By definition, a cake must be beautiful. And as beauty is in the eye of the beholder, any cake made with love qualifies. When all is said and done, a good cake is not just one you want to look at—a good cake is one you want to eat.

Good to Know . . .

— Make sure your oven temperature is precise. An oven thermometer can help if you aren't sure.

— When preparing cake pans for baking, you can butter and flour the pan, being sure to knock out any excess flour by turning the pan upside down over the sink and tapping it several times. Or you can coat the pan with a thin, even layer of vegetable oil spray (such as Pam). And to prevent sticking, I always place a round of parchment paper (cut to fit) on the base of the pan. If using a parchment round, you don't even have to grease your pan. Just run a spatula or small knife around the sides of the cake before unmoulding.

— Unless otherwise stipulated, always let ingredients come to room temperature before beginning the recipe.

— Always use large eggs and unsalted butter for cakes.

— Be sure your baking powder and baking soda are fresh and still active.

— Be diligent. Avoid diverging from the pan size stipulated in the recipe, as using a different-size pan will affect baking times. And don't just blindly follow the baking time; instead, follow these suggestions to check doneness: a skewer or toothpick inserted into the thickest part of the cake (usually the center) should come out clean; the cake should bounce back when pressed lightly with your fingers; the cake should begin to pull away from the sides of the pan. Use your senses to determine when a cake becomes more fragrant at the end of its baking time, which is a good indication that it's almost done. Be careful not to over-bake cakes, or they will dry out and become bitter.

— Always keep your cake wrapped well in plastic wrap once it has cooled to avoid it drying out. And if you aren't using it the same day, keep it refrigerated or frozen.

— Make sure when storing cream cakes in the refrigerator that the fridge does not smell of onions or yesterday's leftovers; the cake will absorb these odours.

— Cakes are adaptable. An 8-inch (20cm) cake can serve 8 to 10, but you can easily stretch it out to 12 portions by adding fresh fruit and/or ice cream. And as many are requesting smaller portions lately, I prefer to leave guests asking for more instead of saddling them with too much of a good thing.

LE WEEKEND AU CITRON

This simple French pound cake is called le weekend *because it remains fresh and delicious all weekend long. It's dense and buttery, best served in thin slices as a teatime treat, or dressed up with fresh fruit for a simple summer dessert. As for the flavouring, lemon is classic, but my favourite is a lemon-lime weekend topped with chopped pistachios.*

Cake

¾ cup plus 3 tablespoons (180g) granulated sugar

1 teaspoon finely grated lemon or lime zest, or a combination of the two

¾ cup plus 2 tablespoons (1¾ sticks/200g) unsalted butter

5 large eggs

1⅓ cups (185g) pastry flour

Glaze

¾ cup (90g) icing sugar

2 tablespoons fresh lemon juice or lime juice

- Preheat the oven to 400°F (200°C). Butter and flour an 8 × 4 × 2½-inch (20 × 10 × 6-cm) loaf pan.

- Rub the granulated sugar together with the zest to release the essential oils of the zest and flavour the sugar.

- In a small saucepan, melt the butter over high heat and bring to a boil. Remove from the burner and set aside.

- In a medium bowl using a handheld mixer or a whisk, beat the eggs and the sugar-zest mixture on high speed until well combined, about a minute. Add the flour all at once and beat until you get a smooth batter, scraping down the sides as you go. Pour in the hot butter, a quarter at a time, mixing well until smooth after each addition before adding the next. Scrape down the sides one last time and give the batter a final whisk to make sure it's smooth.

- Pour the batter into the prepared pan and bake for 45 to 50 minutes, until a toothpick inserted into the center comes out clean. If the top appears to be getting too dark, cover the cake lightly with aluminum foil for the last 10 minutes of baking.

- Meanwhile, make the glaze: Sift the icing sugar into a small bowl and whisk in the lemon juice. The texture should resemble heavy cream. Keep covered until ready to use.

- When the cake is finished baking, remove from the oven and let cool in the pan for 5 minutes, then unmould onto a wire rack. With a pastry brush, brush half the glaze over the top and sides of the hot cake. Wait 10 minutes, then repeat the operation with the remaining glaze. One layer may seem to be enough, but the glaze flavours the cake, so it really does need two.

- Let cool completely before cutting into thin slices, preferably with a bread knife. Wrapped well, the cake will keep at room temperature for several days; avoid freezing or refrigerating it or the glaze will melt.

VANILLA BEAN CHEESECAKE

SERVES 8 TO 10

I'm not the biggest fan of cheesecake, but this one is lighter and creamier than most. It's also a cinch to make, avoiding the tedious step of a water bath when baking. You can also make it with a chocolate wafer crust, or add a layer of raspberries before pouring in the batter. But don't overdo it. I serve it simply, with strawberry coulis alongside. I like to make this with a vanilla bean, but as they have become increasingly expensive and hard to find, lemon juice and zest are a great substitute. You could use orange as well, or lime. But if you spring for a vanilla bean, be sure to save the scraped bean to make vanilla sugar (see page 51).

Crust

1 cup (120g) graham cracker crumbs

Pinch of fine sea salt

3 tablespoons brown sugar

3½ tablespoons (50g) unsalted butter, melted

Filling

2 (8-ounce/225g) packages cream cheese, at room temperature

⅔ cup (135g) granulated sugar

½ cup (125g) sour cream

1 vanilla bean, split lengthwise and seeds scraped out, or 1 tablespoon pure vanilla extract, or 2 tablespoons fresh lemon juice and 2 teaspoons grated lemon zest

3 large eggs, lightly beaten

→

- **Prepare the crust:** Preheat the oven to 400°F (200°C).

- In a small bowl, combine the graham cracker crumbs, salt, and sugar and mix in the melted butter until the mixture begins to stick together. Press the mixture firmly into the bottom of an 8- or 9-inch (20 or 23cm) springform pan, reaching up the sides by about an inch (2.5cm). Set aside.

- **Prepare the filling:** In a large bowl using a handheld mixer, or in the bowl of a stand mixer fitted with the paddle attachment, beat the cream cheese with the sugar on medium-high speed until smooth. Blend in the sour cream and the pulp from the vanilla bean. Beat well until smooth and silky. Slowly beat the eggs into the cheese mixture, scraping down the sides of the bowl as needed, until well combined. Do not overmix.

- When everything is ready, bake the crust for 5 minutes, or until it begins to brown around the edges. Remove from the oven and immediately pour the filling over the crust. Using the back of a spoon, even out the filling to make sure it's not thicker in the center.

Topping

1 cup (250ml) sour cream

⅓ cup (75ml) whipping cream

3 tablespoons (45g) granulated sugar

1 teaspoon vanilla extract

Fresh berries of choice or orange suprêmes, for decoration

Strawberry Coulis (page 308), for serving

Place back in the oven for 5 minutes, then turn off the heat and leave the cheesecake in the closed oven for 45 minutes, until firm. Do not open the oven! The cheesecake might crack, but not to worry. (If ever it is not firm after 45 minutes, leave the cake in place, turn the oven on to 300°F/180°C, and bake for another 10 minutes.) Set the pan on a wire rack and let cool for 20 minutes.

• **Make the topping:** Preheat the oven to 350°F (180°C).

• In a medium bowl, whisk together the sour cream, whipping cream, sugar, and vanilla. Pour the mixture onto the cooled cheesecake and spread with a spatula into an even layer. Bake for 8 to 10 minutes, until the topping starts to pull away from the sides of the pan, then remove from the oven and let cool to room temperature.

• Refrigerate, covered, for about 4 hours (or better yet, overnight) before removing the sides of the springform pan. Decorate with fresh berries or orange suprêmes, and serve with the coulis. Always cut cheesecake with a hot knife, wiped clean after each slice.

On Icing and Decorating Cakes

Like rolling pie dough, stress levels escalate when inexperienced cooks are faced with icing a cake. Sure, you can watch hundreds of how-to videos online, but when it comes to doing it yourself, chances are your first cake won't look great. Nor your second. But by the time you get to your third, the cake will probably be a little straighter and prettier than the last. If you try piping with a pastry bag, that will improve the result. Like with everything else, practice is what makes all the difference between turning out a good-looking cake and a great-looking one.

Good to Know . . .

— The easiest cream to ice a cake with is whipped cream, so start with cakes like the French Strawberry Shortcake (page 309) or Black Forest Cake (page 310) to get a feel for how you can move the cream around with a spatula over a cake.

— About spatulas: You can definitely ice a cake with a butter knife, but a spatula, either straight or offset, will help you achieve smooth and straight sides on your cake and an evenly iced surface.

— To keep your serving plate clean, slide several long pieces of parchment paper between the cake and the plate. These will be removed once the cake is fully iced.

— Be sure when icing a cake that you spread the icing or cream all the way to the sides of the cake instead of mounding it all in the center. Most often when a cake ends up looking like a volcano, that's the problem.

— I always place a cardboard of the same size as my cake under the base to be sure I can pick it up to transfer it to a serving plate once it is iced. Otherwise, you might end up damaging the cake when moving it.

— A turntable really can help you ice a cake, and you can purchase an inexpensive rotating cake stand or turntable for as little as $20. You'll be a cake decorator in no time.

— When assembling your cake, it's always best to work with a day-old cake, as fresh cakes are often too soft and spongy to slice with ease. If you need to cut your layers into halves, begin by making a horizontal mark (or marks) on the side of your cake to know exactly where you'll be slicing before proceeding. Always use a serrated bread knife to cut your cake (the longer the blade, the better), using a back-and-forth sawing motion, and it's crucial to keep the blade as straight as possible while you slice, so get right down to the level of the knife to make sure it is always kept straight. And be careful—those serrated knives are sharp! To keep your iced cakes straight, stack the layers in the same order and position they were in when you originally sliced the cake.

— Piping with a pastry bag is intimidating, but practice makes perfect. Begin with a #2 or #4 star tip and practice on a plate before tackling your cake.

— When piping, never fill the bag more than halfway, and twist the bag to close as you don't want cream coming out the top. Starting from that twisted closure, hold the bag in the hand you write with to apply pressure and guide the tip with the other. Apply even pressure from the top of the bag so that the cream pipes out evenly.

— Always make sure your star tip is open before you start piping. The "teeth" should be in a straight line with the tube, not curved inwards as it is when you buy it. To open it up, insert a smaller tip inside and push the teeth out until they are straight.

— Ultimately, if your cake looks a bit lopsided, fret not. Homemade cakes are very much on trend, and don't hesitate to use fruit, flowers, chocolate shavings, or sprinkles to hide any mishaps. As for any thin-looking icing on the sides, just remember that naked cakes (lightly iced cakes) are also all the rage. It's the picture-perfect cakes that look commercial of late, so let your creative juices flow. Watch and learn. There are plenty of how-to videos on cake decorating and piping online. And if you have kids looking for something to do, get them in on the action, too. It's fun!

GENOISE

Genoise is the classic sponge cake used in a myriad of French cake recipes. It's a simple cake, which means it's easy to mess up, but be gentle with the folding and you will be fine. Keep in mind that this is a cake used primarily as a building block for other cakes, and is a great soaker-upper of flavoured syrups, but a little bland on its own. This recipe can easily be halved or doubled.

1½ cups minus 1 tablespoon (200g) all-purpose flour

6 large eggs

1 cup (200g) sugar

2 tablespoons unsalted butter, melted

- Preheat the oven to 350°F (180°C) and place the baking rack in the middle position. Butter a 9 × 3-inch (23 × 7.5cm) round cake pan and line the bottom with a round of parchment paper cut to fit. Lightly butter the paper, then flour the pans, knocking out the excess flour.

- Sift the flour onto a sheet of parchment or into a small bowl. In the bowl of a stand mixer fitted with the whisk attachment, or in a large, heat-resistant bowl, whisk the eggs and sugar together until well blended. Set the bowl over a pot of simmering water and whisk the mixture continuously until it becomes warm (not hot!) and smooth to the touch. You shouldn't feel the sugar crystals between your fingers when it's ready. Meanwhile, pour the melted butter into a small bowl and have a whisk at the ready.

- In the bowl of the stand mixer or with a handheld mixer, beat the egg mixture on high speed for 5 minutes until it has tripled in volume. Reduce the mixer speed to medium and beat for another 3 minutes. The mixture should reach "ribbon" consistency, meaning it develops into a thick foam that forms a ribbon when it falls from the beaters or whisk.

- Using a large rubber spatula, fold the flour gently into the egg mixture, a third at a time. Do not overmix or the batter will deflate. Scoop out about ½ cup (125ml) of the batter into the bowl of melted butter and whisk until smooth, then fold that gently back into the rest of the batter.

- Pour the batter into the prepared pan, spread it out evenly, and immediately place in the oven. Bake for 40 to 45 minutes, until the cake bounces back when pressed with your fingers and begins to pull away from the sides of the pan.

- Let cool in the pan for 10 minutes, then unmould and cool completely on a wire rack. Wrap the cooled cake well to store in the refrigerator for a couple of days or in the freezer for up to 1 month.

- For a chocolate genoise: Reduce the quantity of flour to 1¼ cups (175g) and add 3 tablespoons (20g) best-quality unsweetened cocoa powder. Be sure to sift the flour and cocoa powder together before incorporating into the batter.

CRÈME CHANTILLY (SWEETENED WHIPPED CREAM)

MAKES 2 CUPS (500ML)

1 cup (250ml) whipping
cream

3 tablespoons icing sugar

1 teaspoon vanilla extract

• Chill a large bowl and the beaters of a handheld mixer
for 15 minutes. Combine the cream, sugar, and vanilla
in the chilled bowl and beat on medium speed until
the cream holds stiff peaks. Cover and refrigerate until
ready to use, up to 8 hours.

* **Note:** For a more pronounced vanilla flavour, bring the
cream to a simmer with the sugar and the seeds scraped
from half a vanilla bean (add the scraped pod as well).
Remove from the heat and let steep until it cools to
room temperature, then chill completely. Remove the
vanilla pod before whipping.

SIMPLE SYRUP

MAKES ABOUT ¾ CUP (180ML)

½ cup (125ml) water

½ cup (100g) sugar

• In a saucepan, combine the water and sugar and whisk.
Bring to a boil over high heat, then turn off the heat and
let cool completely. Strain into a clean jar with a lid,
cover, and keep refrigerated.

STRAWBERRY COULIS

MAKES ABOUT 1½ CUPS (375ML)

*While the kirsch in this recipe enhances the flavour
of the strawberries, it is entirely optional.*

2 cups (about 300g)
strawberries, washed,
stemmed, and sliced

2 tablespoons sugar

1 tablespoon fresh lemon
juice, or 1 tablespoon
kirsch

• Put the strawberries in a medium bowl. Sprinkle the
sugar and lemon juice over the berries. Stir and then
refrigerate for a few hours. Puree in a blender or food
processor until smooth. Strain if you want, but it's not
necessary. Refrigerate until ready to serve or freeze for
up to 2 months.

FRENCH STRAWBERRY SHORTCAKE

SERVES 10

*A French shortcake, using a genoise sponge, is easy to pull together
in summer. The key is to use the most gorgeous strawberries
available and serve them drowned in a fresh berry coulis.*

½ cup (125ml) Simple Syrup (page 308)

1 tablespoon fresh orange juice or orange liqueur (such as Grand Marnier)

1½ cups (175ml) whipping cream

¼ cup (60g) mascarpone cheese, crème fraîche, or sour cream

1 teaspoon vanilla extract

6 tablespoons (40g) icing sugar

About 2 cups strawberries, sliced. Reserve 10 for decoration if you wish

1 (9-inch/23cm) Genoise (page 306)

Edible flowers, mint sprigs, and icing sugar (optional)

Strawberry Coulis (page 308), for serving

- Combine in a small glass or measuring cup the syrup with the orange juice or the liqueur (or both!).

- To make the cream, in a cold bowl using chilled beaters, whip together the cream and mascarpone with the vanilla and icing sugar until it holds stiff peaks. Refrigerate until ready to use.

- Place the genoise upside down on a serving plate and peel off the parchment. Using a serrated knife, cut the cake in half horizontally, turn over the top layer and place it next to the cake, cut-side up. Brush half the syrup over the base layer of the cake, going right to the edges. Spread half the cream evenly over the top of the cake and then cover the entire surface with the sliced strawberries in an even layer. Spread half the remaining cream over the strawberries, pressing it in between the berry slices. Brush the remaining syrup over the crumb side of the top layer, then turn it over, crust-side up, and place it on the cake. Now you can spread the remaining cream on the top of the cake in a wavy pattern and decorate with the reserved berries. Or, for something more formal, place the remaining cream in a pastry bag fitted with a star tip and pipe 10 rosettes around the circumference of the cake to mark the portions. Dust the whole cake with icing sugar and then place the 10 reserved berries on each rosette.

- Serve immediately, with berry coulis, or refrigerate and serve within the hour.

BLACK FOREST CAKE

SERVES 12

A victim of its success, the mighty Black Forest cake has been diminished by versions made with artificial whipped topping, cheap chocolate, and Day-Glo cherries. Yet having tasted one brought to me from the region of the Black Forest in Germany, I can vouch that when made with quality ingredients, this cake is downright luscious, as the cherry-and-chocolate combo is hard to beat. This is definitely a project cake, so read the recipe a few times before starting, don't stress out, and you will be fine. Use plenty of kirsch—enough so that kids make a face when they eat it. Regarding the cherries: avoid those dreary canned Bing cherries in favour of bottled sour red cherries (Hungarian brands are great), available in many supermarkets and specialty food stores. Fresh cherries can be used for decoration but not in the cake as they are too mild in flavour. Avoid maraschino cherries altogether, because they belong in a cocktail, not a cake.

1½ cups (about 375g) pitted red sour cherries in light syrup, drained

3 recipes Crème Chantilly (page 308)

1 (9-inch/23cm) chocolate Genoise (see page 307)

½ cup (125ml) Simple Syrup (page 308)

¼ cup (60ml) kirsch (see Notes)

About ¾ cup chocolate shavings and ¼ cup chocolate curls (see Notes), for garnish

Sifted icing sugar, for dusting

- Set aside 12 cherries to decorate the finished cake. Coarsely chop the remaining cherries and place them in a large bowl.

- Make the Chantilly cream and whip until it holds firm peaks. Transfer 2 cups of the cream to the bowl of chopped cherries and fold them together. Refrigerate both the remaining cream and the cherry cream.

- Cut a thick round of cardboard to the same size as the Genoise (I use the cake mould to trace the circle). Place the Genoise top-crust-side down on the circle of cardboard and peel off the parchment paper. Using a serrated bread knife, slice it horizontally into three equal layers, leaving the base layer on the cardboard and placing the other two layers in front of it in the order they were cut (for a straight cake, try to keep the layers in the same order and position they were in when you originally sliced the cake).

- Combine in a small glass or measuring cup the simple syrup and kirsch and, using a soft pastry brush, brush the base layer with about ¼ cup (60ml) of the kirsch syrup. Next, spread half the cherry cream evenly over the base layer. Cover with the middle layer of cake, lightly pressing down to make it even, then brush it with syrup as well. Spread over the rest of the cherry cream and then soak the last cake layer with the remaining syrup before placing it over the cream, again pressing down lightly to even out the cake as much as possible.

- With a large, straight spatula, ice the cake with the remaining whipped cream, beginning with the top of the cake and continuing around the sides, spreading it evenly. If the cream coating looks thin, you can ice it a second time. Slip a spatula or knife under the cardboard to lift up the cake by placing your hand under the board, and refrigerate the cake while you clean up your work surface.

- Lift the cake again and, working quickly, pick up the chocolate shavings with your other hand and press them onto the sides of the cake, going right up to the top ridge. Do not hold the shavings in your hand too long or they will melt.

$\longrightarrow$

- Place your cake on a serving plate and, using a pastry bag, pipe 12 rosettes of cream about an inch (2.5cm) from the rim of the cake to mark the portions. If you don't have a pastry bag, you can spoon 12 dollops of cream around the rim, or decorate the top of the cake by swilling the cream over the top. Sprinkle the remaining chocolate shavings (or larger chocolate curls) inside the ring of rosettes and place a reserved cherry on each rosette. Refrigerate the cake for up to 8 hours before serving. Just before serving, sift icing sugar over the chocolate curls in the center of the cake.

* **Notes**: If you prefer to make your cake without alcohol, substitute the bottling syrup from the cherries for the kirsch.

* You can purchase chocolate shavings and curls, but it's less expensive to make your own: For shavings, grate a large (about 3½-ounce/100g) semisweet chocolate bar on the large holes of a box grater (the same holes you would use to grate cheese). For larger curls to decorate the top of the cake, run a vegetable peeler along the flat side of a thick chocolate bar. Keep the shavings and the curls refrigerated until you're ready to decorate the cake.

LE CHOCOLATE CAKE

SERVES 12

As much as I love a good layer cake, many are too dry, too sweet, or just plain dull. Happily, that's not the case with this cake, which I call Le *Chocolate Cake because it meets all my chocolate cake expectations.*

2 cups (230g) pastry flour

½ cup (50g) unsweetened cocoa powder

¾ teaspoon baking soda

1 teaspoon baking powder

½ teaspoon fine sea salt

½ cup (1 stick/110g) unsalted butter, at room temperature

1½ cups (300g) granulated sugar

½ cup (100g) light brown sugar

2 large eggs

1 teaspoon vanilla extract

¾ cup (175g) sour cream

⅔ cup (160ml) boiling water

Ganache Icing (page 317)

- Preheat the oven to 375°F (190°C). Place the oven rack in the middle position. Grease two 9 × 2-inch (23 × 5cm) cake pans and line the base of each with a round of parchment paper cut to fit.

- Sift together the flour, cocoa powder, baking soda, baking powder, and salt into a medium bowl.

- In the bowl of a stand mixer fitted with the paddle attachment, or in a large bowl using a handheld mixer, beat together the butter, granulated sugar, and brown sugar for a good minute until well blended. Add the eggs one by one, followed by the vanilla, then beat a few minutes more, scraping down the sides as needed. The mixture should look light and fluffy.

- Add half the dry ingredients and beat on medium speed to combine, then add half the sour cream, followed by the rest of the dry ingredients, then the rest of the sour cream. Blend until you no longer see either the flour mixture or any streaks of sour cream. Then, with the mixer running, gradually pour in the boiling water. Scrape down the sides of the bowl and blend for 30 seconds more, until the batter is an even consistency.

- Divide the batter between the prepared pans and spread it out evenly, being sure it's the same thickness on the sides as in the middle. Bake for 30 minutes, or until the cakes bounce back when pressed lightly

→

and a toothpick inserted into the center comes out clean. Place the pans on a wire rack and let cool almost completely before unmoulding.

- Ice the cake (see the icing tips on page 302): Place one layer crust-side down on your serving plate or cardboard round (you might want to put a spoonful of icing on the base to "glue" the cake to the surface and prevent it from moving around). To keep your serving plate clean, slide pieces of parchment between the cake and the plate (these will be removed once the cake is fully iced).

- Peel the parchment from the cake and spread about a third of the icing evenly over the surface of the cake. Cover with the second layer, crust-side down, and peel off the parchment. Ice the sides of the cake first and then scrape the remaining icing onto the top. Spread the icing over the top and then ice the entire cake as evenly as possible, swirling the icing into a decorative pattern. It doesn't have to look perfect, so once it looks good, resist swirling too much as the icing begins to set.

- This cake keeps, covered, at room temperature for up to 5 days.

GANACHE ICING

You can make the base ganache ahead of time, but it's essential to finish the icing right when you are ready to ice the cake because it firms up quite quickly and is difficult to spread afterwards. This recipe makes just enough icing for one chocolate cake.

6 ounces (170g) semisweet chocolate (no more than 70% cacao)

¾ cup (180ml) whipping cream

4 tablespoons (½ stick/ 55g) unsalted butter, at room temperature

½ cup (60g) sifted icing sugar

- Chop the chocolate into small pieces and place in a small bowl. In a small saucepan, bring the cream to a boil, and pour over the chocolate. Count to 30 and then stir the mixture until it's smooth and shiny (if you have any pieces of unmelted chocolate, place over a water bath to heat the mixture and stir until it is lump-free). Let cool to room temperature, about 30 minutes.

- With a handheld mixer, beat the butter into the ganache on high speed, a tablespoon at a time, followed by the icing sugar. Beat until the icing holds a firm peak. Use immediately.

PASTRY:
PRACTICE MAKES PERFECT

PASTRY:
PRACTICE MAKES PERFECT

As the choice of commercial pies and tarts is far from inspiring, I decided long ago that it's better to make them myself. Since then, making pies has become one of my great pleasures. Yet sadly, the mention of pastry strikes fear in the hearts of many, even experienced home cooks. Pastry is the most technical branch of the cooking realm, and those techniques can be tricky.

We aren't all pastry chefs, but by succumbing to our cooking insecurities, we deprive ourselves of some of the best homemade foods. The reassuring truth is, with a few simple guidelines and plenty of practice anyone can whip up an impressive *tarte*.

Good to Know . . .

— For pâte brisée, generally referred to in English as shortcrust pastry or simply "pie dough," use butter for flavour and vegetable shortening—or lard—for flakiness. The ideal proportion for this dough is 2 parts butter to 1 part shortening. Feel free to make this entirely with butter if you prefer to avoid shortening.

— Make sure all ingredients are very cold before making pie dough, especially the butter. If the butter is not cold and firm, it will meld into the flour and you will finish with a tough crust with little flakiness. For a sweet shortcrust pastry, as the texture resembles a shortbread cookie, you start with room temperature butter because you want a crumbly rather than flaky consistency.

— Always work your doughs with a light hand to prevent the formation of gluten, a protein found in flour that gives doughs an elastic texture when activated by excess manipulation. For pâte brisée, do not panic if you see little pieces of butter in the dough, as they help make the crust flaky.

— Always refrigerate dough thoroughly (overnight is ideal) before rolling, which gives it a more homogeneous consistency and relaxes the gluten developed as it's made.

— Rest, rest, rest! To prevent your pie from shrinking during cooking, chill for at least 30 minutes before continuing with the recipe to relax the gluten activated by the rolling.

— Wrapped well, pie dough will keep in the refrigerator for up to 3 days and can be frozen for up to 3 months. Be sure to defrost it in the fridge rather than at room temperature.

— A good quiche is a bit tricky to make with homemade dough, but the results are worth it. The dough needs to be blind-baked before the filling is added, or you will end up with the dreaded "soggy bottom." This is also the case for any pie with a liquid filling, like pumpkin pie, or any sort of flan.

— Be careful not to underbake your pies. The pie is cooked when the crust is a beautiful golden brown—not pale gold or chocolate brown.

— Yes, you can buy commercial pie dough, but few are any good. The exception being puff pastry, which takes a bit of skill to master. Look for all-butter dough, usually sold in pastry shops. Puff pastry made with anything else is tasteless.

— If you are really put off by the idea of rolling the dough (like many people . . .), try grating refrigerated sweet pastry on a cheese grater and then pressing it evenly over the bottom and up the sides of your pie plate. It's an easy technique that produces excellent results.

— For the recipes in this book, I use round and rectangular French tart tins with removable bottoms, because I prefer unmoulding my tarts to serve, and I like their straight sides and sharp edge. You can also use glass pie plates. Not only do they conduct heat very well, they give a nice homey look to your pies.

Let's Get Rolling!

When it comes to rolling the dough, here are the rules:

— Beginners should start with pâte brisée, which is less delicate and less prone to stick when being rolled.

— Buy yourself a good rolling pin, and by that I mean a large one. Mine is 14 inches (35cm) long and 2¾ inches (7cm) in diameter. I prefer a pin with handles over the French straight ones because it gives me leverage and is easier to use.

— It's essential to keep your dough cold and put it back in the refrigerator the minute it no longer feels cool to the touch.

— Always flour your work surface and the top of the dough lightly and evenly, and move the dough around often to help keep it from sticking. Think of the rhythm in your head: roll, roll, turn . . . roll, roll, turn . . .

— Aim for a uniform thickness of between 1/10 and 1/8 inch (2.5 to 3mm) for the dough before lining your tin. A good tip to gauge thickness is to roll until you see the pattern of the countertop through the dough.

— To avoid an uneven crust, be sure to roll from the center all the way to the ends, always finishing in an upwards motion to avoid squashing the edges.

— On warm days, aim to roll out your pastry in the morning or late at night when your kitchen is at its coolest. If you can't do that, or your counters are warm, place an ice pack on the counter beforehand to cool down the surface.

— While you can roll out scraps of pâte brisée several times if necessary, sweet pastry absorbs flour every time you roll it out, thus becoming drier and more fragile. You can roll it out once or twice, but after that it tends to fall apart.

— All doughs roll out better the day after they are made, so keep that in mind before choosing to make a tart.

Blind-Baking

Many pies, like cream pies, fresh fruit pie, or lemon pie, require a fully baked pie shell. Others, like quiches and pumpkin pie, require that the pastry be almost fully baked before being filled and put back in the oven; otherwise, the base and sides will never cook through. The only pies I make that require a raw pastry base are pecan pie, frangipane pies, and covered pies like apple pie or potpies.

This prebaking technique is called blind-baking. Always blind-bake at 375°F (190°C), and turn your pie shell halfway through the baking to prevent hot spots.

To keep the base and sides from shrinking or puffing up, the raw crust must be lined with a sheet of parchment paper or aluminum foil larger than the tin and filled with enough pie weights, baking beans, dried beans, rice, or even white sugar to cover the base and come three-quarters of the way up the sides (I've been using the same dried chickpeas to blind-bake for years). This keeps the shell in place, preventing it from shrinking or puffing up while baking. Avoid having the baking weights, beans, or rice in direct contact with the dough, or they will bake into the pie shell.

Once the edges begin to colour, after about 25 minutes, remove the pie shell from the oven, wait a few minutes, then carefully lift out the paper and the weights and place the crust back in the oven to bake for about 5 minutes more, until cooked through. It's often recommended to prick the base of a tart made with pâte brisée with a fork (docking) to avoid it puffing up.

PÂTE BRISÉE (FLAKY PIE DOUGH)

MAKES ABOUT 12 OUNCES (335G), ENOUGH FOR
ONE 9-INCH (23CM) TART SHELL

This is an all-purpose dough that can be used for either sweet or savoury tarts. If making a savoury tart, add just a pinch of sugar or leave it out altogether. I add a touch of vinegar to the dough to keep it from oxidizing, but it's optional.

1⅓ cups (185g) all-purpose flour

2 teaspoons sugar

¼ teaspoon fine sea salt

⅓ cup (75g) cold unsalted butter, cut into small cubes

3 tablespoons (40g) cold shortening, cut into small pieces

¼ cup (60ml) ice water

¼ teaspoon white wine vinegar (optional)

- Pour the flour into a large bowl, or directly onto your counter, and stir in the sugar and salt. Add the butter and shortening and toss to coat with the flour. Using your fingers, break up the butter and shortening, at first pinching it and then breaking it up further into pea-size pieces in the flour, trying your best not to squish the butter right into the flour. You can stop when most of the fat is broken up, but it doesn't matter if you have a few larger pieces in the mix. Make a well in the center and pour in the ice water and vinegar (if using). Using your fingers, slowly incorporate the liquid into the flour mixture until a dough begins to form. If the dough seems dry, you can add a tablespoon of water, but add it a bit at a time; it's preferable if your dough is just a bit crumbly, and in no way sticky.

- Using the palm of your hand, knead the dough until smooth, four or five times, being careful not to overwork it or it will be tough. Ideally you will still see small bits of butter in the dough. Shape the dough into a flat disc, tucking under the edges to make it smooth, as this will facilitate rolling later on. Wrap in plastic wrap and refrigerate until ready to use. This dough must be chilled completely for a few hours before rolling; overnight is even better.

- **Food processor method**: Combine the flour, sugar, and salt in a medium bowl. Toss the butter and shortening into the dry ingredients. Place the bowl in the freezer to firm up the butter, at least 30 minutes.

- Transfer the mixture to a food processor and pulse-chop for a few seconds (8 to 10 pulses), until the butter is in tiny pieces and the mixture has the texture of coarse cornmeal or couscous. Add the ice water and vinegar (if using) and process just until the dough comes together. Turn out onto the counter and knead to form a smooth dough. Wrap well and refrigerate for a few hours before rolling.

RED PEPPER AND CHEDDAR QUICHE

I like this quiche in the summer. Here I've made it with red peppers, but it's also great with sautéed mushrooms, spinach, or grilled zucchini, served warm or at room temperature, with a salad alongside and some white wine. If you make it in advance, be sure to reheat it in the oven, NOT the microwave, or the crust will become soft.

1 recipe Pâte Brisée (page 326)

1 red bell pepper

¾ cup (175ml) milk

½ cup (125ml) whipping cream

1 large egg

3 large egg yolks

Fine sea salt and freshly ground black pepper

Pinch of grated nutmeg

⅔ cup (60g) grated aged Cheddar cheese

- Roll your dough out to about an eighth of an inch thickness (2 to 3mm) and transfer it to a 9-inch (23cm) pie plate or tart pan (with a removable bottom), making sure the top rim of the tart isn't too thin and trying to form a border that goes beyond the edge of the mould. Chill for at least 30 minutes.

- Preheat the oven to 375°F (190°C). Place the oven rack in the middle position.

- When the tart shell is chilled, line it with parchment paper and baking beans (or weights) and blind-bake for about 25 minutes, until the edge begins to brown. Cool for 5 minutes, then remove the paper and the beans, lightly prick the base of the dough with a fork (this will prevent it from rising up) and bake for a further 5 minutes, until the dough is almost cooked through. Let cool.

- Meanwhile, grill the bell pepper over a live (gas) flame or under the broiler until charred and then wrap it snugly in a paper towel and let cool. Rub off the charred skin, remove the seeds and membranes, and slice the flesh into thin strips. Pat dry.

- In a small bowl, whisk together the milk, cream, egg, egg yolks, a large pinch each of salt and pepper, and the nutmeg. Set aside.

- When ready to bake the quiche: Place 2 tablespoons of the milk-egg mixture in the base of the shell and brush it over the entire surface, getting into the holes. Bake for about 5 minutes, until the liquid is set (this will seal the crust and prevent it from leaking). Remove from the oven, cool slightly, and then arrange half the sliced pepper over the base of the tart. Sprinkle over three-quarters of the cheese, then arrange the remaining pepper slices over the top. Place the tart shell on a baking sheet, then carefully pour over the remaining liquid, being very careful that it does not overflow. Sprinkle over the remaining cheese.

- Bake for 35 to 40 minutes, until the filling begins to rise around the edges and the topping is golden and set in the middle.

- Let cool and serve warm or at room temperature.

PÂTE SUCRÉE (SWEET SHORTCRUST PASTRY)

MAKES 1½ POUNDS (735G), ENOUGH FOR TWO 9-INCH (23CM) TART SHELLS

*Keep in mind that you will only need half of this dough to make one
tart shell. Wrap and refrigerate or freeze the extra dough for a future
use. If you're not an experienced pastry maker, try the grating method
described on page 322. It takes a bit of patience, but it works well.*

1 cup (2 sticks/220g) unsalted butter, at room temperature

¾ cup (90g) icing sugar, sifted

Pinch of fine sea salt

3 large egg yolks

2 tablespoons ice water

2½ cups (350g) all-purpose flour

• Beat the butter, icing sugar, and salt until smooth and creamy. Blend in the egg yolks one by one, followed by the water. Stir in the flour until you have a ragged dough, then turn it out onto a lightly floured counter and crush with the base of your palm until the dough has a uniform consistency without overworking it. Divide in half, shape into two discs, wrap in plastic wrap, and refrigerate for at least 2 hours before rolling (or 4 hours before grating.)

• Remove the dough from the refrigerator, cut into large pieces, and, working quickly, squeeze them in your hands, like Play-Doh, to soften. Press them together into a ball and then flatten into a disc, tucking under the edges to make them smooth. You want your dough to be malleable but still cool.

• On a lightly floured surface, roll the dough out into a large round, keeping the counter and the surface of the dough lightly floured at all times and turning the dough a quarter turn every few rolls. Continue rolling out until it reaches about an eighth of an inch thickness (2 to 3mm), or until you just begin to see the pattern of your counter through the dough. Give your dough a final turn, flour it lightly, carefully roll it onto the rolling pin, and then unroll it onto a 9-inch (23cm) tart mould (with a removable bottom).

Carefully press the dough into the mould, being sure to get it right into the corners and trying to keep the sides as high as possible so they won't sink down when baking. If you end up with any holes or cracks, use any extra dough to patch it together. Make sure the top rim of the tart isn't too thin and try to form a border that goes beyond the edge of the mould. Chill for about 30 minutes before baking.

- Keep any extra dough refrigerated. It can be incorporated into fresh dough for your next crust.

- **Grating method:** When dough is very cold, grate the dough using the medium holes of a box grater. Sprinkle half the grated dough around the sides of a 9-inch (23cm) French tart mould (with a removable bottom), pressing the dough evenly onto the sides and well into the corners. Then press the remaining dough evenly over the base, making sure the entire surface of the mould is evenly covered by about an eighth of an inch (3mm) of dough and that there aren't any holes. Chill the tart base until firm, at least 30 minutes, before baking.

RASPBERRY TART

SERVES 8 TO 10

I could not write a chapter on tarts without including my favourite:
a fresh raspberry tart. Filled with a light custard cream that can be
flavoured with kirsch or orange liqueur, it's also delicious made with
strawberries. When I'm feeling especially rebellious, I like to turn the
raspberries upside down and scatter over some blueberries to give the tart
a completely different look. If you're up for extra raspberry flavour, try
spreading a bit of raspberry jam between the tart shell and the cream.

1 cup (250ml) whipping cream

1½ tablespoons granulated sugar

1 teaspoon vanilla extract

1 recipe Pastry Cream (page 334)

2 tablespoons kirsch or orange liqueur (optional)

1 (9-inch/23cm) Pâte Sucrée tart shell (page 330), fully blind-baked

About 3 cups (450g) fresh raspberries

Icing sugar

• In a small bowl, whip the cream with the granulated sugar and vanilla until it forms firm peaks. In a larger bowl, whisk the pastry cream vigorously until it reaches a lump-free consistency. Add the kirsch (if using), as well as a large spoonful of the whipped cream, whisk until smooth, and then fold in the rest.

• Spoon the cream into the cooled pastry shell and spread it into as even a layer as possible, getting right into the corners. Arrange the berries over the top of the tart in concentric circles or pile them in a heap, which can look pretty, too—just do your best to cover as much of the cream as possible. Using a fine sieve, sprinkle over a light dusting of icing sugar and serve immediately, or refrigerate for up to a day.

PASTRY CREAM

Pastry cream (or custard) with fruit is a pairing I adore. For another delicious dessert, combine equal amounts of pastry cream and Chantilly cream (see page 308), and serve atop sugared berries or baked stone fruit in a decorative glass. For the adult version, whisk in 1 tablespoon Cointreau or kirsch.

1 cup (250ml) milk

¼ cup (50g) sugar

1 teaspoon vanilla extract, or ½ vanilla bean, split lengthwise and seeds scraped out

3 large egg yolks

3 tablespoons cornstarch

2 teaspoons unsalted butter

- In a small saucepan, whisk together the milk, half the sugar, and the vanilla (or vanilla pulp and pod) and bring to a boil.

- Meanwhile, in a small bowl, vigorously whisk together the egg yolks and the remaining sugar until smooth and pale in colour. Add the cornstarch and whisk until you have a smooth paste.

- Pour half the scalded milk into the egg mixture, whisk until smooth, then whisk it back into the pot of hot milk. Whisking all the while, bring the mixture back to a boil for about 30 seconds until smooth and thick. Remove from the heat, then whisk in the butter. Transfer to a clean bowl (remove the vanilla pod, if using) and cover with plastic wrap, pressing it directly against the surface of the cream, then immediately refrigerate to cool. Pastry cream keeps refrigerated for 5 days.

LEMON TART

This lemon tart recipe is composed of many parts: a lemon curd recipe of mine along with techniques inspired by Parisian pastry chefs Pierre Hermé and Jacques Genin. It all comes together to make an amazing tart, which can be served solo or with a sprinkling of fresh raspberries in summer or chopped toasted hazelnuts in winter. This recipe makes enough filling for a 9-inch (23cm) tart, but if you're making a smaller tart, you can keep any extra lemon cream refrigerated. It's great on scones, spooned over fresh blueberries, or spread between layers of cake.

1¼ cups (250g) sugar

Grated zest of 2 lemons

Grated zest of 2 limes, divided, plus a bit more for garnish

1¼ cups (310ml) lemon-lime juice (from 3 or 4 lemons, plus the 2 zested limes)

1¼ cups (2½ sticks/280g) unsalted butter, at room temperature

4 large eggs

2 large egg yolks

1 (9-inch/23cm) Pâte Sucrée tart shell (page 330), fully blind-baked

- In a small bowl, combine the sugar, lemon zest, and half the lime zest. Rub the sugar and zest together to release the essential oils in the zest and flavour the sugar.

- In a nonreactive medium saucepan, combine the lemon-lime juice, half the sugar mix, and about a quarter of the butter and bring to a boil over medium-high heat. Meanwhile, in a small bowl, beat the eggs and egg yolks together with the remaining sugar.

- When the lemon juice mixture is boiling, pour one-third of it over the egg mixture, whisking continuously, then pour it back into the pot. Reduce the heat to medium and whisk the mixture until the white foam on the top disappears and the cream visibly thickens and just begins to bubble around the edges. Do not let it come to a rolling boil! Strain immediately into a blender or into a tall container if using an immersion blender (I use a large measuring cup for this). Place a thermometer in the cream and let cool to 113°F (45°C), stirring every so often to help it cool down. When it's ready (it should be warm, not hot, to the touch), begin blending in the remaining butter in small pieces on high speed, until the

$\longrightarrow$

cream is silky smooth and all the butter is incorporated. Blend for a minute more to aerate the mixture. Drop in the remaining lime zest and blend for a few seconds more. Pour the cream directly into the baked tart shell, spreading it out into the corners. If you'd like, grate over a little bit of lime zest to decorate. Return to the refrigerator to chill for a few hours before serving.

Frangipane Tarts

French-style tarts are not simple to make, yet I find that lining the inside with a base of frangipane simplifies the operation. What is frangipane? Frangipane (almond cream) is a tart filling made with butter, almond flour, sugar, and eggs. Some versions are made with marzipan in place of the sugar and almonds, and pastry cream is often added to make this costly cream go further. It's designed to be baked, resulting in a cakelike filling with a dense texture and subtle almond flavour.

French pastry chefs use it in the classic *tarte aux amandes*, and the British use frangipane inside their famous Bakewell tart. I like almond cream because it works brilliantly with fruit, especially stone fruit, pears, and apples.

If you make a tart with frangipane, it will be an open-faced tart that requires only one sheet of pastry, and that sheet of pastry is in the bottom of the pan so it doesn't have to be perfect. Sweet.

Also, when making a frangipane tart, there's no blind-baking. All you do is fill a raw pastry shell with almond cream, cover with fruit, and bake. Done! You can also spread a layer of jam or marmalade beneath the cream, top it with a handful of slivered almonds, and you have the famous French amandine tart. Add a few sliced poached pears to the amandine and you have the classic *tarte Bourdaloue*. If they aren't too acidic, sliced poached apricots also work brilliantly in a frangipane tart. Another smart way to use it is to buy a sheet of puff pastry, roll it out, dock it (which means prick it all over with a fork), spread over an even layer of almond cream, top with fruit, crimp the edges, and bake. The possibilities are endless.

FRANGIPANE (ALMOND CREAM)

MAKES 1½ CUPS (400G), ENOUGH TO FILL
ONE 9- TO 10-INCH (23 TO 25CM) TART SHELL

7 tablespoons (100g) unsalted butter, at room temperature

¾ cup (100g) almond flour

½ cup (100g) sugar

2 large eggs

1 tablespoon all-purpose flour

1 teaspoon vanilla extract

¼ teaspoon almond extract

- In a medium bowl using a handheld mixer, beat the butter on high speed until smooth and creamy. Blend in the almond flour and sugar. Beat in the eggs one at a time, scraping down the sides as needed, and finally blend in the flour, vanilla, and almond extract. Use immediately, or refrigerate, well wrapped, for up to 4 days.

GASCOGNE APPLE TART

SERVES 8 TO 10

Pâtisserie de Gascogne was a legendary French pastry shop in Montreal, and this lovely tart, with a frangipane filling and apples placed upright in staggered rows, was one of their best-sellers. Over time, the tart was phased out, and sadly, their shops closed in 2018. Still today, I make this tart inspired by the hundreds I made when working there in the '90s. Notice the addition of Calvados to the frangipane, which is optional but adds a nice apple kick if you're up for it. This is best made in a 1½-inch-deep (4cm) French tart mould.

5 cooking apples (such as Cortland, Granny Smith, Golden Delicious)

1 recipe Frangipane (page 340, flavoured with 1 tablespoon Calvados)

1 (9-inch/23cm) unbaked tart shell, made with Pâte Sucrée (page 330) or Pâte Brisée (page 326)

2 tablespoons sugar or cinnamon sugar

Ice cream, sweetened crème fraîche, or Crème Chantilly (page 308), for serving

• Preheat the oven to 375°F (180°C). Place the oven rack in the middle position.

• Peel your apples, stand them upright vertically, slice them straight down in the center, and remove the cores (a small melon baller spoon works well for this). Lay the apple halves down flat on their cut sides and cut them horizontally into about 10 slices, roughly ⅛ inch (3mm) thick.

• Spread the frangipane in an even layer over the base of the raw tart shell. Then, starting at the back of the tart, arrange the apple slices standing upright in staggered rows, moving from left to right, with each slice overlapping the next at the halfway point, and pressing each to about a third of its depth into the cream. Leftover apple slices can be used to fill any gaps, but don't overdo it or you'll ruin your design. Sprinkle the sugar evenly over the surface of the apples and place the tart in the oven. Bake for 50 to 55 minutes, until the apple slices and the frangipane that has puffed up between the apple slices are golden brown. Let cool on a rack.

• Serve at room temperature with ice cream, crème fraîche, or Chantilly cream; I also love this with a drizzle of Salted Butter Caramel Sauce (page 71).

CRISPS, CRUMBLES, AND CUSTARDS: EVERYDAY COMFORT

CRISPS, CRUMBLES, AND CUSTARDS: EVERYDAY COMFORT

A great dessert always offers a myriad of textures and flavours. Over the years, I have developed a deep affection for certain combinations, a favourite being warm fruit with a crunchy topping and custard. What I love is that play between the acidity of the fruit and the richness of the eggy/creamy custard, and the contrast of textures and temperatures in a baked dessert served with cream or—better yet—ice cream. Think of these desserts as a tart—minus the crust. That said, you could also assemble these crisps and crumbles inside of a pastry shell.

Good to Know . . .

— Crisps and crumbles need structure in their filling, and for that reason you need to use a firm base fruit, possibly with a secondary fruit added in for flavour. For example, a raspberry or strawberry crumble would amount to a pan of jam, so you will need a firmer fruit like apples, pears, or rhubarb to use with most berries (the exception being blueberries, which work well alone).

— There are no hard rules on what makes a crisp or a crumble, but for me, a crisp topping includes oats and/or chopped nuts, whereas a crumble is just sugar, butter, and either almond flour or regular flour.

— If you're not a fan of custard sauce, serve your crumbles with lightly whipped cream, crème fraîche, frozen yogurt, ice cream, or just a light dusting of icing sugar.

— Crumble and crisp toppings are also great sprinkled atop muffins. An open-faced fruit tart can also benefit from a generous crumble topping. Baked crumble can also be used as a garnish. Spread out on a sheet of parchment paper on a baking sheet and bake at 350°F (180°C) for 20 to 25 minutes, until golden. Chill and use to top ice cream or any kind of cream dessert to add a welcome bit of crunch. You might even want to substitute other nut flours, like hazelnut or walnut, for the almond.

— Fruit crumbles taste great at room temperature, and any leftovers can be enjoyed right out of the fridge for a sweet breakfast the next day. If you prefer them warm, they can be reheated just before serving, but be careful not to dry them out.

— As crisp and crumble toppings keep well refrigerated for about 10 days in an airtight container or zip-top bag, consider making a large batch to have on hand for making last-minute desserts.

— For a dinner party, crisps and crumbles can be assembled beforehand, but try to bake it as your guests are eating the main course to let the aroma give them a taste of what is to come.

— Feel free to butter your baking dish when making a crumble, but it isn't necessary.

BASIC CRUMBLE

MAKES 3 CUPS (400G)

1 cup (100g) almond flour

½ cup (100g) sugar

⅔ cup (90g) all-purpose flour

7 tablespoons (95g) unsalted butter, at room temperature, plus more for greasing

- In a large bowl, combine the almond flour, sugar, and all-purpose flour and add the butter in small pieces. With your hands, rub everything together slowly until it turns into mealy dough (you can also do this in a stand mixer with the paddle attachment on low speed). Squeeze bits of the dough together to make marble-size balls. Toss the mix a few more times to aerate, then spread out onto a tray and refrigerate until needed.

BASIC CRISP

MAKES 2½ CUPS (360G)

½ cup (75g) almonds or walnuts

¾ cup (105g) all-purpose flour

¼ cup (30g) rolled oats

¼ cup (50g) brown sugar

2 tablespoons granulated sugar

Pinch of fine sea salt

¼ teaspoon ground cinnamon

6 tablespoons (¾ stick/ 80g) cold unsalted butter

- Preheat the oven to 350°F (180°C). Toast the nuts on a baking sheet for 7 to 10 minutes, until fragrant. Let cool and chop coarsely by hand into small pieces.

- In a large bowl, combine the flour, oats, brown sugar, granulated sugar, salt, and cinnamon and with your fingers or a pastry blender, cut the butter into the mixture until it resembles a coarse meal and begins to hold together. Squeeze it together lightly to form a few larger clumps. Stir in the cooled nuts. Keep chilled until ready to use.

CRÈME ANGLAISE

MAKES 3 CUPS (750ML)

2 cups (500ml) milk

½ cup (100g) sugar

2 teaspoons vanilla extract, or ½ vanilla bean, split lengthwise and seeds scraped out

5 large egg yolks

- Fill a large bowl of ice, set a smaller bowl on top, and set a strainer in the smaller bowl. Have a wooden spoon (and a candy thermometer, if desired) at the ready as well.

- Pour the milk and half the sugar into a medium saucepan with the vanilla (or vanilla pulp and scraped pod). Whisk the mixture set over high heat until the sugar is melted, and let it come to a boil.

- Meanwhile, in a medium bowl, whisk the remaining sugar energetically into the egg yolks until the mixture has a creamy texture. Slowly whisk half the scalded milk into the egg yolk mixture, lower the heat to medium, then whisk the egg mixture back into the pot of milk. Using the wooden spoon, stir the sauce in figure-eights until it is thick enough to coat the back of the spoon and leave a trace when your finger is drawn through it. (Alternatively, stir the sauce until it reaches 185°F/85°C on a candy thermometer.)

- Remove from the heat and immediately strain the mixture into the chilled bowl. Whisk every so often to release the heat. When the sauce is cool, cover and refrigerate for up to 3 days.

- **For vanilla ice cream:** Make the crème anglaise following the directions above, but once the sauce is cooked to the right temperature, remove it from the heat and immediately whisk in ½ cup (125ml) whipping cream. Strain and chill thoroughly (overnight is best), then churn in an ice cream machine following the manufacturer's instructions.

FRUIT CRUMBLE

SERVES 6 TO 8

*You can make several variations of the fruit crumble theme, which I have
listed on page 351, but the method remains the same. I bake it in an
8 × 12-inch (20 × 30cm) or 9 × 13-inch (23 × 33cm) gratin dish, but
you can adapt the amount of crumble to the size of the dish you have.
They can even be made in individual portions. Add some more fruit if
you like . . . some spice . . . a vanilla bean. Feel free to experiment.*

About 2½ pounds (1kg)
fruit and/or berries

Grated zest and juice of
½ lemon or orange or
1 lime

¼ to ½ cup (50 to 100g)
sugar (see Note)

1 to 2 tablespoons all-
purpose flour or cornstarch
(see Note)

1 recipe Basic Crumble
(page 346)

- Preheat the oven to 375°F (190°C).

- Wash, peel, hull, and slice your fruit as needed, and
place in a large bowl. With your hands, toss in the citrus
zest and juice, then add the sugar and flour and mix
until the fruit is well coated. Transfer the mixture to an
8 to 10-cup gratin dish. Pour the crumble over the top
and spread it evenly. Place the dish on a baking sheet
(to catch any spills) and bake the crisp for 45 to
55 minutes, until the topping is evenly browned and
the fruit juices are bubbling. If the topping is browned
before the fruit is cooked, lay a piece of aluminum foil
loosely over the top of the dish.

* **Note:** For these measurements, it is best to taste your
fruit. If it's very ripe and sweet, add the lesser amount
of sugar. If it is very juicy, add more flour or cornstarch
to bind the juices. I would always suggest adding a bit of
citrus zest and juice, preferably lemon, but orange and
lime are also excellent. Spices work well, too.

PLUM CRUMBLE

2.2 pounds (1kg) plums, or mix of about 1 pound (500g) plums and about 1 pound (500g) other fruit, like pears, blackberries, raspberries, blueberries, peaches, or nectarines

Grated zest and juice of ½ orange

¼ cup (50g) sugar

1 tablespoon all-purpose flour

½ teaspoon ground cinnamon

Seeds of 1 star anise pod, ground

1 recipe Basic Crumble (page 346)

PEAR AND GINGER CRUMBLE

8 ripe (but not too soft) pears, such as Bosc or Anjou, peeled, cored, and sliced into wedges

4 baking apples, peeled, cored, and sliced into wedges

Grated zest and juice of 1 lemon or 2 limes

½ cup sugar or vanilla sugar

½ cup chopped crystallized ginger (preferably organic)

1 recipe Basic Crumble (page 346, with ½ teaspoon ground ginger added to the dry ingredients)

PEACH AND AMARETTO CRISP

8 to 10 medium peaches, blanched, peeled, and sliced into wedges

3 tablespoons amaretto

2 tablespoons all-purpose flour

2 tablespoons sugar

1 recipe Basic Crisp (page 346)

BLUEBERRY NECTARINE CRUMBLE

3 cups (about 1 pound/450g) blueberries, rinsed and picked over

4 large nectarines, pitted and sliced into wedges

Grated zest and juice of 1 small lemon

½ cup (100g) sugar, or a mix of ¼ cup sugar and ¼ cup vanilla sugar

2 tablespoons all-purpose flour

1 recipe Basic Crumble (page 346)

RHUBARB-STRAWBERRY CRISP

1½ pounds (750g) rhubarb, tips trimmed, peeled (if needed), and chopped into 1-inch (2.5cm) pieces

2 cups (350g) hulled strawberries, sliced

Grated zest and juice of ½ orange

½ cup (100g) sugar or vanilla sugar

2 tablespoons all-purpose flour or cornstarch

1 recipe Basic Crisp (page 346) or Basic Crumble (page 346)

PART 5

FEAST!

MY FEAST OF CHOICE:
THANKSGIVING

MY FEAST OF CHOICE:
THANKSGIVING

For me, nothing defines the word "feast" more perfectly than Thanksgiving. The mere notion of giving thanks by feasting on nature's bounty is enough to make my heart and taste buds cry out for seconds.

Thanksgiving is a holiday that's not especially popular in the French Canadian community where I live in Montreal, Quebec. And I'm sure that indifference is shared by many. But, in all humility, I would like to reverse that trend with the following collection of "Best of Thanksgiving" recipes, if only to gather every-one around the table to celebrate the bounty of the harvest.

Of course, the crowning glory of this most North American of feasts is the most North American of birds: the turkey—which might explain a certain lack of enthusiasm for this holiday. I love turkey, will eat it in just about any shape or form, but can't deny it can sometimes be as dry and tasteless as an old cheese sandwich.

After slaving over countless Thanksgiving feasts, I've concluded that brining the turkey is the way to go. Not only is it juicier, it's roasted on high heat so the cooking time is cut down considerably. And because it's brined, the risk of dry-ing it out is close to nil. It's also easier to carve, and with the recipe on page 362, you can use the drippings to make gravy that won't be overly salty. It's win-win all the way.

Another thing I love about Thanksgiving is the predictability of the menu. I tend to make the same dishes year in year out, including roast turkey, gravy, stuffing, cranberry sauce, mashed potatoes, rutabaga and carrot puree, and a heaping mound of Brussels sprouts. For dessert, it's always pumpkin pie and, if I need a second, it's usually an apple-almond tart (see page 341). Sometimes I'll add some green beans, but that's about it. No cheese, no appetizer, not even a canapé to begin.

As for recipes, I've decided things are best kept simple. For the Brussels sprouts I steam them, sauté them in butter, season with salt and pepper and *finito*. No pancetta, no Parmesan cheese, no chestnuts. For the stuffing, I used to make it with sausage, but no longer, because it's not worth the added expense or hassle. Regarding the cranberry sauce and pie, however, I insist on homemade because homemade is better.

Cooking up a full Thanksgiving meal is a pleasurable though exhausting experience, so try to find shortcuts where possible. Prep as much as possible in advance, ask friends and family to bring a vegetable dish or dessert . . . Enlist family members to help wash dishes, set the table, peel carrots, chop onions, etc. Because as great as it is to enjoy a Thanksgiving feast, if you're the one doing all that cooking, chances are you'll be too tired when it's all over to do anything but pass out on your plate.

Don't ask me how I know that . . . !

On Roasting a Turkey

There are so many factors involved when roasting a turkey that it's difficult to offer exact cooking times. I've had good results roasting turkeys at 350°F (175°C) to 400°F (200°C). I've flipped turkeys over, covered the breast with foil, started at high heat and finished low and vice versa. I've roasted wet-brined turkeys, dry-brined turkeys, turkeys rubbed with butter, and turkeys injected with margarine. All these variables make a difference. What's crucial, though, is knowing when your turkey is done.

The best way to judge whether your turkey is cooked is with a meat thermometer that, when inserted in the thickest part of a thigh (without touching bone), should read 165° to 170°F (73° to 77°C). Rest time is essential with a turkey, so be sure when the cooking is completed to tent with foil and let rest at least 20 minutes and up to an hour before carving.

Size and Timing

According to the Canadian Turkey Marketing Agency, for turkeys smaller than 16 pounds, estimate 1 pound (450g) per serving (this accounts for bone weight). For larger birds, a bit less is fine as they have a higher meat-to-bone ratio. But if your goal is to have ample leftovers (which I highly recommend!), aim for 1½ pounds (750g) per person whatever the turkey's size.

The following chart gives you an idea of the size of turkey to purchase, as well as an estimated cooking time to consider when planning the timing of roasting your bird:

For 8 people, buy a 12-pound (5.5kg) turkey, and plan on a 2½- to 3-hour cook time

For 10 people, buy a 15-pound (6.8kg) turkey, and plan on a 2½- to 3½-hour cook time

For 12 people, buy an 18-pound (8.2kg) turkey, and plan on a 3½- to 4½-hour cook time

For 14 people, buy a 20-pound (9kg) turkey, and plan on a 4½- to 5-hour cook time

ROAST TURKEY WITH GRAVY

SERVES 8 TO 10

This recipe, inspired by many I have used over the years, is the one I now use for roast turkey. To brine the bird, use either an immaculately clean bucket or a large (about 25L/6.5-gallon) stockpot. It shouldn't be a tight squeeze but if the container isn't deep enough, the liquid might not cover the turkey. This amount should be adequate for a bird up to 15 pounds and if not, just add enough cold water to cover. As the instructions are quite long, gravy included, it's best to read through the recipe a couple of times before starting. But don't worry, it's really not all that complicated.

Brine

1 cup (200g) sugar

½ cup (135g) fine sea salt

2 red onions, quartered

Stems from ½ bunch parsley

Handful of fresh thyme

2 tablespoons whole black peppercorns

Handful of torn celery leaves

3 bay leaves

1 large orange, quartered and squeezed

1 cinnamon stick

4 star anise pods

1 finger-size piece fresh ginger, peeled and coarsely chopped

→

- **Make the brine:** Fill a large stockpot (or very clean bucket) with the cold water. Add the sugar and salt and whisk to combine. Add the onions, parsley, thyme, peppercorns, celery leaves, bay leaves, orange, cinnamon stick, star anise, and ginger. Give the mix another good whisking to be sure the salt and sugar have dissolved. Remove the neck and giblets from the cavity of the turkey, set aside, then immerse the turkey breast-side down in the brine mixture. If necessary, add enough cold water to cover the bird, then place a dinner plate upside down to keep it immersed. Cover and set in a cold place (even on a back porch in cold weather or a cool cellar) for about 24 hours, but no longer than 2 days.

- To roast: Approximately 4 hours before dinner, remove the turkey from the brine, letting as much liquid run off the bird as possible, then place the turkey breast-side up on a V-rack or sturdy wire rack in your roasting pan. Pat dry, tuck the wing tips under the turkey, and let it come to room temperature.

1 (13-pound/about 6kg) fresh turkey, preferably organic

6 tablespoons (¾ stick/ 80g) unsalted butter, melted, for basting

Gravy

1 medium onion, chopped into large pieces

4 garlic cloves, halved

1 large carrot, chopped into large pieces

2 celery stalks, chopped into large pieces

Stems from ½ bunch parsley

Sage stems (reserved from making Stuffing, page 366)

3 tablespoons all-purpose flour

3 cups (750ml) unsalted turkey stock or Chicken Stock (page 82)

- After 30 minutes, preheat the oven to 400°F (200°C). Place the oven rack in the lowest position.

- Lift the turkey on the rack out of the roasting pan and pour out any liquid that may have accumulated, then scatter the gravy aromatics: the onion, garlic, carrot, celery stalks, parsley, and sage stems all over the pan. Pour over 1 cup (250ml) water and then set the turkey on the rack back in the pan. Brush the bird all over with about a third of the melted butter and place in the oven.

- Roast the turkey until the skin begins to brown, about an hour. Always be sure there is some liquid at the base of the pan, and if it gets too dry, pour more water in as needed. Remove from the oven and, if you can manage it, flip the turkey breast-side down on the roasting rack, then baste the underside. (If you are not able to flip the turkey, it's not the end of the world, but it is a great way to assure even roasting.)

- Roast for another hour, then flip it breast-side up again, pouring out any juices that have accumulated in the cavity into the roasting pan. Baste again, and if the skin is looking too dark at this point, cover loosely with foil. Roast for another 30 minutes.

- At this point, the turkey is either cooked or might need another 30 minutes or so, depending on the size of the bird. The juices should run clear and the legs should move easily, with the skin starting to recede on the drumsticks. But to be extra sure, check the internal temperature by inserting a meat thermometer into the thickest part of the thigh (without touching bone); it should read 165° to 170°F (73° to 77°C).

→

- When it's done, carefully remove the turkey from the roasting rack and transfer to a large cutting board. Let it rest for at least 20 minutes and up to an hour before carving. For longer wait times, tent with foil and then cover with a couple of dish towels to keep warm.

- **Make the gravy:** Strain the aromatics and drippings from the roasting pan through a sieve and into a large measuring cup and place the roasting pan on the stovetop over one or two burners. Press on the vegetables to release any juices, then scrape any accumulated vegetable puree from the underside of the sieve into the liquid. Discard the used vegetables. Ideally this liquid should be poured into a fat separator, but if you don't have one, carefully spoon the fat off the top (reserve it for another use), keeping the brown liquid beneath (this is the good stuff!).

- Heat the roasting pan over medium-high heat, add the flour, then using a whisk, stir it around the pan, scraping up any browned bits as you go. When the flour is well coated in the pan scrapings, pour in the brown liquid drippings and whisk until smooth, then gradually whisk in the stock. Bring to a boil, then remove from the heat.

- Strain the gravy into a small pot, bring back to a boil, and reduce the heat to maintain a simmer. After a few minutes, check the consistency and either add a bit more stock (or water) if it looks too thick or reduce it for a few minutes more if it looks a bit thin.

- Carve the turkey and serve with the gravy in a heated gravy boat alongside.

STUFFING

*You can use this recipe to stuff a large turkey or, my preference, to fill a 9 ×
13-inch (23 × 33cm) gratin dish to bake on its own. As for bread, I go for the day-
old unsliced loaves of pain au levain sold at my supermarket instead of the often
tasteless sliced sandwich bread. This recipe should be started either the night
before or the early morning of the meal. Stuffing is traditionally served with
turkey but it's also great with roast chicken or pork. If you like a bit of a tang in
there, I'd suggest adding 1 cup of chopped dried apricots, cranberries, or apples.*

1 unsliced loaf good-quality
white bread

½ cup (1 stick/110g)
unsalted butter, plus
2 tablespoons, and more
for greasing the pan

2 cups (about 275g)
chopped yellow onion

2 to 3 celery stalks,
chopped (about 1 cup)

½ leek, washed and
chopped (about 1 cup)

2 tablespoons chopped
fresh sage leaves (reserve
the stems for making gravy,
see page 363)

2 teaspoons chopped fresh
thyme leaves, or 1 teaspoon
dried

Fine sea salt and freshly
ground black pepper

8 ounces (225g)
mushrooms, cleaned and
finely chopped

• The night before or morning of the day you make
the stuffing: With a sharp bread knife, slice off the
outer crust from the bread and set aside for another
use. Then slice the bread into about ¾-inch (2cm)
slices and then each of those into ¾-inch (2cm) cubes.
You should end up with about 8 cups of cubed bread.
Spread them out in an even layer on a baking sheet to
dry out at room temperature overnight, or in your
oven at the lowest setting for a couple of hours. When
they have dried out considerably, transfer to a large
bowl.

• In a large skillet, melt the ½ cup of butter over medium-
high heat, then add the onion, celery, and leek. Fry
together until they have softened without colouring,
about 10 minutes. Add the sage, thyme, and a teaspoon
each of salt and pepper and fry for another couple of
minutes, then add the mushrooms and fry until all the
liquid they give off evaporates, about 5 minutes more.
Remove from the heat and scrape the mix into the bowl
of bread cubes. Add the parsley, stir to combine, and let
cool slightly. Grease a 9 × 13-inch (22 × 33cm) baking
pan with butter and set aside.

→

½ cup finely chopped fresh
flat-leaf parsley

2¼ cups (560ml) Chicken
Stock (page 82) or store-
bought

2 large eggs

- Stir in 1 cup (250ml) of the stock and mix well (you can
  use your hands here). Wait 15 minutes for the bread
  to absorb the liquid. While waiting, whisk the eggs
  with another cup (250ml) of the stock in a small bowl
  or measuring cup, then add it to the mix and stir to
  moisten everything equally. Pick up a bit of the stuffing
  and squeeze to determine whether it's dry and if so,
  add the last ¼ cup (60ml) stock. The texture should be
  damp not wet or, on the flip side, crumbly. Season to
  taste, then transfer the mixture into the prepared pan
  and spread it out evenly. Finally, take the remaining
  2 tablespoons butter and break it into bits to scatter
  over the surface of the stuffing. Cover with a sheet of
  aluminum foil and refrigerate until ready to bake.

- A half hour before your turkey is done, take the stuffing
  out of the fridge and place it on the counter so it comes
  to room temperature. When the turkey comes out, set
  the oven temperature to 400°F (200°C) and bake the
  stuffing for 30 minutes. Remove the foil and bake for
  10 to 15 minutes more to crisp up the topping. If it
  still looks a little pale, set the oven to broil to speed up
  the browning process for the last few minutes. Serve
  immediately.

CRANBERRY COMPOTE

MAKES ABOUT 2 CUPS ([TK METRIC])

I dislike the sweetness of canned cranberry sauce and prefer this recipe, which includes orange juice, wine, and less sugar than most.

1 (12-ounce/340g) bag fresh or frozen cranberries

½ cup (125ml) fresh orange juice

½ cup (100g) sugar

½ cup (125ml) red wine or water

2 tablespoons grated orange zest

- In a medium saucepan over medium heat, combine the cranberries, orange juice, sugar, red wine, and zest and bring to a boil. Simmer until thick, stirring occassionally, about 20 minutes.

- Transfer the mixture to a serving bowl and let cool, then chill for at least an hour before serving.

PUMPKIN PIE

When making the tart shell, be sure to patch any holes or cracks before baking as the filling could end up leaking out and cause everything to stick. This tart is best served at room temperature with whipped cream. You could do ice cream, but really it needs little in the way of enhancement.

1 (9-inch/23cm) unbaked tart shell, 1½ inches (4cm) deep, made with Pâte Brisée (page 326) or Pâte Sucrée (page 330)

1¾ cups (395g) pure pumpkin puree (canned is fine)

½ cup (100g) granulated sugar

¼ cup (50g) brown sugar

½ teaspoon fine sea salt

1 teaspoon ground cinnamon

½ teaspoon ground ginger

2 large eggs

1 cup (250ml) whipping cream

Scant ½ cup (110ml) milk

2 tablespoons brandy, bourbon, or whisky (but not a peaty whisky!)

- **Bake the crust:** Preheat the oven to 375°F (180°C). Place the oven rack in the middle position. Line your chilled tart shell with parchment paper and baking beans (or weights) and bake for about 20 minutes, until the edge of the shell begins to brown. Remove the paper and the beans and set aside to cool slightly. Reduce the oven temperature to 350°F (175°C).

- **Make the filling:** In a blender or food processor, combine the pumpkin puree, granulated sugar, brown sugar, salt, cinnamon, ginger, eggs, cream, milk, and brandy and blitz at high speed for a minute until well blended. Place your tart shell on a baking sheet and return to the oven for 5 minutes. Remove from the oven and pour in the filling. With the back of a spoon, swirl to spread it into the corners of the shell.

- Bake for 45 to 50 minutes, until the filling is set in the center and the edges just begin to rise. Let cool on a wire rack to room temperature before slicing.

TURKEY POTPIE

SERVES 6 TO 8

This is my first choice for using up turkey leftovers. I even include the extra gravy because I always have some left over and it really boosts the flavour. You can make the filling ahead of time, but then increase the baking time by about 10 minutes, or until the sauce is bubbling beneath a golden crust. Feel free to mix up the vegetable content, but don't forget the pie will bake for a long time so avoid putting anything in the mix that will become too mushy. This recipe also works well with chicken for a chicken potpie.

1 recipe Pâte Brisée (page 326)

6 tablespoons (¾ stick/80g) unsalted butter, divided

⅓ cup (45g) all-purpose flour

3 cups (750ml) cold turkey stock or Chicken Stock (page 82)

½ cup leftover gravy (see page 364; optional)

½ cup (125ml) whipping cream

1½ teaspoons fine sea salt

1 teaspoon freshly ground black pepper

1 medium onion, or 2 large French shallots, finely chopped

3 medium carrots, cut into small dice

→

- On a lightly floured surface, roll out the pâte brisée to a rectangle of about 11 × 15 inches (28 × 38cm), transfer to a parchment-lined baking sheet, and chill while you make the filling.

- Preheat the oven to 400°F (200°C). Place the oven rack in the middle position.

- In a small pot, melt 4 tablespoons (55g) of the butter over high heat, then add the flour and whisk to make a paste. Cook for a minute while whisking, then gradually whisk in a third of the stock. Whisk until smooth, then gradually whisk in the rest of the stock, along with the gravy (if using) and cream. Season with the salt and pepper and bring to a boil, then reduce the heat to maintain a simmer.

- In a large skillet, melt the remaining 2 tablespoons of butter over medium-high heat, then add the onion, carrots, leek, and celery. Sauté for 5 minutes to soften the vegetables, then add the sliced mushrooms and thyme. Sauté until the mushrooms are softened, about 3 minutes more. Add the peas, stir, then pour over the thickened sauce. Stir well and add the parsley. Bring to a boil.

1 leek, white part only, washed and thinly sliced

2 small celery stalks, finely chopped

2 cups (about 200g) button mushrooms, cleaned and sliced

1 teaspoon chopped fresh thyme leaves, or ½ teaspoon dried

1 to 2 cups (170 to 340g) frozen green peas

3 tablespoons chopped fresh parsley

4 cups (about 500g) cubed cooked turkey meat

1 egg, beaten

- Scatter the turkey pieces over the base of a 9 × 13-inch (23 × 33cm) gratin dish, then pour over the sauce and vegetables and stir a bit in the dish to make sure everything is evenly distributed. Using a pastry brush, brush some water between the stew and the rim of the pan (this will help the pastry stick), then take the pastry out of the fridge and lay it over the top of the turkey stew, letting the pastry touch the mixture while slightly going up the moistened sides of the dish. Press the pastry lightly against the sides of the dish and cut a small hole in the center of the pastry, then brush with the beaten egg.

- Place in the oven and bake for 10 minutes, then reduce the oven temperature to 350°F (180°C) and bake for 40 to 45 minutes more, until the pastry is golden and the filling beneath it is bubbling. Serve hot.

ONE FINAL RECIPE . . .

In the past couple of years, the world was struck by the COVID-19 pandemic. Overnight, we went from travelling, food shopping, dining in and out with friends and family to a literal lockdown.

Within days of the news, schools were closed, and those who could worked from home, while doctors, nurses, and essential workers kept the world going. Restaurants not shuttered put out takeout menus to keep afloat. The usually busy city streets were close to deserted while we waited to hear what would happen next. How long would we be talking to our parents and grandparents via computer screen . . . how long until our children were back behind their desks . . . how long before we could speak to a neighbour face to face? How long until we could shake a colleague's hand or kiss a loved one's cheek?

With so much sorrow and suffering around us, as well as a deep sense of uncertainty, this was an experience like no other for our generation. As I was writing the French edition of this book, my days were spent worrying about my kids, my work, and my family members, both close and far away. Every morning I opened my eyes and remembered we were in the middle of a pandemic, and that dreaded feeling washed over me like a cold wind.

As many of us were at home trying to keep busy and distracted from the daily news, we were glued to the TV, cleaning closets, raking leaves, or reorganizing the Tupperware drawer. And cooking our hearts out. Bread making became the national pastime, as did everything from cake baking to comfort food cooking. Never before had feeding my family felt more like the best outlet to keep me going, without a consideration that it be low-cal, healthy, quick, or inexpensive. It just had to be delicious and, most important, comforting.

Our planet changed so drastically in the time it took to write this book, which I began by asking the question: "Does the world need another cookbook?" When I ask myself the same question today in unimaginably different circumstances, without hesitation I'd say YES! In this time of uncertainty, one thing many of us yearn for now more than ever is the company of our loved ones around a crowded dinner table! I feel certain this newfound interest for cooking will carry over for years to come.

To finish, I include a recipe not planned in the original manuscript but one I enjoy greatly in times of deep anxiety. Funny enough, it's for a dish that I never cared for before: rice pudding. But it seemed the ideal simple dish we all ate as kids that you suddenly find yourself craving when life seems overwhelming.

You can eat this as is, or drizzled with caramel sauce (see page 71), "burnt" with brown sugar like a crème brûlée, or sprinkled with caramelized pecans. Or why not try it the way I like it best: in the morning, right out of the fridge, with a few sips of hot coffee.

LUKE'S RICE PUDDING

SERVES 4 TO 6

I named this recipe for my son Luke, who ate all the test
batches and chose this as the BEST. What a trooper!

½ cup (100g) short-grain white rice, such as Arborio

2 cups (500ml) milk

1 tablespoon vanilla extract, or ½ vanilla bean, split lengthwise and seeds scraped out

1 to 2 strips of orange or lemon zest

¼ cup (50g) sugar, plus more if needed

Good pinch of fine sea salt

3 large egg yolks, or 1¾ ounces (50g) chopped white chocolate

¾ cup (180ml) whipping cream (optional)

Ground cinnamon (optional)

- In a small saucepan, bring 2 cups (500ml) water to a boil. Add the rice, bring back to a boil, reduce the heat to low, and simmer for 10 minutes. Drain, rinse lightly with cold water, and set aside.

- Meanwhile, in a heavy, medium saucepan, combine the milk, vanilla (including the pod, if using a vanilla bean), orange zest, sugar, and salt. Bring to a boil over medium-hight heat, add the rice, and bring back to a boil. Reduce the heat to low and simmer, stirring occasionally, until the rice is cooked and the milk has thickened, about 20 minutes.

- Increase the heat to high and add the egg yolks. Whisk vigorously and bring it all up to a boil for 10 seconds, then remove from the heat. (If using the white chocolate, no need to recook the mixture—just add it to the hot rice and whisk until melted.) Pour the mixture into a shallow, six-portion serving dish. Remove the vanilla pod and orange zest. Cover with plastic wrap and refrigerate.

- When the rice mixture is cold, you could cover it with a thin layer of sugar and caramelize it with a blowtorch as you would a crème brûlée. Or, to make a creamy pudding, whip the cream in a small bowl to firm peaks, mix a third into the rice mixture to lighten it, and then fold in the rest.

- Eat as is, or with a sprinkling of cinnamon. Some say rice pudding is even better the next day, so feel free to keep it refrigerated in an airtight container for a day or two.

ACKNOWLEDGEMENTS

As much as cooking is often a solo undertaking, pulling together a cookbook is anything but.

First, thanks to Les Éditions Cardinal's general director, Antoine Ross-Trempe, and former éditorial director, Emilie Villeneuve, for accepting my original pitch and not batting an eye when I submitted a very different book. I appreciate you giving me that freedom to "find" the book inside me after all these years on the food beat. Thanks also to coordinators Jeannie Gravel and Mathilde Bessière, as well as my editor, Joëlle Landry, who worked her magic on the manuscript so intelligently and patiently, and to translator Vincent Fortier, for meeting the challenge of preserving my voice.

Photographer (and gourmand!) Maude Chauvin made all my dishes shine. Book designer Catherine Gravel added her great taste and discipline to the mix.

And to Justine Villeneuve, the kitchen assistant I wish was at my side every day.

Thanks also to my former editors at the *Montreal Gazette*, Evangeline Sadler, Jordan Zivitz, and Enza Micheletti, as well as editor in chief, Lucinda Chodan. And to Julian Armstrong, for years of advice, as well as countless colleagues from the food-writing world who set the bar so high.

Special thanks to Marc Bourg and Naomi Duguid, as well as chefs Jean-Francois Vachon, Danny St Pierre, Hubert Streicher, Mike Forgione, Vikram Vij, and especially James MacGuire, for allowing me to share their recipes in these pages. And to Jean-Paul Grappe, for his constant support.

An extra-special thank you to my family, starting with my sons, Max and Luke Bazin, who always gave me an honest opinion on what they ate, and their dad, Bertrand Bazin, for the inspiration and never-ending pastry advice.

Thanks to my sister, Lorraine Holl, who helped me forge ahead when words failed me, and my mother, Sylvia Chesterman, my #1 fan now and forever. And to Jean Aubry, for the unconditional love and support.

And finally, to my readers and listeners from over twenty years in the food media in Quebec and Canada. Thanks for letting me into your kitchens. There's no place I'd rather be.

For the English edition: A special thanks to my editor Kirsten Hanson for taking on this project and for her precious guidance, as well as the entire team at Simon & Schuster Canada. To my good friend, Laura Calder, for setting the wheels in motion. And also to all my English readers for their patience.

*   *   *

Thanks to:

Boutique VdeV and
La Maison Milan

Who so kindly loaned certain
items for the photo shoots

INDEX